Serious Poetry

SERIOUS POETRY

Form and Authority
from Yeats to Hill

PETER McDONALD

CLARENDON PRESS · OXFORD

OXFORD

UNIVERSITY PRESS

Great Clarendon Street, Oxford OX2 6DP

Oxford University Press is a department of the University of Oxford.
It furthers the University's objective of excellence in research, scholarship,
and education by publishing worldwide in

Oxford New York

Auckland Bangkok Buenos Aires Cape Town Chennai
Dar es Salaam Delhi Hong Kong Istanbul Karachi Kolkata
Kuala Lumpur Madrid Melbourne Mexico City Mumbai Nairobi
São Paulo Shanghai Singapore Taipei Tokyo Toronto
and an associated company in Berlin

Oxford is a registered trade mark of Oxford University Press
in the UK and in certain other countries

Published in the United States
by Oxford University Press Inc., New York

British Library Cataloguing in Publication Data

Data available

Library of Congress Cataloging in Publication Data

Data available

ISBN 0–19–924747–1

1 3 5 7 9 10 8 6 4 2

Typeset in Garamond
by Kolam Information Services Pvt. Ltd, Pondicherry, India
Printed in Great Britain
on acid-free paper by Biddles Ltd, Guildford and King's Lynn

For
PATRICK and CASSY O'BRIEN

Foreword

Several chapters in this book, or portions of them, have appeared in earlier versions in the following publications, to whose editors I am indebted: *English*, *The Irish Review*, *Metre*, *Princeton University Library Bulletin*, *Proceedings of the British Academy*, *Thumbscrew*, and *Yeats Annual*. I have taken care to ensure that all quotations from copyright material fall within the definition of fair dealing for the purposes of criticism.

A number of the chapters might not have been begun without invitations to speak in public, and I am grateful to Ron Schuchard, George Watson, and the organizers of the Yeats Summer School in Sligo; Ralph Pite of Liverpool University; Andrew Benjamin and Michael John Kooy of the University of Warwick; and to Edna Longley and Fran Brearton of Queen's University, Belfast, for their hospitality and interest.

I have incurred many intellectual debts, and must thank my creditors for their forbearance: none should be held responsible either for my arguments or my mistakes. I am very grateful to the Dean, Canons, and Students of Christ Church, Oxford, and to the Trustees of the Estate of the late Christopher Tower, for their practical support, and to my students in the University of Oxford for listening good-naturedly as some of the arguments in this book took shape. I am grateful also to Lesley Bankes-Hughes, who kept things running on the Tower Prize with tact and efficiency while I hid from the phone. Some chapters were written while I was a member of the English Department in the University of Bristol; I am immeasurably indebted for their support and good counsel to my friends there: George Donaldson, Tim Kendall, John Lyon, and Carol Meale.

Above all, I have been helped and encouraged by my wife Karen, and my daughter Louisa.

P.McD.

Woodstock, Oxfordshire,
Summer 2001

Contents

CHAPTER 1

'Rather than words':
The End of Authority?

'Authority' is a chilly word, at least in literary criticism: it suggests all kinds of unwelcome things, and makes far too many assumptions. On its own, it seems to be in need of an adjective—'monolithic', perhaps, or 'overbearing', even 'academic'. 'Authority' is something that tries to tell you what to read, or what to think, and has views about that; 'authority' says one thing is better than another, and that some things take more work than others; 'authority' is on your case. So, it is both easy and advantageous to say that we need to get away from 'authority', get over it and beyond its reach into a more friendly world in which literature, like the other good things in life, is simply there, endlessly diverse, and without any obvious ill intent: it's affirmative, it's warm, and it won't demand anything of you, or make you feel small.

This would not matter much, if the plurality and infinite devolution of a literature freed from the structures of authority were really all they claim to be. But in fact, the actual structures and operations of critical and academic authority are as strong as ever; one set of authors changes for another set, and one group of friends replaces another group of friends in the world of mutual reviewing and praise, but the literary landscape in Britain remains in essence the same as that of fifty years ago. Now, as then, access to publication is limited to a small number of individuals identified not by work but by affiliation; now, as then, poetry occupies a minute and necessarily marginal place in most readers' minds; now, more than then, the political temper of the time sets the tone of poetry's meaning, content, and reception. That temper is plainly against words like 'authority', but it is still assiduous in the backing and maintenance of authority's actual functioning.

According to the *Oxford English Dictionary* (itself an authority, at least in so far as its acts of witness to usage should carry interpretative weight), one definition of 'authority' (5b) may be given as 'Power over, or title to influence, the opinions of others; authoritative opinion; weight of judgement or opinion, intellectual influence.' This covers a wide canvass, but it begins at the central point, with 'Power', before moving to matters of 'opinion' and 'judgement'. Just as it would be possible to read the speeches and listen to the interviews of Britain's most powerful individuals without encountering the term 'power' once, so one might easily think that literary power had been devolved, and taken out of the hands of a narrow elite. According to Simon Armitage (a celebrated poet) and Robert Crawford (a celebrating academic), in the Introduction to their *Penguin Book of Poetry from Britain and Ireland since 1945*, 'A sense of local accents, dialects, languages attaining their own authority, at the same time as ideas of absolute central authority dissolve, characterizes the poetry of the period and plays a strong part in the evolution of the democratic voice.'[1] The appeal here, from political (or cultural) model to poetic judgement and critical rule, is direct and obvious. If readers are unsure about how to recognize 'the democratic voice', they may consult the anthology's list (authoritative in its size and inclusiveness) of 141 poets.

   It should be possible to ask critical questions about the ways in which 'the weight of ... opinion' is exerted upon poetry, or in poetry, or even by poetry. 'Authority' (whatever it changes its name to) will always be an indispensable aid for those who want to know what they should think, and here opinion's weight counts for much. And opinion (*OED* 1b: 'what is generally thought about something') is a strong, but not an accountable thing: 'Opinion is a powerfull, bould, and unmeasurable party' in Florio's Montaigne, as cited by the *OED*; in more modern times, it has remained 'unmeasurable' in its reach, and continues to exercise power through consensus and—the other side of the coin— through the anxiety not to be left out of this consensus. Opinion's most winning ways suggest that those with a special interest and the pretence of authority in a subject have been outstripped by you and me, or have got wrong what we agree we have got right. Samuel Johnson on Gray's 'Elegy' is the most sprightly instance of this attractive sentiment:[2]

In the character of his *Elegy* I rejoice to concur with the common reader; for by the common sense of readers uncorrupted with literary prejudices, after all the

---

[1] Simon Armitage and Robert Crawford (eds.), *The Penguin Book of Poetry from Britain and Ireland since 1945* (Harmondsworth: Penguin, 1998), p. xxiv.

[2] Samuel Johnson, Life of Gray, *Lives of the English Poets*, ed. George Birkbeck Hill (Oxford: Clarendon Press, 1905), iii. 441.

refinements of subtilty and the dogmatism of learning, must be finally decided all claim to poetical honours. The *Church-yard* abounds with images which find a mirrour in every mind, and with sentiments to which every bosom returns an echo.

This is bold, certainly; and in British criticism, its influence is unmeasurable. Johnson's voice here is one which has haunted many exponents of even 'the dogmatism of learning' over the years; it has sounded loudly, too, in the ears of those critics willing to make popular acclaim their last refuge of value. But Johnson's 'concur' does not concede much, or greatly, to 'the common reader'; rather, this reader is being congratulated for returning the correct verdict, and Johnson sets out to describe the reason behind this correctness. Yet the famous judgement carries authority of another, and blunter, kind. One common reading makes this a charter for 'common sense' and plain dealing, the warm endorsement of the unreasoned opinion of contemporary readership as the true measure of literary worth.

It is clear that, in contemporary British culture, literary worth and opinion are intimately bound together. As the 1990s came to an end, and even into the following decade, the thirst for definitive statements of worth seemed to intensify: few Sunday papers could go for long without a list of the top ten or top 100 examples of a particular art or genre of art. Perhaps millennial anxiety sharpened the journalistic and critical need to issue posterity with clear instructions; but even so, it is tempting to wonder how Johnson might have complied with the request to name his fifty favourite moments in Shakespeare, or 100 favourite words. Top poets and poems (if less good than top films or pop stars) still make good copy, and the criteria of mirroring minds, and re-echoing bosoms, continue to be useful in drawing up these lists. By the 1990s, even 'the dogmatism of learning' was streetwise, and played along for all it was worth.

Writing on his 'Books of the Century', Oxford's Merton Professor of English came to Philip Larkin, an author to whom the few years since his death had not been kind, and around whom there still drifted the thick smoke of political unacceptability. The Samuel Johnson defence came immediately to hand:[3]

Readers of Larkin's poetry tend to feel they have a personal relationship with him. That is unusual, and unfashionable. T. S. Eliot decreed that poems should

---

[3] John Carey, 'John Carey's Books of the Century', *Sunday Times*, 28 Nov. 1999, 'The Culture', p. 48.

be impersonal. But Larkin's often read like diary entries. When his letters were published, some readers, discovering that his political views differed from theirs, felt betrayed. That was simple-minded, of course. Yet it tells us something about the poems. The personality they project—wry, unpretentious, adult—gains our trust. It needs to do so, because, despite his reputation as Mr Glum, he is a didactic poet, teaching us how to survive.

As a specimen of the ways in which the academy tries to relate to the world beyond itself, this is invaluable; John Carey's prose gets rid of Eliot's troublesome decree about 'impersonality' as though it were widely enforced, and as if what we are reading this Sunday were indeed both unusual and unfashionable. The Merton Professor is sticking his neck out here, he wants us to know: but this is all because he is one of us, not one of them—those, that is, who deplored the evidence of Larkin's political views when they read the letters, and who did not understand the simple-mindedness of their objections about things as petty as 'political views'. Poor old Larkin, mauled after his death by a pack of academics and media politicos; it could happen to any of us. Rightly, Carey directs attention to the poems, rather than what is recoverable of the poet; but this leads us straight back, not to Larkin's poetry but to 'The personality they project', which 'gains our trust'. The first-person plural here is collusive: it is all 'we' want to be—'wry, unpretentious, adult'—and marks out the ground on which the critic and the common reader may rejoice to concur. If Larkin really is capable of 'teaching us how to survive' (and Carey is, one assumes, speaking metaphorically, since otherwise Philip Larkin would make a very bad example indeed), our survival is identified with the survival of all those commonsensical and 'adult' traits of personality in the face of 'simple-minded' demands made on us by life. We are all grown-ups here.

Something has coarsened in the transition from Johnson to Carey; something has thickened. Something is pushing the Merton Professor to the side of his own profession, where 'the refinements of subtilty', like 'the dogmatism of learning' are so much guff to be seen through. For the author of 'Books of the Century', or at least for his projected readership, it's important to remember that 'Books are a load of crap'[4]—in comparison, at least, with 'The personality they project'. But the pretended eccentricity is—'of course'—a fiction: the *Sunday*

---

[4] The last line of 'A Study of Reading Habits', from *The Whitsun Weddings*; repr. in Philip Larkin, *Collected Poems*, ed. Anthony Thwaite (London: Marvell Press and Faber and Faber, 1988), 131.

Times did not solicit opinions from the common reader, but from an Oxford Professor, and Carey's resistance to the deprecation of Larkin's views is self-consciously conclusive, full of the sense of its own consequence. The weight of the critic and the weight of opinion are at one here. 'Larkin' becomes a name for the unchallengeability of what 'we' know and agree upon, and the Professor joins in an anti-elitist show of strength, miming perfectly along to 'the democratic voice' perhaps, to salvage poetry from politics by proving that it's all a matter of 'personality' in the end.

Another approach can be taken—though this is truly, and not in sham, an 'unusual, and unfashionable' one. The merest smattering of literary biography will show that poets have written, and often still write, poetry which has more resource, complexity, and imagination than they could themselves demonstrate as men and women. Taking poetry seriously can also mean taking poetry seriously as an authority: the unique property of a real poem is its capacity to work against the grain of opinion, or in complex and guarded relation to it, so as to create an original order in which language overpowers the 'weight of judgement or opinion' through an individual (and essentially unrepeatable) form. However, this way of approaching poetry puts poetic form in the place that 'personality' in fact tends to occupy; and that is only the beginning of its disadvantages in terms of what is presently sayable and thinkable in literary criticism and academic discussion. For where would the promotion of contemporary poetry be without personalities to push? And where would academic study of modern writing find itself if the props of opinion, and the 'Power over, or title to influence, the opinions of others' were located elsewhere?

But 'serious' is, in its turn, a problematic term, another word that feels unwelcome in the domains of 'the democratic voice'. First of all, there is more than a smack of the humourless about it, a suspicion of dour intensity and prim high-mindedness: serious poetry, in this light, is something read by desiccated intellectuals in cold houses without television, and it sits on their shelves along with volumes of F. R. Leavis and Raymond Williams. Overtones of 'elitist' are all too easy to detect in the word; what is worse, it seems almost the perfect opposite of 'playful' (or, in some company, 'ludic'), an approved and assured virtue. 'Now often, concerned with the grave and earnest sides of life as opposed to amusement or pleasure-seeking,' says the *OED* right at the start of things (1a), and there is no doubting the accuracy of this in terms of

contemporary usage. For all that, form is the serious heart of a poem—
an amused or amusing poem as much as a troubled or perplexed one—
where such 'authority' as poetry bears must reside. In this sense, the
poem is a serious business, however the poet chooses to run his
business in broader senses.

    In his volume *The Less Deceived* (1955), Larkin himself took the weight
of 'serious' with telling accuracy and effect. 'Church Going' surveys a
country churchyard of its own, though inevitably with Gray somewhere
in the background, and Dr Johnson on Gray somewhere in the air. A
good deal has changed, of course, since the eighteenth century; the
scene is a bit different, and the pieties voiced by the poet have a new
language; most importantly of all, the poet is himself on view, and
posing carefully for just that purpose. Larkin's first-person narrative
has a novelist's eye for detail ('Hatless, I take off | My cycle-clips in
awkward reverence') which makes it clear that we are dealing here with
an identifiable person. But this first-person candour moves up a gear as
Larkin's poem comes to its conclusion, and the first-person singular
swells up into the plural:[5]

> It pleases me to stand in silence here;
>
> A serious house on serious earth it is,
> In whose blent air all our compulsions meet,
> Are recognised, and robed as destinies.
> And that much never can be obsolete,
> Since someone will forever be surprising
> A hunger in himself to be more serious,
> And gravitating with it to this ground,
> Which, he once heard, was proper to grow wise in,
> If only that so many dead lie round.

'Serious' echoes through this final stanza to problematic (and ingenious)
effect; 'A serious house on serious earth it is' seems already to be
standing at an angle to some proposition—'it is', at the end of the line,
is an acknowledgement of something that is not being said for the first
time here, and feels like both an endorsement and a qualification of that
remark. 'It is' says with a tone of deliberation, 'Yes, that's right, "serious" ': the word itself is being agreed with, but not necessarily in the
sense that it was first uttered. So, as the stanza works round to its close,

---

[5] Larkin, *Collected Poems*, 98.

Larkin can speak of how 'someone will forever be surprising | A hunger in himself to be more serious', revisiting the word with a resigned awareness of its relation to human need; on this encounter, 'serious' becomes an irreducible constant, to be discovered by most with surprise, and something far more simple than it might seem. Essential to the effect of this is Larkin's shift from the first-person singular to the plural in just one line, where 'all our compulsions meet'. This moment helps to make 'someone' into everyone—all of us in the same boat—and allows the poet to close his poem with the generalities that might otherwise risk bathos or obviousness. The poem's 'I' has been so convincingly (and winningly) presented that to resist the conclusion, and the assumptions in 'our', seems either churlish or tone-deaf. Yet there is another telling moment in the stanza, when Larkin's voice prepares for the conclusion, in the flat-footed iambics of 'And that much never can be obsolete': at this point, metrical regularity trammels the speaking voice into a cadence that rings false, protesting too much. The hollow sound made by this line gives the game away, as far as the poem's relation to form is concerned: at points of stress in the argument, the regular tramp of metrical progress becomes too audible, and form is not the poem's rationale but the mode of enforcement for its thought.

This seems harsh, and perhaps appears at first to over-read the merest accidentals in the form and execution of Larkin's poem. But the things 'Church Going' is serious about are the things that regard precisely such details as accidental, marginal, or unimportant. All of this is entirely in tune with Carey's reading of Larkin in relation to 'us' and 'our' concerns, for which poetry is fundamentally a vehicle. The 'personality' that hitches a ride there becomes ours in giving itself to us, and offers in the process that most exquisite *frisson* of contemporary literature, the feeling that the 'personality' and the reader are on intimate terms, and are even, for the moment, united. If words are not the obedient vehicles of this thrill, they are simply getting in the way.

One of Larkin's most celebrated poems, 'High Windows', surprises a hunger in itself to be more serious. In terms of its influence on British poetry, this short lyric is extremely important, containing within itself a potent combination of the attitudes and stylistic resources which go into much contemporary writing. The poem's gruff, unillusioned, and 'adult' opening lines ('When I see a couple of kids | And guess he's fucking her and she's | Taking pills or wearing a diaphragm...') lead in to a meditation on generations, freedom, and restraint, in which Larkin's

first-person lyric voice, enviously contemplating the sexual liberty of the
1960s, mimics the voices of his own elders looking enviously at what
seemed the freedoms of his own youth (*'He | And his lot will all go down the
long slide | Like free bloody birds'*).[6] The situation which the poem presents,
then, is one of a fairly simple irony: I look at younger people, and envy
'everyone young going down the long slide | To happiness, endlessly',
just as my elders envied me. Even allowing for Larkin's attunement to
Thomas Hardy, this seems little more than one of life's little ironies; and
Hardy, indeed, might well have left it at that. But 'High Windows' wants
to be something more, and its importance as a model is in the way in
which it moves from a closed loop of ironic observation into a final
moment of epiphany:

> And immediately
>
> > Rather than words comes the thought of high windows:
> > The sun-comprehending glass,
> > And beyond it, the deep blue air, that shows
> > Nothing, and is nowhere, and is endless.

The stylistic shift is so sudden as to be disruptive: Larkin's 'immediately'
is the warning of something startling to come. But what does come here
is, of course, the very opposite of startling, since it assuages and reassures:
the final lines settle into a smooth rhythm to deliver images in and for
themselves, that offer another way out of the poem in a vision that is
beyond the bickering and gabble we have been hearing just a few lines
before. Barbara Everett has written of how the 'Symbolist logic' here
'finally embodies and resolves all its impossibilities', and of the 'extremity
of style' in the poem as a whole, 'that violent flatness of its opening which
modulates into the exaltation of the close'.[7] But the resolution, as much
as the modulation, is something willed upon this poem by such readings,
and is not actually work done in or by the poem itself. This resolution is a
final epiphany that costs Larkin nothing (it does not make earlier
thoughts in the poem problematic or painful, nor indeed try to make
sense of them in any way), and its celebration of a luminous 'Nothing'
wants to make something out of the dead end which the poem had
reached. In so bluntly demotic a poem, the final lines take on a faintly

---

[6] Larkin, *Collected Poems*, 165.

[7] Barbara Everett, *Poets in their Time: Essays on English Poetry from Donne to Larkin* (London:
Faber and Faber, 1986; repr. Oxford: Clarendon Press, 1991), 242.

reverential tone, and build to a final 'endless' which is something quite distinct from an ironic echo of the church's 'World without end', or even T. S. Eliot's 'Humility is endless', and more like a successful attempt to add the weight of these things to its own tone of reverence.

The last lines do, of course, come claiming to be images pure and simple, and are presented as coming 'Rather than words'. The phrase is not meant to be thought about, or taken all that seriously; but it is more revealing than Larkin (or Larkin's admirers) might think. For a poem to gesture beyond its own capacities, and beyond its own language, is a trope which (with Eliot lending his authority) passes into the mainstream of British poetry; its success there is owing partly to the degree to which readers (and poets) would much rather not be tied down by language's limitations and liabilities; partly, too, it is a result of a common sense of poetry as a private haven from language's unreasonable demands, demands that so often pay no heed to what we want to say or to hear being said, and intrude public concerns on our private intensities. Words, if they are not just vehicles, get in the way.

The stereotypical short lyric poem from Britain in contemporary writing inherits much from all this. Such a poem will be in the first person (at least to begin with); it will demonstrate wry knowledge of what is most current in speech or reference (a contributor to *Poetry Review* in 2001 claimed that poetry was '*au fait* with the zeitgeist');[8] it will tell some kind of anecdote or story, and point out the irony of the situation it describes; finally, it will find an image or images that transcend the situation, and that constitute an unspecific, apparently secular, epiphany. The poem will cultivate a knowing irony in relation to everything but its own control of language. If such a poem succeeds, the reader will remember most of all the appeal of the personality projected there, and be able to identify with it, as with a character on stage or screen. The poem's seriousness, like its humour, will relate finally to the 'personality'; the poet will have put him- or herself into words, and the words will bring the poet vividly to life. We will be able to identify with this poetry, and see our lives in its life.

Poems, and 'personalities', that make themselves 'ours' present a much more appealing, and less forbidding, subject than a series of works that rely on form for authority. But there is a problem with 'ours', and this problem hinges on the very authority which much critical

---

[8] Roddy Lumsden, 'Ready Salted', *Poetry Review*, 91/1 (Spring 2001), 108.

writing renders invisible. Who are 'we'? And, more problematically still, *When* are 'we'? For John Carey and many like him, the answers to such questions are so obvious that asking them is proof of either academic obfuscation and vested interests, or a more fundamental obtuseness and possibly stupidity. Nevertheless, one must take one's chances.

In a long footnote, the poet and critic Geoffrey Hill quotes a blurb from the 1980s for a series of critical publications on contemporary authors, in which the editors speak of 'some of the most important writers of our time', and of 'the vitality of a living literature which, because it is contemporary, is especially ours'. Hill's protracted—pitiless—meditation on this is not widely enough known, but should be a key critical document:[9]

'Especially ours' elides the indeterminate commonality of 'our time' with the elusive determination of 'our wish'. It is 'our wish' to oblige the clichés of current conversation ('we live in a major creative time', 'the works of major post-war writers'); it is also 'our' wish to present such authors as Margaret Drabble and John Le Carré as 'most important writers'. '*Our*' time must here mean '*your* time made placable to *our* cultural scenario'. If they truly meant 'our time' they would have to take account of e.g. *my* time. Margaret Drabble and John Le Carré do not figure among the most important writers of my time, but my scepticism, and the views of those who might share my scepticism, are effectively excluded from consideration from being included in the complacent locution.

Hill's step-by-step exposure of the relation between complacency in language and the enforcement of authority in literary judgement has consequences far beyond his specific example. Nor is the phenomenon Hill targets one confined to the 1980s; indeed, the complacency of locution in these matters has, if anything, increased in much contemporary discussion and promotion of literature. The definition of a consensus is more than ever a pressing business for the enforcers of a contemporary British 'cultural scenario', especially as this affects literature; and the coercive force of consensus is unmeasurable. The *OED*'s citation from 1874 of being 'sustained by a great consensus of opinion' (Consensus, 2b) still catches accurately the foundations of much critical authority. Hill continues by invoking Johnson on Gray:

This appeal to the supposed consensus seems to me in direct conflict with Dr Johnson's meaning when he wrote that Gray's 'Elegy' 'abounds with images

[9] Geoffrey Hill, *The Enemy's Country: Words, Contexture, and other Circumstances of Language* (Oxford: Clarendon Press, 1991), 105–6.

which find a mirrour in every mind, and with sentiments to which every bosom returns an echo', though Bradbury and Bigsby doubtless 'rejoice to concur with the common reader' according to their understanding of that term. To the suggestion that Johnson's statement is itself merely a matter of opinion delivered with aplomb I would reply that his priorities strike me as being right and that he avoids blurring or eliding the implications of his words. For Johnson it is the *poem* that establishes and maintains the tone; the sensibility of the 'common reader' may be judged by his or her capacity to echo or reflect its intrinsic qualities.

Hill corrects the complacent appropriation of Johnson by insisting on the formal qualities in writing to which 'the common reader' can indeed respond. The assumptions themselves behind Hill's critique are the opposite of what is often called 'elitist'; like Johnson, Hill presupposes no intermediary agents of 'opinion' through whom alone poems can communicate to the reader: poetry itself, in its own resources of form and expressive language, its 'intrinsic qualities', is capable of setting up the resonance with the reader on which all such art finally depends.

But in quoting Hill at this point, and at this length, I will seem to have given the game away, for Hill's name has resonances of its own in the present 'great consensus of opinion', and his criticism (and, latterly, his poetry) have aroused grave suspicions among those most committed to testing 'personality'. Put bluntly, Hill has committed the sin of being less forthcoming, less complaisantly accommodating, and pleasantly affirmative than the other widely read poets of his generation and after. Read in terms of a projected 'personality', there is either not enough to go on, or a positively unwelcome presence to be detected; Hill's insistence on words as something other than simple vehicles under the control of a self-depicting author is doubly unwelcome, and spoils the party for too many critics. Where Larkin has been forgiven or tolerated, Hill is beyond much critical forgiveness or even, increasingly, toleration. Given all this, it is interesting to read Hill on Larkin—a poet whose brief tangle with the politically correct was resolved by the likes of Carey and the big guns of 'our' opinion. Responding in part to Christopher Ricks's positive judgement of Larkin, Hill writes:[10]

I must conclude that there is a tone that Larkin represents which is stronger even than Ricks's acute sense of pitch; and what Larkin represents is an

[10]   Geoffrey Hill, 'Dividing Legacies' [review of T. S. Eliot, *The Varieties of Metaphysical Poetry*, ed. R. Schuchard (1993)], *Agenda*, 34/2 (Summer 1996), 27–8.

assumption, a narrow English possessiveness, with regard to 'good sense' and 'generous common humanity'. 'Good sense', so propertied, so keen to admit others, at a price, to its properties, strikes me as a deplorable kind of *bienséance*. During his lifetime Larkin was granted endless credit by the bank of Opinion and the rage which in some quarters greeted his posthumously published *Letters* was that of people who consider themselves betrayed by one of their own kind. In fact Larkin betrayed no-one, least of all himself. What he is seen to be in the letters he was and is in the poems. The notion of the accessibility of his work acknowledged the ease with which readers could overlay it with transparencies of their own preference.

The degree to which the poem is held to speak to 'us', and for 'us', and is written by a 'personality' with whom 'we' can identify, is significant in assessing the force and direction of Hill's argument here. Hill is striking at the root of much contemporary authority in matters of poetry, by insisting on its identification with opinion. Beyond this, his critique of Larkin takes the measure of the critical desire to have something 'Rather than words' in poetry—a desire which many poets can learn to share.

As the makers and moulders of 'authority' (still a small band, still mostly known to one another, still delighted to find that talent runs in families) know less and less, so language and knowledge become more threatening to them, and need more to be kept at arm's length by art. New terms of abuse arise: 'academic', for example, puts knowledge in its place. 'Personality' assumes more significance in this scenario, and human interest stories are at a premium. The media feeding-frenzy that accompanied the publication of Ted Hughes's *Birthday Letters* in 1998 was, in many respects, both prurient and in bad taste; whether or not Hughes's poetry had encouraged this, it was significant that the British critical and literary establishment rushed on publication to declare the arrival of a timeless classic, and to identify the worth of the poetry with the intensity and newsworthiness of the story it told. Sheer personality, and a literary love affair of the century, won Hughes an instant ticket to posterity among the all-time greats. Criticism does not want to get left behind by the news; it is, on the whole, less worried about being deficient in attention to words and form than it is anxious to make the leap from the book supplements into the features pages. In such a context, Hill's points about Larkin have special force; they are also, from the point of view of that kind of criticism, either risible or monstrous.

Sometimes the underlying issues come to the surface, and what is usually kept out of sight comes into view. In recent years, Hill has tended to provoke such moments. Reviewing Hill's poetry of the late 1990s, James Wood writes with a useful directness:[11]

> Unfortunately, Hill's most recent poetry is also his most abstract and rebarbatively academic. It is, above all, the author's authority that far too much of the verse in *Canaan* and *The Triumph of Love* asserts. ... Such academicism, which perhaps flows from a misreading of Eliot, is an unhappy perversion of the modern poet's status, not his glorious culmination. What was the natural inheritance of Wordsworth, or even of Hopkins, became the struggle of Eliot, and is now the academic fusillade of Hill. He twitches quickly from model to model, like a man with too many alibis; his allusion is merely allusive, the crust of something dead, or kept alive artificially, leaving the reader to register not what is alluded to, but the existence of the allusive. This has become the mark of authority, and we notice only after we have been beaten over the head with it that Hill's tradition and his models of high literacy are as personal as anyone else's. And if Hill, like anyone else, is shut out of a common high culture, it is because there is no longer such a thing.

Quite apart from one's view of the poetry, or of Hill, this comes clean about the challenge which contemporary opinion gives to the literary and critical intellect and imagination. They will have to go. Wood can only see Hill's learning in terms of a supposed personality—the 'academic' side of Hill will not do as it is told, and it is thus rebarbative—and adduces a revealing genealogy for this 'unhappy perversion', in which other poets are seen as points in a graph of decline, of which Hill marks the nadir. Most revealingly of all, Wood complains about 'the mark of authority': we are, he assures the reader knowingly, all far too grown up for that kind of thing. Hill's learning is a social *faux pas* based on an embarrassing fallacy: 'there is no longer such a thing' as 'a common high culture'. What *is* common to Wood's scenario is the ability to sniff out such awkward and cringe-making mistakes. What we know or don't know is—of course—less important than knowing how to behave.

It is instructive to compare the late 1990s with the early 1960s in this regard. In the second edition of Kenneth Allott's *Penguin Book of Contemporary Verse*, the editor found himself embarrassed, and again this time by the then much younger Geoffrey Hill. The problem in 1962 was not about 'high culture', but about simple (and comic) incomprehension, for which Hill had provided the occasion. Allott wanted to include poems

[11] James Wood, review of Geoffrey Hill, *Canaan* and *The Triumph of Love*, in *London Review of Books*, 1 July 1999, p. 25.

from Hill's *For the Unfallen* (1959), but the poet preferred more recent work. Allott, however, was all at sea with this: 'I find the darkness of many of the later pieces,' he wrote in his introductory note, 'so nearly total that I can see them to be poems only by a certain quality in their phrasing.'[12] Allott's note reports how he has 'come down on the side' of representing Hill by recent work:

I have chosen the latter course because I think Mr Hill is a poet. I understand 'Annunciations' only in the sense that cats and dogs may be said to understand human conversations (i.e. they grasp something by the tone of the speaking voice), but without help I cannot construe it. Mr Hill has kindly supplied the following comment on his poem:

Two full pages of 'comment' follow, in which Hill patiently takes the measure of words and phrases, only to end with 'I feel dubious; and the whole business is dubious.'[13] This comic non-meeting of minds is one between a critic who lives by 'tone' and a poet who lives intensely, uncertainly, and often self-checkingly in words. For Allott, the two 'Annunciations' poems are just so many words, leaving him in the position of 'cats and dogs'. Being a happy pet is made to seem the more comfortable option, as perhaps it is; but Hill's performance neverthe-less disrupts the domestic surroundings of Allott's anthology in the early 1960s, much as he continues to prove an impossible house-guest at the best literary addresses of the twenty-first century.

'Authority' is not something that, like 'a common high culture', may be said to come to an end; although its name might not be spoken, or might change, it is always a basic condition of any contemporary literature. But poetry's dealings with authority, in this sense, are seldom straightforward. One kind of poetry—which will always, in any age, be the vast bulk of poetry—wants approval, and knows very well how authority can help; it absorbs opinion, and wants to get the weight of consensus behind its effort: some of this will be praised, and accounted a success. Another kind of poetry knows too much to play by these rules, and is not abject in relation to the authority of its time; it accepts form as its *sine qua non*, and puts up with the finally uncontrollable difficulty and complexity of language; it knows that words, not 'personality', are what survive or perish. The critical task of telling one kind of poetry from

<hr>

[12] Kenneth Allott (ed.), *The Penguin Book of Contemporary Verse 1918–1960* (Harmondsworth: Penguin, 1962), 391.
[13] Ibid. 393.

another is never simple, and can never be performed with completeness; indeed, it is probably misleading to suggest that poets necessarily conform entirely to one or the other of these patterns, for many careers mix both kinds of ambition, and both kinds of achieved writing. For all that, it is a critical task which a number of poets, as well as critics, have attempted, and which still pays certain dividends, both critical and creative, in contemporary writing.

Form itself is a word long under suspicion in academic circles. However, poets themselves are unlikely to worry about the consequences, in the politics of the academy, of any supposed 'formalism'. A respect for poems, and a respect for poems' workings, negotiations with language and each other, and economies of meaning, image, and expression, is the common currency of poetic influence; without these things, talk of 'intertextuality' remains mere academic chatter. It may be significant that this creative fascination with form is so often combined with a sceptical attitude to the received shapes of authority in the literary, cultural, and political spheres, at least amongst the best and most enduring poets. Because of this acceptance of form's authority, real poets know (as they have always known) that poetry cannot work to extra-poetic agendas: this applies to someone like W. H. Auden or Louis MacNeice in 1940, under attack for desertion and political backsliding; but it applies also to contemporary poets faced with a British cultural agenda of openness and availability, in which poetry is replaced with poetries, and 'the democratic voice' calls the tune.

In the present book, only a few poets are the objects of sustained attention: among them Yeats, Eliot, Auden, MacNeice, and Hill. By this, I do not intend to launch a radically truncated list of who matters in twentieth-century verse; but I do wish to use these poets as points of attention for critical evaluation that can extend beyond them and their work into the realm of modern poetry in general. If Yeats weighs more heavily than the other names here, this reflects a deliberate recognition of his pre-eminence as a twentieth-century poet; I am not unaware that such a recognition is sometimes viewed (in Britain at least) as another of those embarrassing *faux pas* that simply give the game away: increasingly, an admiration for, or interest in, Geoffrey Hill's work is another sure-fire indication of poor literary breeding. For myself, I do not know (and do not expect ever to know) the identities, still less the ranking, of all the twentieth-century poets who are most important; but I write in the belief that such importance can be felt in the end only through the degree to which their poetry centres itself on form, and remains open to the complexity of the language it uses: in this sense, form is a real poem's final, and binding, authority. In the end, there is nothing a good poem would rather be than the words it is. If learning to live with this, as readers and critics, has some serious difficulties, it is not without its serious rewards.

CHAPTER 2

Yeats and Remorse

Near the end of July 1915, Henry James was busy soliciting on behalf of
Edith Wharton, and addressed Thomas Hardy with a request for a poem
to be written, sent, and received in just under a fortnight. Asking Hardy
'if you *can* manage between now and the 10th to distil the liquor of
your poetic genius, in no matter how mild a form, into three or four
blest versicles', James reassured the poet that 'It is just the stray sincerities and casual felicities of your muse that that intelligent lady [Edith
Wharton] *is* all ready to cherish', and urged him finally to 'overflow, no
matter into how tiny a cup'.[1] Responding (as requested) 'gently and
helpfully', Hardy poured out a generous enough measure for *The Book
of the Homeless*, Wharton's charity venture in aid of Belgian refugees: 'Cry
of the Homeless', which was later to carry the subtitle 'After the
Prussian Invasion of Belgium', filled up three eight-line 'versicles', two
of them voicing the curses of the War's victims on the 'Instigator of the
ruin— | Whichsoever thou mayest be | Of the mastering minds of
Europe | That contrived our misery'.[2] In the final stanza, after the
bitter wish from the 'victims', ' "May thy dearest ones be blighted | And
forsaken... And thy children beg their bread" ', Hardy spoke in an
authorial first-person voice, modulating the poem's curses into something more subtle:

> Nay: too much the malediction.—
> Rather let this thing befall
> In the unfurling of the future,
> On the night when comes thy call:
> That compassion dew thy pillow
> And absorb thy senses all

[1] Henry James, *Letters*, iv: 1895–1916, ed. Leon Edel (Cambridge, Mass.: Harvard University
Press, 1984), 773.
[2] Thomas Hardy, 'Cry of the Homeless', in Edith Wharton (ed.), *The Book of the Homeless*
(New York: Charles Scribner's, 1916), 16.

For thy victims,
Till death dark thee with his pall.

Whatever the extent of this poem's 'casual felicities', its concluding
stanza appears to mark a moment when 'stray sincerities' enable the
voice to return on the rhetoric it has entertained, and concede that it is
in some ways 'too much'. In wishing 'compassion' on what this poem
calls simply the 'Enemy', Hardy allows himself his own instant of
corrective reflection. Writing to James on 8 August (two days ahead
of his deadline), Hardy held on to his misgivings: 'I send the enclosed
page, for what it may be worth, as not quite the right thing.... Anyhow
I hope it may help, though infinitesimally, in the good cause.'[3]

By the time he published it in his volume *Moments of Vision* (1917),
Hardy evidently felt that not every detail of his poem was 'quite the right
thing', having refined the curses of its first two stanzas so that 'thy
dearest ones' (now simply 'thy loved') are no longer just 'blighted | And
forsaken', but 'slighted, blighted | And forsaken', thus giving a full
measure of insult to the original injury.[4] Moreover, the final stanza is
now voiced by the 'victims' rather than the poet, and instead of going
back on a malediction that was 'too much', offers 'a richer malediction'
in a future of 'compassion' that will no longer 'dew' but now 'bedrench
thy pillow'. Although the poem's level of vitriol rises in revision, Hardy
makes his own position more difficult to determine by assigning the last
'malediction' to voices not his own. Other contributors to *The Book of the
Homeless* shared Hardy's revisionary impulse: W. D. Howells, for
example, seems to have had early qualms about his 'The Little Children',
where hapless infants are seized by 'The master-spirit of hell':[5]

through the shuddering air
Of the hope-forsaken world
The little ones he hurled,
Mocking that Pity in his pitiless might—
The Anti-Christ of Schrecklichkeit.

Perhaps feeling that this too was 'too much', Howells attempted to
withdraw the poem shortly after dispatching it; yet the situation was too

---

[3] Thomas Hardy, letter of 8 Aug. 1915, quoted in Thomas Hardy, *Complete Poetical Works*,
vol. ii, ed. Samuel Hynes (Oxford: Clarendon Press, 1984; corr. repr. 1987), 505.

[4] Thomas Hardy, 'Cry of the Homeless: After the Prussian Invasion of Belgium', ibid. ii.
296–7.

[5] William Dean Howells, 'The Little Children', in Wharton (ed.), *The Book of the Homeless*, 17.

late to mend, as Edith Wharton was able to report:[6] 'He sent a ringing little poem to Mr. James, and when he wrote to recall it, Mr. James flatly refused, to my eternal gratitude. The poem is just what I wanted—and curiously enough, it is very much like the one which Mr. Hardy has written for me.' Whatever Howells's second thoughts about his shrill verses in the cause of 'Pity', the 'ringing little poem' fitted in well to the scheme of *The Book of the Homeless*, and was duly printed there, joining Hardy, James himself, and many others, among them W. B. Yeats.

Unlike Hardy (and Howells), Yeats provided a poem which, rather than just prompting later reconsideration, was *already* a kind of recantation of poetic 'meddling' with the times. The six lines, as they appeared in Wharton's book, carried the title 'A Reason for Keeping Silent':[7]

> I think it better that at times like these
> We poets keep our mouths shut, for in truth
> We have no gift to set a statesman right;
> He's had enough of meddling who can please
> A young girl in the indolence of her youth
> Or an old man upon a winter's night.

Sending the poem to the editor, Yeats regretted only that it was not longer;[8] in a letter copying the verses to James, he added some brief reflections:[9]

It is the only thing I have written of the war or will write, so I hope it may not seem unfitting. I shall keep the neighbourhood of the seven sleepers of Ephesus, hoping to catch their comfortable snores till bloody frivolity is over.

Yeats's 'I hope it may not seem unfitting' is in a different key to Hardy's more diffident 'not quite the right thing', for 'It is the only thing I have written of the war or will write' gives the poet's 'hope' a certain air of confidence. The appropriateness of 'A Reason for Keeping Silent' to

[6] Edith Wharton, letter to Sarah Norton, 10 Sept. 1915, quoted in Alan Price, *The End of the Age of Innocence: Edith Wharton and the First World War* (London: Robert Hale, 1996), 66.

[7] W. B. Yeats, 'A Reason for Keeping Silent', in Wharton (ed.), *The Book of the Homeless*, 45.

[8] See Price, *The End of the Age of Innocence*, 63.

[9] W. B. Yeats, letter to Henry James, 20 Aug. 1915, *The Letters of W. B. Yeats*, ed. Allan Wade (London: Rupert Hart-Davis, 1954), 599–600. It is interesting to compare this with opinions expressed in a letter to the poet from his father J. B. Yeats, on 25 Apr. 1915: 'On two subjects I want to share with you some of my wisdom, war versus art. The ego in man, the undying worm from whose [*word indecipherable*] he escapes in the mad and at heart utterly frivolous excitement of war or in the sane and beneficent and profoundly wise excitement of art and poetry.' See Richard J. Finneran, George Mills Harper, and William M. Murphy (eds.), *Letters to W. B. Yeats*, vol. ii (London: Macmillan, 1977), 313.

The Book of the Homeless is not, however, of the same kind as that of Howells's poem, or of Hardy's; the silence it keeps about 'times like these', and the distance it puts between itself and what the letter calls 'bloody frivolity', might constitute not responsible detachment but culpable uninterest.

If Yeats was in some sense in error in the tone of his contribution to Edith Wharton's book, his mistake was not one which acts of local revision could make good. Nor is 'A Reason for Keeping Silent' an isolated occurrence, a freakish mismatch between Yeats's particular kind of imagination and the prevailing circumstances, for another short poem, explicitly addressing the War, shares the same attitude towards acts of 'bloody frivolity':[10]

A Meditation in Time of War

> For one throb of the artery,
> While on that old grey stone I sat
> Under the old wind-broken tree,
> I knew that One is animate,
> Mankind inanimate phantasy.

The determined abstraction of this poem, which sends the reader directly to Yeats's more esoteric concerns with its shorthand mixture of Blake and Neoplatonism, may sit uncomfortably with the facts from which it seems to avert its gaze. All the more so, perhaps, when one sees that the poem's first draft is in a notebook immediately beneath a memorandum of a prophecy made by Olivia Shakespear:[11]

---

[10] W. B. Yeats, *The Variorum Edition of the Poems of W. B. Yeats*, ed. Peter Allt and Russell K. Alspatch (London: Macmillan, 1956), 406.

[11] This note, with a draft of the poem lower on the same page, is in a notebook given to Yeats by Maud Gonne in 1912, and now in the National Library of Ireland (NLI 30, 358 fol. 58ʳ). A photographic reproduction of the page, with a transcription of the poem only, is given in *Michael Robartes and the Dancer: Manuscript Materials*, ed. Thomas Parkinson with Anne Brennan (Ithaca, NY: Cornell University Press, 1994), 194–5. My transcription of Yeats's memorandum about Olivia Shakespeare and her prophecy differs slightly from that given by John Harwood in his *Olivia Shakespeare and W. B. Yeats: After Long Silence* (London: Macmillan, 1989), 138. It is worth noting that the date 'Nov. 9, 1914' appears directly under the memorandum in Yeats's notebook (where the context does seem to make a dating of the prophecy necessary); Harwood takes this to be the date for Yeats's note, and not for the poem which follows. Parkinson and Brennan, perhaps agreeing with this, do not include the date in their transcription of the poem. The other draft of a poem contained in this notebook (on fol. 68ᵛ) is for 'The Rose Tree', and is dated 'April 7. 1917', so 'A Meditation in Time of War' might have been composed around this time. However, 'A Meditation in Time of War' has been dated as 9 Nov. 1914 by some of Yeats's editors, following Richard Ellmann's 'Chronology of the Composition of the Poems' in his *The Identity of Yeats* (London: Macmillan, 1954; 2nd edn.

A few days ago Mrs Shakespear said 'I was praying for the happiness of the souls of those that die in battle' (she had I know been moved by the preyeirs for this object ordered by the Grand Lama) & got the impression 'Peace on Feb 14' I want you to make a note of it

The prophecy was recorded on 9 November 1914; many more 'souls of those that die in battle' were to come to account before Yeats published 'A Meditation in Time of War' in *Michael Robartes and the Dancer* (1921). Whether Yeats took a just measure of such facts has seemed debatable, and it is still possible to find critics who take this poem, together with 'A Reason for Keeping Silent', as powerfully negative evidence against the Yeats 'who had denied a high degree of reality to the Great War, and who refused to write a poem about it on request'.[12]

In the weeks shortly before the Armistice, Yeats's American patron John Quinn wrote to the poet on the subject of the War, and on his part in its literature—too small a part, in Quinn's view:[13]

I never said to you before what I have said frequently to your father, and that was how much I regretted that you had not taken some part on the side of what I have always felt to be justice and right in this war, or at least have spoken some word for France or for the justice and right....I do not mean anything like making a propagandist of yourself or a journalist or anything of that sort, nor the reshaping of your mind and style. I merely mean some expression as an artist in the form either of prose or verse that your genius might take—some token that you felt that in this, perhaps the greatest struggle of all-time, you had been on the side of justice and right.

Although Quinn did not demand any 'reshaping of your mind and style', he thought that change of some kind was in order for Yeats. Quoting the remark of Abbey Theatre actor J. M. Kerrigan that too many Irishmen are 'grave worshippers', Quinn urged Yeats to 'forget' those specifically Irish things which prevented a fuller act of contemporary remembrance:

London: Faber and Faber, 1964), 290: see for example A. Norman Jeffares, *A New Commentary on the Poems of W. B. Yeats* (London: Macmillan, 1984), 207, and *W. B. Yeats: The Poems*, ed. Daniel Albright (London: Dent, 1990), 238. If this short poem was composed *after* 1914, and perhaps a considerable time afterwards (Yeats did not include it in either the 1917 or 1919 vesions of *The Wild Swans at Coole*), then it may be in part a meditation also on the hopes for peace (however oddly received and expressed) of 1914, in the light of later events; its abstractions would be therefore abstractions made *after* the facts, rather than in advance (and innocence) of such things.

[12] Declan Kiberd, *Inventing Ireland* (London: Jonathan Cape, 1995), 246.

[13] John Quinn, postscript of 22 Oct. 1918 to letter dated 2 Oct. 1918, *The Letters of John Quinn to W. B. Yeats*, ed. Alan Himber (Epping: Bowker, 1983), 192.

It is sometimes the highest wisdom to be able to forget. Of course some artists simply cannot make themselves over. For example Joseph Conrad, whose heart is, I know, all in the struggle on the side of right and justice. He has not given any artistic expression to it, except in the one contribution of 'Reminiscences in Poland in War Time' which was published in a book that Mrs. Wharton got up for France. I have not overlooked your little contribution to that book, but those five or six lines were quite unworthy of you and the occasion.

'A Reason for Keeping Silent' is much concerned with worthiness, both to itself and to its occasion; Quinn's criticisms here impugn that sense of what is appropriate in a fundamental way. The question of the War provokes for Quinn the imperative of artists having to 'make themselves over', a phrase which one would not address to W. B. Yeats without a degree of critical deliberation. As Quinn would have known well, Yeats's *Collected Works* of 1908 had included an epigraph in which the poet boasted of his powers of self-reinvention:[14]

> The friends that have it I do wrong
> When ever I remake a song
> Should know what issue is at stake:
> It is myself that I remake.

This friend, however, was quarrelling with Yeats's *failure* to make himself over in relation to the War, and thought he saw specifically Irish reasons for the poet's unwillingness to speak. Quinn's suspicion has been shared by Yeats's critics, and is voiced clearly in Denis Donoghue's declaration that 'The plain fact is that Yeats did not feel inclined to put his genius to work in England's cause.'[15]

Although it is perfectly possible to argue for the profound long-term effects of the First World War on Yeats's poetry, it would be hard to make a case for his having accepted Quinn's advice to provide some immediate 'token' of his support for 'justice and right' or to have 'spoken some word' that might not be construed as equivocal at the time. Yeats did, in fact, remake 'A Reason for Keeping Silent', but he altered the poem only in the direction of stiffer rhetorical grandeur, having the lines now announce themselves as 'On Being Asked for a War Poem', and disposing of 'We poets keep our mouths shut' in favour of 'I think it better that in times like these | A poet's mouth be silent'.[16]

[14] Yeats, *Variorum Poems*, 778.
[15] Denis Donoghue, *We Irish: Selected Essays*, vol. i (Brighton: Harvester, 1986), 185.
[16] Yeats, *Variorum Poems*, 359.

There is just one poet now, and the added sense of dignity, of the poem's worthiness of the poet, could have done little to increase Quinn's admiration of its appropriateness for the times. In fact, far from setting itself to be worthy of its occasion, the poem in question had always adapted occasions to suit itself: Yeats already had the lines when James wrote on behalf of Edith Wharton in July 1915, having written them early in February, with the title 'To a friend who has asked me to sign on his manifesto to the neutral nations'.[17] Some time after *The Book of the Homeless*, a holograph copy made its way into a college library in Massachusetts, as part of the response to an appeal on behalf of 'The Fatherless Children of France'.[18] In 1917 and 1919, the poem took its place in the two versions of Yeats's collection *The Wild Swans at Coole*. In all these (and, it could be said, in subsequent) appearances, the six lines spoke to different occasions; but the poetic stance, for all the poet's minor revisions, remained constant and unapologetic.

Ten years after the end of the War, Yeats embroiled himself in controversy when he rejected Sean O'Casey's play *The Silver Tassie* for the Abbey Theatre, and his reasons for dealing this blow to the playwright developed and consolidated those which had conditioned his writing a decade earlier. In what he described as 'a hateful letter to write', the poet did not flinch from spelling out the grounds of his condemnation:[19]

The mere greatness of the world war has thwarted you; it has refused to become mere background, and obtrudes itself upon the stage as so much dead wood that will not burn with the dramatic fire. Dramatic action is a fire that must burn up everything but itself ... Among the things that dramatic action must burn up are the author's opinions; while he is writing he has no business to know anything that is not a portion of that action.

O'Casey himself was unable to forget or forgive this: remembering Yeats's assertion in the letter that 'You are not interested in the Great War; you never stood on its battlefields', his indignation in the autobiography *Rose and Crown* (1952) was still fresh:[20]

---

[17] See W. B. Yeats, The Wild Swans at Coole: *Manuscript Materials*, ed. Stephen Parrish (Ithaca, NY: Cornell University Press, 1994), 219.

[18] See ibid., p. xiii for details of manuscript in the Dinand Library, College of the Holy Cross, Worcester, Mass.; another holograph fair copy was made by Yeats, and is now in the Burns Library of Rare Books and Special Collections at Boston College (see ibid., p. xii).

[19] W. B. Yeats, letter to Sean O'Casey, 20 Apr. 1928, *Letters*, ed. Wade, p. 471.

[20] Sean O'Casey, *Rose and Crown* (1952), in *Autobiographies*, vol. ii (London: Macmillan, 1981), 275.

Oh, God, here was a man who had never spoken to a Tommy in his life—bar Major Gregory; and to him only because he was an artist as well as a soldier— chattering about soldiers to one who had talked to them all . . . *Not interested* to one who had talked and walked and smoked and sung with the blue-suited, wounded men fresh from the front; to one who had been among the armless, the legless, the blind, the gassed, and the shell-shocked!

O'Casey's outrage, burnt in rather than burnt away with the passing of time, assumes that Yeats has wronged the plain facts of experience; Yeats on the contrary decided that the matter of fact had overcome the artist in O'Casey. Yeats's 'Pages from a Diary in 1930' returns to the controversy, now even more certain of its ground:[21]

The war, as O'Casey has conceived it, is an equivalent for those primary qualities brought down by Berkeley's secret society, it stands outside the characters, it is not part of their expression, it is that very attempt denounced by Mallarmé to build as if with brick and mortar within the pages of a book. The English critics feel differently, to them a theme that 'bulks largely in the news' gives dignity to human nature, even raises it to international importance. We on the other hand are certain that nothing can give dignity to human nature but the character and energy of its expression. We do not even ask that it shall have dignity so long as it can burn away all that is not itself.

The implied violence of Yeats's recurring metaphor, 'burn away', replies to the rejected violence of the War as part of another tit-for-tat exchange in the poet's late manner between the English and 'We Irish'.

Yeats's later pronouncements regarding the War were not to change matters, and his most notorious remarks, in the Introduction to *The Oxford Book of Modern Verse* (1936) revealed an attitude hardened by the years, for which 'passive suffering is not a theme for poetry', and in which the situation of the war poets excluded from his anthology was reshaped as 'some blunderer has driven his car on to the wrong side of the road—that is all'.[22] The poetry of war, it seemed, was anywhere but in the pity. Privately, Yeats was no more accommodating, and wrote of Wilfred Owen as 'all blood, dirt and sucked sugar-stick', conceding only that 'There is every excuse for him, but none for those who like him.'[23] Yet there were those who were unable to excuse Yeats for this, especially

[21] W. B. Yeats, *Explorations* (London: Macmillan, 1962), 339–40.

[22] W. B. Yeats (ed.), *The Oxford Book of Modern Verse 1892–1935* (Oxford: Clarendon Press, 1936), p. xxxiv.

[23] W. B. Yeats, letter to Dorothy Wellesley, 21 Dec. 1936, *Letters*, ed. Wade, p. 874.

as another War cast its shadow over his words, and Stephen Spender's declaration that 'Yeats wrote by saving himself from the mud of Flanders'[24] was one sign of a reaction against his perceived irresponsibility. In 1915 and after, the poet had found his reasons for keeping silent; when the opportunity for redress offered itself, in the anthology twenty years later, Yeats only exacerbated the original affront.

On the face of things, Yeats emerges in this respect as a writer who is singularly lacking in the capacity for conceiving and articulating regret. However, the registers of regretful memory, or retrospective doubt and qualm, are central to a great deal of Yeats's best poetry, and find their focus in his poetic vocabulary with the word 'remorse', a term which denotes something *more* than regret, though also one which suggests significance other than the purely occasional or personal for that regret. For Yeats, remorse exists in the most intimate relation to the poetic impulse, and happens even in the textures of the poetry itself, in the soundings of words' returns on themselves and their sounds, through the structures of rhyme and of repetition; at the same time, remorse is a force against which the poetry exerts its own rhetorical counter-pressures. Sometimes, a victory of sorts is achieved, as in the concluding stanza of 'A Dialogue of Self and Soul':[25]

> I am content to follow to its source
> Every event in action or in thought;
> Measure the lot; forgive myself the lot!
> When such as I cast out remorse
> So great a sweetness flows into the breast
> We must laugh and we must sing,
> We are blest by everything,
> Everything we look upon is blest.

'When such as I cast out remorse...': the reaction of an O'Casey to that 'such as I' may be readily imagined, and would not be disallowed completely by the knowledge that 'I' here does not represent (all of) the poet W. B. Yeats. 'Cast out' poses its own problems: one might cast out devils, but an emotion like remorse is not commonly understood as devilish, and Yeats's voice here seems all too ready to perform its own acts of self-forgiveness and exorcism in a manner quite incompatible

---

[24] Stephen Spender, 'Tragedy and some Modern Poetry', *Penguin New Writing*, 4 (Mar. 1941), 147.
[25] Yeats, *Variorum Poems*, 479.

with actual sorrow or regret. In his account of his own early writings in
The Trembling of the Veil (1922), Yeats identified remorse as a problem:[26]

For ten or twelve years more I suffered continual remorse, and only became
content when my abstractions had composed themselves into picture and
dramatization. My very remorse helped to spoil my early poetry, giving it an
element of sentimentality through my refusal to permit it any share of an
intellect which I considered impure.

When Yeats recalls his own younger sense of the inappropriateness of
poetic abstraction to the matter of life and plain facts, he identifies a
disabling remorse there; and this puts him in good poetic company,
since he had claimed Edmund Spenser as 'the first poet struck with
remorse' in his selection from that poet in 1906, where the demands of
Elizabethan religion and policy were seen as responsible for the remorseful impulse to allegorize of 'the first poet who gave his heart to the
State'.[27] The word 'remorse' sounds through much of the later Yeats,
and in *The Winding Stair*, where the Self casts out remorse in its dialogue
with the Soul, there is also 'The Choice', with its presentation of the
alternatives of 'The day's vanity, the night's remorse',[28] and the poem
'Remorse for Intemperate Speech', with its final acknowledgement of
the Irish 'Great hatred, little room' that 'Maimed us at the start'.[29] At the
beginning of the sequence 'Vacillation', the destructive 'brand, or flam-
ing breath' is given a double identification: 'The body calls it death, |
The heart remorse.'[30] Announcing 'The first principle' in 'A General
Introduction for My Work' (1937), Yeats declares that 'A poet writes
always of his personal life, in his finest work out of its tragedy, whatever
it be, remorse, lost love, or mere loneliness.'[31] The very late play
Purgatory ends with the bleak prayer to God to 'appease | The misery
of the living and the remorse of the dead'.[32] The meaning of Yeatsian
remorse is clearly something other than simple regret, and its function
is quite distinct from that of apology or reparation. The definition of
remorse offered by the *OED* (*sb.* 2a), 'A feeling of compunction, or of
deep regret and repentance, for a sin or wrong committed', introduces

[26] W. B. Yeats, *Autobiographies* (London: Macmillan, 1955), 188.
[27] W. B. Yeats, 'Edmund Spenser', *Essays and Introductions* (London: Macmillan, 1961), 373.
[28] Yeats, *Variorum Poems*, 495.
[29] Ibid. 506.
[30] Ibid. 500.
[31] Yeats, *Essays and Introductions*, 509.
[32] W. B. Yeats, *Collected Plays* (London: Macmillan, 1952), 689.

elements that seem almost completely absent from Yeats's uses for the word. Most importantly, remorse for the later Yeats is something which has its dealings with the dead, and which can also describe the dead's business with the living.

To define Yeats's remorse in this way is to claim an intimacy between the word and those obsessions with spiritualism, magic, and esoteric and arcane traditions which run through almost the whole of the poet's writing life. However, such a definition also helps to locate this remorse historically, for it is during the First World War that Yeats, at the same time as he makes the breakthrough effected by and in the automatic script of his wife George, discovers remorse as a potent term in his imaginative vocabulary. If specific War casualties were bearing in on Yeats at this time—Sir Hugh Lane, perhaps, or later Major Robert Gregory—a much more numerous army of 'those that die in battle' could no more be ignored by the poet than they were by a public eager for the consolations of a belief in the afterlife, as exercised in the church or the seance-room. In the light of this, it is possible to see Yeats's writing about the War as including *A Vision* (1925) along with the many poems which, remorsefully and remorselessly, speak to, for, and some-times against the dead.

By the time Lady Gregory's son Robert was killed in action on 23 January 1918, Yeats was already absorbed creatively in the dynamics of death and remorse. In his attempt at a pastoral elegy for Robert, 'Shepherd and Goatherd', Yeats had to hand a developed theory of the 'dreaming back' of the dead. In the poem, the process is misleadingly (though understandably in the circumstances) consolatory in its effect:[33]

> Jaunting, journeying
> To his own dayspring,
> He unpacks the loaded pern
> Of all 'twas pain or joy to learn,
> Of all that he had made.
> The outrageous war shall fade ...

Behind this is a theme which, although it becomes elaborate in the automatic writings of 1917 and afterwards, had roots deep in Yeats's customary preoccupations. In *Per Amica Silentia Lunae*, finished just before George's communications began, Yeats gives the idea a high rhetorical polish, writing that 'The toil of the living is to free themselves

---

[33] Yeats, *Variorum Poems*, 342.

from an endless sequence of objects, and that of the dead to free themselves from an endless sequence of thoughts.'[34] In 'Shepherd and Goatherd' Robert Gregory dreams back his life without pain or remorse, but Yeats knew that other thoughts beside these could be assigned to his ghost, and was to write a poem in 1920 in which these 'second thoughts' could be spelled out. By this time, Yeats is able to confront the dead with history, and demand remorse from both the dead and the living.

To measure the distance between Yeats's writings at the beginning of the War, and his attitudes by 1920 and the writing of 'Reprisals', is to encounter a number of plain facts lodged in history, which affected the poet in more and less profound ways. Of course, the significance of such historical matter is nothing like so plain: that the most catastrophic event in Irish history in the year 1916, for example, should have been ignored by Yeats seems unlikely. And yet the dead from the Irish and Ulster Divisions at the Somme are silent in Yeats's writing, and are silenced in much Irish history, while the dead of the Dublin insurrection of 1916 enjoyed, and continue to enjoy, a much more active afterlife. By the time of the poem 'Reprisals', the War had come to Ireland in the shape of the Black and Tans; Yeats voices anger and bitterness, forcing Gregory's ghost to face the brutal matter:[35]

> Yet rise from your Italian tomb,
> Flit to Kiltartan Cross and stay
> Till certain second thoughts have come
> Upon the cause you served, that we
> Imagined such a fine affair:
> Half-drunk or whole-mad soldiery
> Are murdering your tenants there ...

[34] W. B. Yeats, *Mythologies* (London: Macmillan, 1959), 353–4.

[35] The text of 'Reprisals' quoted here is that of the typescript which Yeats sent to Lady Gregory in a letter of 26 Nov. 1920, as reproduced in The Wild Swans at Coole: *Manuscript Materials*, ed. Parrish, p. 423. The textual history of the poem is an involved one: its first publication was posthumous, in *Rann: An Ulster Quarterly of Poetry* (Autumn 1948), in a text deriving from a MS fair copy in Yeats's hand (NLI 13,358), which went on to be the basis of the text of 'Reprisals' in *Variorum Poems* and some subsequent editions. The typescript sent to Lady Gregory is regarded as more authoritative by Richard J. Finneran in *Editing Yeats's Poems: A Reconsideration* (London: Macmillan, 1990), 147–151, where the matter of the poem's early history is discussed in detail. It appears that a third version of the poem was available to T. R. Henn, whose 1965 lecture 'Yeats and the Poetry of War' quotes in full a text 'taken down from [Peter] Allt himself, in 1947, which seems to me far more Yeatsian' (*Proceedings of the British Academy*, 51 (1965), 310, repr. in T. R. Henn, *Last Essays* (Gerrards Cross: Colin Smythe, 1976), 89). However, Henn's lecture seems now to be the only source for this text of 'Reprisals'.

A note in Yeats's hand on a draft of the poem records a remark made by Gregory to the poet, that 'I see no reason why anyone should fight in this war except friendship', and that 'The England I care for was dead long ago'.[36] When he instructs Gregory's ghost to 'stay | Till certain second thoughts have come', Yeats does so in the context of rethinkings of his own, most clearly expressed in the opening of a manuscript version of the poem:[37]

> Some nineteen German planes, they say,
> You had brought down before you died.
> We called it a good death. To day,
> Can ghost or man be satisfied?

To go back over things is not the same as being able to go back on them: 'We called it a good death'—and yet, as the poem ruthlessly records, we were wrong. What is more (and what is worse), there is no going back open to the voice in this poem, just as there is no possibility of regret open to the ghost itself. A last couplet instructs Gregory to 'stop your ears with dust and lie | Among the other cheated dead', advice which echoes the bitter send-off given to Parnell in 'To a Shade' (1913), 'Away, away! You are safer in the tomb'.[38]

In appearing to demand remorse from its subject and then, failing to elicit this, giving him his marching orders, Yeats's 'Reprisals' follows a remorseless rhetorical course. In this sense, at least, it needs to be distinguished from the poet's other Gregory poems, as Yeats himself knew: it was written to the moment, and for a purpose, 'because I thought it might touch some one individual mind of a man in power'.[39] The atrocities which the poem bridles at are those it hopes it might help put an end to; bound originally for *The Nation*, and then for *The Times*, 'Reprisals' was written as a provocative poem, but the poet hoped that it would also provoke remorse among at least some of its English readership. Yeats was pleased with the poem, and had to have second thoughts forced upon him by Lady Gregory:[40]

---

[36] This note is on the verso of a MS fair copy (NLI 13,583), and is quoted by Finneran in *Editing Yeats's Poems: A Reconsideration*, 150.

[37] NLI 13,583, reproduced in The Wild Swans at Coole: *Manuscript Materials*, ed. Parrish, p. 422.

[38] Yeats, *Variorum Poems*, 293.

[39] W. B. Yeats, letter to Lady Gregory, 3 Dec. 1920, quoted in Finneran, *Editing Yeats's Poems: A Reconsideration*, 151.

[40] *Lady Gregory's Journals*, vol. i, ed. Daniel J. Murphy (Gerrards Cross: Colin Smythe, 1978), 207.

I cannot bear the dragging of R., from his grave to make what I think a not very sincere poem—for Yeats knows only by hearsay while our troubles go on—and he quoted words G.B.S., told him and did not mean him to repeat—and which will give pain—I hardly know why it gives me extraordinary pain and it seems too late to stop it...

It was not too late; the poem was stopped; and Yeats himself (whether remorsefully, regretfully, or forgetfully) did not include it in a future collection. Whatever the reasons for this occlusion, 'Reprisals' is a poem in which Yeats's imagination allows itself to become opportunistic, and in which the dead (whether Gregory in his 'Italian tomb' or the victims of the Black and Tans) are too simply pressed into service. There is a damaging sense in which 'Reprisals' cheats on the dead when it declares them to have been 'cheated', and the distortion which its (proper) outrage at the news from Ireland forces on the War is a part of that cheating which no amount of just intentions on the poet's part can make good. Lady Gregory thought it better that, in times like those, poets should keep their mouths shut—at least, if their words were to pay less than respect to either the truth or the dead—and Yeats may have come to agree with her. At any rate, the passive suffering which 'Reprisals' tries to force on Gregory's ghost was not a theme for Yeats's best poetry.

When Yeats wanted to engineer remorse in a public register, he insisted on 'second thoughts' as the trigger, and his own more private experiences lay behind this, suggesting as they did the possibilities (and the liabilities) of going back over the past. Again, the point at which the dynamics of personal regret and self-doubt begin to charge Yeats's work with energies of remorse comes during the War, in the flurry of ultimatums and decisions surrounding his marriage in 1917. Certainly, the Yeats who wrote to Lady Gregory on 19 September of that year was burdened by worries, about his love life, the reasonableness of his own behaviour, and the intrusiveness upon all this of the War. With Maud Gonne and her daughter Iseult excluded from Ireland under the Defence of the Realm Act, the poet found himself in 'rather a whirlpool':[41]

Poor Iseult was very depressed on the journey and at Havre went off by herself and cried. Because she was so ashamed 'at being so selfish' 'at not wanting me to marry and so break her friendship with me.' I need hardly say she had said nothing to me of 'not wanting.' Meanwhile she has not faltered in her refusal of me but as you can imagine life is a good deal at white heat. I think of going to

[41] W. B. Yeats, letter to Lady Gregory, 18 Sept. 1917, *Letters*, ed. Wade, p. 632.

Mrs. Tucker's on Monday but may not as I am feeling rather remorseful especially now that this last business of the defence of the realm act has come.

The next day, Yeats reported that 'I am going to Mrs. Tucker's in the country ... and I will ask her daughter to marry me.'[42] Even this decisive (and successful) proposal did not put an immediate end to the poet's personal remorsefulness, and a honeymooning Yeats found himself 'in great gloom', and 'saying to myself "I have betrayed three people" '.[43] It is easy to say grandly of Yeats that 'The transformations of art ... are closely bound up with betrayal',[44] but the enduring costs of such 'transformations' are more difficult to account for; and here, certainly, the meaning and role of remorse are at issue. With three people betrayed (Maud, Iseult, and his bride George), it is understandable that a pair of short poems from Yeats's period of 'gloom', subsequently titled 'Owen Aherne and his Dancers' (and thus put within the fictional orbit of *A Vision*), should figure remorse prominently:[45]

> A strange thing surely that my Heart, when love had come unsought
> Upon the Norman upland or in that poplar shade,
> Should find no burden but itself and yet should be worn out.
> It could not bear that burden and therefore it went mad.
>
> The south wind brought it longing, and the east wind despair,
> The west wind made it pitiful, and the north wind afraid.
> It feared to give its love a hurt with all the tempest there;
> It feared the hurt that she could give and therefore it went mad.

In these lines, from the first of the poems, the Lover's dilemma is to be cornered by fear of emotional facts that are all too plain, and the Heart's apparent madness is presented as the result of being put in an impossible position. However, Yeats provides a companion poem, in which the Heart can have its say, this time in open opposition to the earlier verses assigned to the voice of the Lover. Now, the attitude is one that mocks the Lover's responsible worries: 'Let the cage bird and the cage bird mate and the wild bird mate in the wild.' Yeats begins and ends this second poem with the Heart's reckless dismissal of the Lover's misgivings, but he lodges a stanza of remorse, voiced for the lover, in the poem's midst:

---

[42] Yeats, letter to Lady Gregory, 19 Sept. 1917, ibid. 633.
[43] Yeats, letter to Lady Gregory, 29 Oct. 1917, ibid. 633.
[44] Stan Smith, *The Origins of Modernism: Eliot, Pound, Yeats and the Rhetorics of Renewal* (Hemel Hempstead: Harvester Wheatsheaf, 1994), 179.
[45] Yeats, *Variorum Poems*, 449–50.

'You but imagine lies all day, O murderer,' I replied.
'And all those lies have but one end, poor wretches to betray;
I did not find in any cage the woman at my side.
O but her heart would break to learn my thoughts are far away.'

'Owen Aherne and his Dancers' is not an overbalancing or a lopsided dialogue; although the Heart has the last word, it does not refute the Lover's accusation that 'You but imagine lies'. Instead, the Heart retorts by bringing to bear other home truths:

'Speak all your mind,' my Heart sang out, 'speak all your mind; who cares,
Now that your tongue cannot persuade the child till she mistake
Her childish gratitude for love and match your fifty years?
O let her choose a young man now and all for his wild sake.'

The air is thick with 'lies' in this debate, where each participant tries to force second thoughts upon the other. The poem's final exultation, in other words, resonates also with the echoes of self-doubt and remorse. The effect achieved by Yeats here has been described as 'disturbed and disturbing',[46] and this accounts accurately for the relative states of the two voices, one stricken with paralysis, the other goading and relentless in its mockery. Each side alleges facts against the other, and the facts lie plainly on both sides of the argument. However uncomfortable Yeats might have felt, his poetry was able to thrive in such an impossible position, and he sent the paired poems to Lady Gregory with the comment that 'they are among the best I have done'.[47]

In biographical terms, the breaking of this particular stalemate in Yeats's emotional life might seem miraculous; the poet himself would have applied that term, though in doing so he might have been rather more literal in intent, for George's automatic writing, which constituted the otherworldly intervention in 1917, did something decisive with some all too recalcitrant facts. Not least, the messages which George supplied spoke directly to Yeats's sense of remorse, and about it, in an idiom which enabled the poet to construct a system in which that remorse might find its place. On a personal level, George encouraged the poet to inspect his past—and especially the 'Crisis Moments' in his emotional past—in the light of ideas of character, fate, and passion which are developed from themes already present in his writing. One

---

[46] Elizabeth Butler Cullingford, *Gender and History in Yeats's Love Poetry* (Cambridge: Cambridge University Press, 1993), 105.

[47] Yeats, letter to Lady Gregory, 29 Oct. 1917, *Letters*, ed. Wade, 634.

early communication enjoins both 'self knowledge' and 'anihilation [*sic*] of the concealed', and recommends 'confession':[48]

[Question] What do you mean by confession.
[Response] Confession is preceded by self knowledge—confession itself implies a need for human sympathy & expansion of the nature—the word is perhaps implying too much the idea of christian conf[ession] & repentance—I mean it as an acknowledgement of weakness or an acknowledgement of the need of all human beings for protection in one side of their nature...

The process of emotional defrosting which George's writing encouraged can be seen here, and its supernatural and symbolic accompaniments need to be understood partly as an idiom of reference which husband and wife shared. If 'repentance' was unhelpful at this stage (and also, in some ways, by this stage pointless), 'acknowledgement of weakness' was an area in which, increasingly, Yeats's creative strength lay. What was more, the crossing of 'self knowledge' with more esoteric concerns gave the poet's habitual preoccupations a new lease of life.

As usual, such vitality in Yeats exists in close proximity to, and attempts to draw its energy from the dead. In *Per Amica Silentia Lunae*, where 'The dead, living in their memories are... the source of all that we call instinct',[49] Yeats had already sketched out the lines connecting the dead, memory, judgement, and the self which George's automatic writing (and, in time, *A Vision*) would elaborate:[50]

We carry to *Anima Mundi* our memory, and that memory is for a time our external world; and all passionate moments recur again and again, for passion desires its own recurrence more than any event, and whatever there is of corresponding complacency or remorse is our beginning of judgment; nor do we remember only the events of life, for thoughts bred of longing and of fear, all those parasitic vegetables that have slipped through our fingers, come again like a rope's end to smite us upon the face...

'Memory' is the medium in which 'passionate moments' come back on the self as they 'recur again and again'; the 'remorse' which figures here in Yeats's prose is the same remorse which becomes part of the process of 'dreaming back' explored in George's automatic script, where the whole

---

[48] George Mills Harper (general ed.), *Yeats's Vision Papers*, i: *The Automatic Script 5 November 1917–18 June 1918*, ed. Steve L. Adams, Barbara J. Frieling, and Sandra Sprayberry (London: Macmillan, 1992), 90. This message is dated 20 Nov. 1917.
[49] Yeats, *Mythologies*, 359.
[50] Ibid. 354.

idea of recurrence is elevated into a central principle of historical as well as personal fate. In the system which George and her husband developed, the destiny of the individual soul is to go back over its lives again and again, and the fate of civilizations is to re-enter cycle after cycle of growth and decay. Both processes are marked by moments of cataclysmic significance, which become the focal points for Yeats's poetic attention. While poems like 'The Second Coming' and 'Byzantium' emerge from Yeats's fascination with points of historical change, and attempt some measure of detachment from the scenes upon which they magnificently spectate, the poet's need to go back over the matter of memory, and the 'passionate moments' which found their place in the more personalized aspects of the symbolic system, make self-scrutiny and unsparing recollection necessary. Above all, in this supernaturally shadowed brooding on 'self knowledge', Yeats is able both to figure remorse in his writing, and to take his writing beyond remorse. Like his efforts to make good a creative detachment from the catastrophes of history, Yeats's inspections of and departures from remorse run the risk of seeming to outrun (culpably, for some of his readers) the plain facts, and to forget too readily or wilfully those loose ends of personal or public history which recur again and again, and come back, as it were, to smite him upon the face.

Yeats saw remorse as something distinct from action, and grew increasingly convinced of the need for art to include and forward action. Passivity, as Yeats understood it, could produce only an art of inertia, and this was a tendency he was able to detect retrospectively in some of his own early writing, and in that of his contemporaries. *The Trembling of the Veil* broods over the fate of a whole 'Tragic Generation' of artists whose defiance of things as they are carries with it a high cost in terms of inaction, self-delusion, and remorse. This is most subtly explored in Yeats's depiction of Oscar Wilde, but is a theme which brings many of his contemporaries into the same fold. Accounting for William Sharp's belief in his own literary alter ego, for example, Yeats recalls how 'he had created an imaginary beloved, had attributed to her the authorship of all his books that had any talent, and though habitually a sober man, I have known him to get drunk, and at the height of his intoxication when most men speak the truth, to attribute his state to remorse for having been unfaithful to Fiona Macleod.'[51] Similar paralysis afflicts Lionel Johnson, 'who could not have written *The Dark Angel* if he did not suffer from

---

[51] Yeats, *Autobiographies*, 341.

remorse', and who, despite the fact of his alcoholism 'showed to friends an impenitent face'.[52] Going over the past in his autobiographical writings, Yeats sees remorse as a state producing paralysed repetition— or in the case of Ernest Dowson paralytic repetition: 'the last time I saw Dowson he was pouring out a glass of whiskey for himself in an empty corner of my room and murmuring over and over in what seemed automatic apology, "The first to-day." '[53] The cast of Yeats's 'Tragic Generation' go over and over the same things, as incapable of action in their lives as they are, being dead, for Yeats in 1922. Thus, when Yeats invokes Matthew Arnold against Owen and other war poets, it is the Arnold of the 1853 Preface, who stands in judgement on his own work, doing away with *Empedocles on Etna* on the grounds that 'the suffering finds no vent in action . . . there is everything to be endured, nothing to be done'.[54] By 1936, Yeats had found plenty for his own poetry to do; and one crucial thing done in the verse was the poet's listening to the sounds of his own endurance, and his ability to go back over those sounds.

It is no more than a truism to say that Yeats's poetry, from a very early stage, tends towards patterns of verbal and rhythmic repetition. However, there is a critical tendency to treat repetition in poetry as a device only, and an unremarkable one at that; whereas for Yeats (as for many other poets) such specifics of poetic texture are never simply formalities. In the matter of memory, with its possibilities of remorse, Yeats's poetry is especially prone and alert to recurring sounds. Even the contrived stasis of an early poem like 'He Wishes for the Cloths of Heaven' depends largely on the surprise effect of having what should be the rhyme words repeat themselves exactly, so that 'Tread softly because you tread on my dreams'[55] comes to possess a certain intransigence of relentless (and perhaps remorse-provoking) suffering. In the later Yeats, such returns of sound carry strong and complex charges. In a draft of section V of the sequence 'Vacillation' (a section that initially bore the title 'Remorse'), the triggers for remorseful memory include 'a sound':[56]

> Blunders of thirty years ago
> Or said or done but yesterday
> Or what I did not say or do

---

[52] Ibid. 312.   [53] Ibid.
[54] Matthew Arnold, Preface to *Poems* (1853), *The Poems of Matthew Arnold*, ed. Kenneth Allott, 2nd edn. ed. Miriam Allott (London: Longman, 1979), 656.
[55] Yeats, *Variorum Poems*, 176.
[56] Quoted in Richard Ellmann, *The Identity of Yeats* (1964), 272–3.

> But that I thought to do or say
> A word or sound and I recall
> Things that my conscience and my vanity appall.

'A word or sound' can be caught up in the patterns of recurrence where
remorse figures, and threatens the paralysis of memories stuck in the
grooves of their own repetition. Again, the crises and resolutions in
Yeats's personal life during the First World War produce poems in
which repetition becomes a major force. In 'Broken Dreams', written
for Maud Gonne in 1915, the element of repetition may be a force for a
profound inertia, and the poem's coda-like conclusion seems to acknowledge as much:[57]

> The last stroke of midnight dies.
> All day in the one chair
> From dream to dream and rhyme to rhyme I have ranged
> In rambling talk with an image of air:
> Vague memories, nothing but memories.

This final line has become a kind of irregularly returning refrain; finishing the poem with the line intensifies a sense that the voice has not gone
beyond this point (nor wanted to get beyond it), and its recurrence
becomes a kind of reassurance, with its internal repetition almost
comforting. This measure of resignation (and, it may be, of passive
suffering) has left behind the raw wounds present in early stages of the
poem's composition, where Yeats remembered 'The lineaments that
peirced [*sic*] my life with pain | Till it could have no life but memories'.[58]
'Broken Dreams', which ranges from repetition to repetition, is a poem
in which Yeats sounds out measures of resignation, but also one in
which he takes the measure of such resignation, and balances against an
imagined afterlife in which Gonne's beauty will be restored the small,
actual imperfections ('Your small hands were not beautiful') which
survive the vagueness of the 'memories'.

   However problematic it may be in its context, the final line of 'Broken
Dreams' echoes into other writings in which Yeats takes the measure of
regret. On the back of one of the pages on which the elegy 'Shepherd and
Goatherd' is composed, a fragment in four-stress couplets begins by

---

[57] Yeats, *Variorum Poems*, 356.
[58] Holograph of 'Broken Dreams' (NLI 30,370 fol. 2ʳ), reproduced and transcribed in The
Wild Swans at Coole: Manuscript Materials, ed. Parrish, pp. 186–7.

hearing again the words and rhythm of 'Vague memories, nothing but memories', and paring them down:[59]

> Memories upon memories
> Have bowed my head upon my knees.
> A dying boy with handsome face
> Upturned upon a beaten place,
> A sacred yew tree on a strand
> A woman that holds in steady hand
> A burning wisp beside a door
> And many and many a woman more[.]
> And not another thought than these
> Have bowed my head upon my knees.

Yeats then alters his final couplet to produce 'Memories upon memories | Have bowed my head upon my knees'. If the fragment has a connection with 'Shepherd and Goatherd' and Robert Gregory (as seems likely), it records a more personal corollary of the 'dreaming back' which the airman's ghost experiences in the poem proper, where 'He grows younger every second', so that 'The outrageous war shall fade';[60] here, powerful and inscrutable symbolic images are canvassed, but the paralysis of passive recollection takes over, leaving the voice to murmur over its 'Memories upon memories'.

There is another context for these lines, or at least a suggestive parallel for them, in Yeats's wartime writings. In the play *The Only Jealousy of Emer*, which was much on the poet's mind in the first year of George's automatic writing, and in fact featured on occasion as the subject-matter of the spirit communications, the character of Cuchulain is depicted in relation to three female figures: his wife Emer, his mistress Eithne Inguba, and the supernatural Fand, a woman of the Sidhe. Given Yeats's anxieties over his having 'betrayed three women', the play's engagement with love, possessiveness, and renunciation is biographically loaded, as its author and his wife well knew. If the play's subject-matter is familiar, so is some of its language, as when Cuchulain's ghostly form converses with Fand:[61]

---

[59] Holograph, Berg Collection, New York Public Library (Quinn (14)). The lines quoted here are on the verso of leaf 4 of the five leaves of draft materials for 'Shepherd and Goatherd': they are reproduced and transcribed in The Wild Swans at Coole: *Manuscript Materials*, ed. Parrish, pp. 418–19.

[60] Yeats, *Variorum Poems*, 342.

[61] Yeats, *Collected Plays*, 291.

Woman of the Sidhe What pulled your hands about your feet,
Pulled down your head upon your knees,
And hid your face?

Ghost of Cuchulain Old memories:
A woman in her happy youth
Before her man had broken troth,
Dead men and women. Memories
Have pulled my head upon my knees.

As his body lies between life and death, Cuchulain's ghost is tempted away from the weight of recollection, the 'memories' which 'Weigh down my hands, abash my eyes'. While there is a recollection of 'Broken Dreams' here (and in the fragment relating to 'Shepherd and Goatherd' obviously related to the play), there is also the most glancing of allusions to another poem of 1915 in the word 'abash'. This poem, 'The People', remembers and restages an argument between Yeats and Maud Gonne, letting Maud's dignified reply face down and cast doubt upon the poet's pride and affected haughtiness; at the poem's conclusion, the voice of the poet is chastened again in its recollection of the original mistake:[62]

> And yet, because my heart leaped at her words,
> I was abashed, and now they come to mind
> After nine years, I sink my head abashed.

'Abashed . . . abashed' taps into the distinctive energies of poetic repetition: the poet is abashed twice—nine years ago and now—but he is also brought up against the word's sound again, and its reiteration makes audible a humiliation that has become a sticking-point. 'Abashed' comes back like a rope's end that smites the poet on the face. The Yeats who wrote these lines (unusually for one of his lyric poems, they are in blank verse) had learned much from listening to Wordsworth, the great English poet of repetition, in Ezra Pound's renditions during the wartime winters spent at Stone Cottage.[63] When 'abash' returns in *The Only Jealousy of Emer*, it comes in a different formal element, the ritualistic rhymed tetrameters in which one world converses with another; now, as Fand woos Cuchulain's ghost away from the vestiges of its humanity, memory must be erased altogether:[64]

---

[62] Yeats, *Variorum Poems*, 353.

[63] James Longenbach, *Stone Cottage: Pound, Yeats, and Modernism* (New York: Oxford University Press, 1988), 142–3.

[64] Yeats, *Collected Plays*, 292.

> *Woman of the Sidhe* Then kiss my mouth. Though memory
> Be beauty's bitterest enemy
> I have no dread, for at my kiss
> Memory on the moment vanishes:
> Nothing but beauty can remain.
>
> *Ghost of Cuchulain* And shall I never know again
> Intricacies of blind remorse?

With 'Memory on the moment vanishes' the rhythm, for a moment, flutters out of its course, and the repetitive, four-beat measure in which memories recur seems, for a breath, to be loosening its grip. Cuchulain's question to Fand is sunk in the rhythm it hopes perhaps to leave behind when it forsakes remorse along with memory. Fand's last lines to Cuchulain promise a remorseless 'oblivion':[65]

> But what could make you fit to wive
> With flesh and blood, being born to live
> Where no one speaks of broken troth,
> For all have washed out of their eyes
> Wind-blown dirt of their memories
> To improve their sight?

Cuchulain, on the verge of vanishing forever with Fand, is reclaimed for humanity only by his wife Emer's last-minute decision to renounce his love. For Yeats, in the process of both inspecting and finding ways around his own 'Intricacies of blind remorse', the scene's incantatory rhyming towards and away from the hold of memory has a certain exploratory significance.

The rhythmic effects of repetition had always, in some obvious senses, been important to Yeats; his early poetry is often essentially incantatory, and years of effort, experiment, and thinking went into his practice, with associated excursions into the speaking of dramatic poetry, and the virtues offered by Florence Farr's psaltery accompaniments. But the question of poetic rhythm's hold on reality changes and deepens as Yeats grows, and by the time of the First World War it has taken on new dimensions. Now the stakes are higher: memory, the dead, betrayal, action, and remorse are all implicit in poetry's rhythmic integrity, or its lack of integrity, but they are also concerns which might find blunter expression in the resistance put up to such poetry by an all too intrusive historical situation. When John Quinn chastised Yeats with

[65] Ibid. 293.

'It is sometimes the highest wisdom to be able to forget', he underestimated the complexity of the ways in which poetry remembers, and of
Yeats's own knowledge (and experience) of this; whatever his *bona fides*
on the subject of Ireland, England, and the War, Quinn's demand that
Yeats do something 'on the side of right and justice' was too confident
of what it took to be the facts of the matter. When Yeats writes 'Easter
1916', a poem in which the historical ironies of the insurrection's self-
consciousness are given full rein, he does so with memory as his subject,
and the poem concludes with the incantatory creation of memory, as the
voice 'murmur[s] name upon name'.[66] 'Easter 1916' takes full measure
of its dead and, in fundamental ways, questions them and subjects them
to the forces of historical chance and irony; in creating their memory as
a historical meaning, the poem shapes the dead into a deliberate, quasi-
liturgical rhythm, sealed up behind the marble walls of the polished and
emphatic refrain that structures and ends the poem. 'Changed, changed
utterly' is built on a dead repetition, one which acknowledges grimly
that, from now on, there will indeed be no change.

    The dead of 'Easter 1916' are not the living men and women of
Yeats's memory; like the dead in the poet's supernatural system, they
have become a force to reckon with, 'living in their memories'. The
poem's Irish context and meanings have this as their starting-point, but
Yeats's procedure here derives also from his protracted encounter with
the special demands of the dead as these presented themselves to him in
wartime. Irish history makes the Dublin dead of 1916 an obvious source
for much subsequent imagination and action; but Yeats's sense of the
dead as a 'source', which conditions the poem, continues to develop in
his writing, in ways which perhaps try to address Quinn's desire for
something 'on the side of justice and right'. Yeats's equivalent to that
phrase, when he describes the abstractions of *A Vision* as elements
which 'have helped me to hold in a single thought reality and justice',[67]
has two sides to it, and summarizes a process in which the dead are both
accommodated and resisted. The place of remorse in this, and of the
sounds and rhythms of remorse in Yeats's poetry, help to explain the
poet's ambivalence about the dead as a 'source'.

    Looking for the source of action was a habit well known to Yeats, and
one which he experienced in both personal and historical speculations.

---

[66] Yeats, *Variorum Poems*, 394.
[67] W. B. Yeats, *A Vision* (London: Macmillan, 1937), 25.

But when, in the Self's final stanza in 'A Dialogue of Self and Soul', 'source' is rhymed with 'remorse', the connection for Yeats is a matter of something more than either chance or convenience, and refigures earlier connections of the idea of 'source' and those of judgement and dreaming-back in *A Vision*. Of the personality at Phase 26, for example, Yeats says that 'His own past actions also he must judge as isolated and each in relation to its source; and this source, experienced not as love but as knowledge, will be present in his mind as a terrible unflinching judgment.'[68] Describing 'The Return', Yeats again fixes on 'the source':[69]

During this state which is commonly called the *Teaching* he is brought into the presence, as far as possible, of all sources of the action he must presently, till he has explored every consequence, dream through. This passion for the source is brought to him from his own *Celestial Body* which perpetually, being of the nature of *Fate*, dreams the events of his life backward through him.

When the Self announces that 'I am content to follow to its source | Every event in action or in thought', it is preparing to quarrel in the most fundamental way with 'a terrible unflinching judgement'; defying the Soul in Yeats's 'Dialogue', the Self will also face down the dead by judging itself, forgiving itself, and casting out remorse. In the stanza's strong and supple *ottava rima*, the rhyme for 'source' is deployed only to be rejected, and the connection of sounds is made only to be superseded by other, liberating forms of rhyming and rhythmic connection.[70]

The stanzaic nature of so much of Yeats's poetry from *The Wild Swans at Coole* onwards offers the poet opportunities of self-dramatization, but also presents him with a medium in which the rhetorical momentum can change in relation to the returns, postponements, confirmations, and surprises of rhyme. If the couplet, for Yeats, sounds out the dynamics of fate and inevitability, then stanzaic structures are those of freedom and action. In one sense, stanzaic forms give opportunities for Yeats to put remorse in its place, and it is this which the Self uses to its own advantage in the 'Dialogue'. In 'The Choice', a single stanza of *ottava rima*, the more expansive range of the 'Dialogue' has been compressed:[71]

---

[68] W. B. Yeats, *A Vision* (1925), quoted from *A Critical Edition of Yeats's* A Vision *(1925)*, ed. George Mills Harper and Walter Kelly Hood (London: Macmillan, 1978), 112.

[69] Ibid. 225.

[70] See Ch. 6 below, 141–2.

[71] Yeats, *Variorum Poems*, 495.

> The intellect of man is forced to choose
> Perfection of the life, or of the work,
> And if it take the second must refuse
> A heavenly mansion, raging in the dark.
> When all that story's finished, what's the news?
> In luck or out the toil has left its mark:
> That old perplexity an empty purse,
> Or the day's vanity, the night's remorse.

Despite the appearance of insistently binary divisions, it is not clear that the poem acknowledges the reality of any choice at all: the intellect is not free to choose, but 'forced' to do so, and the terms of its choice are slewed towards 'the work'. However bitterly, the poem represents 'toil' and its consequences rather than any putative 'perfection of the life', and it follows the traces of this in its chain of rhymes, from 'work' to 'dark', to 'mark', preparing for a concluding couplet in which the plain fact of 'an empty purse' rhymes with 'remorse', and provides its own untranscendent gloss on that term. Furthermore, despite its internal division and balance, the last line presents 'the day's vanity, the night's remorse' not as alternatives, but as aspects of the same thing. 'The choice' is a poem about a choice long made, and not the presentation of a decision still open. Even so, the poem is alert to, and alive with second thoughts, not least in its freeing of the word 'remorse' from the associations with the dead that rhymes like 'source' might conjure. As Helen Vendler has noticed, Yeats opens up the last couplet by making 'perplexity' and 'purse' 'reinscribe the contest between the lofty and the vulgar dictions of the first six lines', whereas 'vanity' and 'remorse' 'belong to a single register of diction' and 'clash in content, but do not clash in plane'. The couplet does not rhyme like with like, and 'remorse' remains to that degree unstable, its work unfinished. On another level, 'The Choice' itself represents a second thought, having been cut away from its original place as a stanza in 'Coole Park and Ballylee, 1931'. This adds its own weight to Vendler's summary of the last line, that 'the work one was so vain about in the daytime turns out to be, in the watches of the night, the cause of remorse'.[72]

The capacity of Yeats's poetry to return upon itself is the measure of its ability to speak to (and sometimes speak against) remorse. The process comes to its most extreme pitch in some of the late poetry, and in 'The

---

[72] Helen Vendler, 'Yeats and *Ottava Rima*', in Warwick Gould (ed.), *Yeats Annual 11* (London: Macmillan, 1995), 216–17.

Man and the Echo', where another dialogue takes place, the ambition to 'measure the lot' results in questions which articulate powerful self-doubt and regret:[73]

> All that I have said and done,
> Now that I am old and ill,
> Turns into a question till
> I lie awake night after night
> And never get the answers right.
> Did that play of mine send out
> Certain men the English shot?
> Did words of mine put too great strain
> On that woman's reeling brain?
> Could my spoken words have checked
> That whereby a house lay wrecked?

The full rhymes and the metronomic regularity of the verse here bring these lines very close to the measures of Yeatsian remorse, just as the poem itself is situated on the border between life and death. Like others of his dialogue poems, 'The Man and the Echo' makes itself listen to the voice of the dead, and here the voice of the Echo is dead indeed, repeating fragments of the living voice exactly. In so far as the poem attends to and joins in this repetition, it gravitates towards the state of remorse which is the domain of the dead; to the extent that it resists the recurrence and reiteration of painful memory, the poem finds an element of freedom and escape from what seem by now all but inescapable conditions. In a prose draft, Yeats pictured himself 'Worn down by my self torturing search', and wrote how 'Among this solitude I seek re-morse', but struck out 'remorse' to replace it with 'escape'.[74] The words are true alternatives: one precludes the other, and Yeats's decision to choose 'escape' is what causes this poem's creative heart to beat. The particular freedom of 'The Man and the Echo' is its willingness to take stock of the worst possible things, the plainest and most humiliating facts, and still recognize that they are not the only facts, and that the living and individual will can yet, even here, pursue its thoughts towards active (and, finally, open) self-judgement. The remorselessness of the poem's self-interrogations is the guarantee of its escape from the deathwards

---

[73] Yeats, *Variorum Poems*, 495.
[74] Transcription of holograph draft in Jon Stallworthy, *Vision and Revision in Yeats's Last Poems* (Oxford: Clarendon Press, 1969), 60.

pull of remorse. The extraordinary conclusion, in which 'I have lost the theme', takes the poem to places wholly unprepared for in its initial scenario of unsparingly ultimate questions:

> But hush, for I have lost the theme,
> Its joy or night seem but a dream;
> Up there some hawk or owl has struck
> Dropping out of sky or rock,
> A stricken rabbit is crying out
> And its cry distracts my thought.

'Seem but a dream' concentrates the grim closeness of the rhymes into a near-jingle, while 'struck' and 'rock', 'out' and 'thought' break free from close rhyme's air of inevitability. The repetition of 'cry' which happens internally in the last couplet is at the same time contrasted by the off-rhyming of 'out' with 'thought' (and also perhaps carries a faint recollection of the 'cry', 'cry' repetition in 'In Memory of Alfred Pollexfen', where the rhyme was—inescapably—with 'die').[75] 'A stricken rabbit is crying out' takes the poem's predominantly trochaic tetrameter (the metre of 'Under Ben Bulben') away from its rhythmic norm just as, at an earlier moment of assertion, the voice stretched the line's confines to accommodate:

> That were to shirk
> The spiritual intellect's great work
> And shirk it in vain. There is no release
> In a bodkin or disease...

Such moments effect releases of their own, and in order to hear them it is necessary also to hear the menacing enclosure and completeness from which they depart. Seamus Heaney has praised the poem's last rhyme, writing that 'The rhyme—and the poem in general—not only tell us of that which the spirit must endure; they also show *how* it must endure.'[76] The poem's final lines are lines enacting this exemplary escape, and not lines of remorse, where, as Jahan Ramazani has well characterized them, 'life disrupts the meditative progression toward death, calling the poet back with a cry of suffering'.[77]

---

[75] Yeats, *Variorum Poems*, 360.
[76] Seamus Heaney, *The Redress of Poetry: Oxford Lectures* (London: Faber and Faber, 1995), 163.
[77] Jahan Ramazani, *Yeats and the Poetry of Death: Elegy, Self-Elegy, and the Sublime* (New Haven: Yale University Press, 1990), 199.

There are, of course, many kinds of suffering, his own and others', to which Yeats might be called back; in his late work especially, he seems to have a high tolerance for the kinds of suffering that can be theorized as conflict and realized as war. The Self in 'A Dialogue of Self and Soul' speaks not just with a sword, but for the sword: ten years after that other dialogue in 'Owen Aherne and his Dancers', it echoes the Heart's 'who cares?' in its principled rejection of remorseful brooding, but adds to this a deliberate belligerence. A very early skeleton of the poem has the Soul as 'He' and the Self as 'Me', with the demand 'What use to you now | love and war[?]' being met with 'only the sword gives truth'.[78] Yeats's actual swashbuckling in 'A Dialogue of Self and Soul' is not, it hardly needs saying, quite so clearly defined as this, and it is an incautious reading of the poem which does not attend to the Soul's protracted silence at the same time as the Self's prolonged aria of victory which that deliberated silence permits. Nevertheless, the casting-out of remorse characterizes a particularly heroic action for the later Yeats, one which he was not reluctant to apply to contemporary events. In 'The Municipal Gallery Revisited', the assassinated Kevin O'Higgins becomes one such heroic figure:[79]

> Kevin O'Higgins' countenance that wears
> A gentle questioning look that cannot hide
> A soul incapable of remorse or rest...

Whatever Yeats's attitudes towards the remorselessness of his friend's actions in the service of the Irish State, the poem takes O'Higgins as an example of the militant encounter of the living with the force of the dead. The otherworldly corollaries of remorse are still present in a draft of the stanza, in which Yeats begins by seeing 'Kevin O'Higgins eyes which on death and birth rest', then asks 'Kevin O'Higgins on what horizon stares?' The historical weight of O'Higgins's example is felt fully when Yeats calls his friend 'That guilty and remorseless man' who 'that weary body bears'.[80] Yeats does not shirk the facts—but nor does his finished version of the lines try to conceal them, insisting as it does

---

[78] Holograph fragment, National Library of Ireland (NLI 13,590 fol. 1ʳ), reproduced and transcribed in The Winding Stair *(1929): Manuscript Materials*, ed. David R. Clark (Ithaca, NY: Cornell University Press, 1995), 22–3.

[79] Yeats, *Variorum Poems*, 601.

[80] Holograph draft in National Library of Ireland (NLI 13,593 (29)), as transcribed by Wayne K. Chapman, '"The Municipal Gallery Re-visited" and its Writing', in Warwick Gould (ed.), *Yeats Annual 10* (London: Macmillan, 1993), 166.

on what cannot be hidden. There is a certain remorselessness in the
poet's returning on the image of O'Higgins: 'guilty' is not summarily
erased from the lines, but is fully absorbed into 'incapable of remorse or
rest': the costs are real, and the poem knows that they have been borne
in full.

If Kevin O'Higgins's heroism consists for Yeats partly in his ability to
resist remorse, and so stare down the dead in his capacity for action, 'The
Municipal Gallery Revisited' constitutes a more complex and ambivalent
'action' in its own right. Here, after all, the figure of the poet is brought
almost literally to his knees by the power of memory:[81]

> Heart-smitten with emotion I sink down,
> My heart recovering with covered eyes;
> Wherever I had looked I had looked upon
> My permanent or impermanent images . . .

At first sight, this comes to within a hair's breadth of remorse, but the
voice keeps itself out of remorse's downward pull; in part, this is
something audible in the lines, which absorb repetition in order to
effect change: 'recovering' and 'covering', 'looked' and 'looked upon',
'permanent' and 'impermanent' may sound like Yeatsian close-textured
incantation, but they are taking the measure of repetition only to deny it
its chance. In a poem concerned with understanding and channelling the
energies of the dead, the inertia of remorse is rejected in both theory and
action. What Yeats presents in the poem are not 'Vague memories,
nothing but memories', or those 'Memories upon memories' that 'Have
bowed my head upon my knees', but ordered, functioning and available
'images' which, at the conclusion, he seems himself to join, sure of the
benevolence of his legacy. If there is a contrast to be noticed between
this and the more ambivalent legacy recorded in 'Easter 1916', where the
verse concentrates into an almost threatening sounding of the dead as a
'source', there is a difference too between 'The Municipal Gallery
Revisited''s achieved and expansive poise and the grim, marching rigour
of other late poems, not least 'Under Ben Bulben'. These things also are
parts of the Yeatsian legacy, and in such contexts the overcoming of
remorse (or the imperviousness to it) may seem too easily achieved.

To judge Yeats in such terms is to set his poetry in relation to a
selection of plain facts, and to fix upon the poet 'that accusing eye'

---

[81] Yeats, *Variorum Poems*, 602.

which, in certain moods, he was happy to invite. Irish criticism and Irish poetry have both registered profound difficulties with Yeats's work, and with the designs it seems to have upon a future which is, in part at any rate, our own time. There are readers of Yeats who regard his writings as a part of Ireland's cultural and political history for which, at this point in the century, critical remorse might be in order. In such arguments, there are always facts to be adduced, facts which Yeats may be said to have ignored, distorted, or wilfully denied. Such objections have ground in common with fundamental literary downgradings of Yeats's work as, in Yvor Winters's phrase 'a more or less fraudulent poetry'.[82] When Christopher Ricks, for example, notes Yeats's refusal to rethink a line from a poem of 1886, where 'peahens dance on a smooth lawn'[83] and then deplores his retort 'As to the poultry yards, with them I have no concern', he flings the plain facts about peahens in the poet's face: 'no amount of high and mighty scorn will undo the fact that a high price is paid by a poetry which invokes poultry and at the same time declares that it has no concern with the poultry yards.'[84] But the fact of peahens' behaviour and the fact of this 'high price' are not obviously facts of the same order, and Ricks's rhetorical sleight of hand itself misses (or bypasses) the facts both of what Yeats said and the context of his saying it. The quoted retort comes from Yeats at the age of 23 (itself a fact of some possible relevance, given the weight being attached to his remark), in a letter to John O'Leary written in the wake of a bloodthirsty review of *The Wanderings of Oisin and Other Poems* in the *Freeman's Journal*. As is fitting in a letter addressed to a much older man, and one whom the young poet regarded as a figure of authority, the tone is one of deference to authorities greater than that of the periodical press:[85]

---

[82] Yvor Winters, *The Poetry of W. B. Yeats* (1960), quoted in Elizabeth Butler Cullingford (ed.), *Yeats: Poems 1919–1935: A Casebook* (London: Macmillan, 1984), 124.

[83] Yeats, *Variorum Poems*, 77.

[84] Christopher Ricks, 'Literature and the Matter of Fact', in *Essays in Appreciation* (Oxford: Clarendon Press, 1996), 304. Ricks's source for his quotation from Yeats is A. Norman Jeffares's *Commentary on the Collected Poems of W. B. Yeats*, in its first edition (London: Macmillan, 1968): although this provides a reference to Yeats's *Letters* for the offending words, it supplies no direct information regarding the date of Yeats's remarks, or their context.

[85] W. B. Yeats, letter to John O'Leary, 3 Feb. 1889, *The Collected Letters of W. B. Yeats*, i: *1865–1895*, ed. John Kelly and Eric Domville (Oxford: Clarendon Press, 1986), 138. As the editors point out, Yeats was correct, in point of fact, on the subject of peahens in Indian literature: 'There are . . . a number of descriptions of peahens dancing in the poems of Kalidasa, the great Sanskrit poet of the fifth century.' If Indian poets do, indeed, 'lie' on this matter, then Ricks has a legitimate quarrel with them as well as with Yeats.

The Freeman reviewer is wrong about peahens they dance throughout the whole of Indian poetry. If I had Kalidasa by me I could find many such dancings. As to the poultry yards, with them I have no concern—The wild peahen dances or all Indian poets lie.... That Freeman review will do no harm—It is the kind of criticism every new poetic style has received for the last hundred years. If my style is new it will get plenty more such for many a long day. Even Tennyson was charged with obscurity...

The facts of literature and the facts of a bad press are not to be reconciled here: Yeats is defiant in settling for literature—for poetry rather than poultry yards—and even dancing himself a little in his rhetorical postures for O'Leary's benefit. Part of the letter's winning quality resides in its boastfulness, and in the temerity of the young Yeats mentioning himself and the (still living) Tennyson in the same breath. It is less remarkable a century later for Ricks to align those two poets, but when he goes on to register an instance of Tennyson's regard for botanical accuracy as a fact which 'seems to me the more honourable position—and to have made for the greater poetry', the critical consequences of this kind of respect for the facts begin to come into view.[86] An older Yeats was even less ready to apologize for this order of mistake, still less to attempt to go back on it, as when he noted that 'Henry More will have it that a hen scared by a hawk when the cock is treading hatches out a hawk-headed chicken', and added the parenthetical remark that 'I am no stickler for the fact'.[87] However, it would be a poor reader who seized on this as evidence of the poet's culpable disregard for the facts, since Yeats's irony (here, indeed, about the poultry yard) is more subtle and more pervasive than a critical demand for indiscriminate verisimilitude can comfortably acknowledge. In Ireland, the facts sometimes adduced against Yeats are different (and, it may be, of a different order), while the canonical consequences are altogether distinct, but the assumption that an 'honourable position' (however that is to be ascertained or assessed) can 'make for the greater poetry' is made in an unreflecting way by many who find Yeats less than satisfactory in relation to the truth as they see it. The kinds of remorse such readers demand are not forthcoming in Yeats's writings, and the remorse he does write of seems to them a hollow mockery of the real thing.

Demands like these tend to coarsen the reading of literature, and in particular of poetry. It needs to be observed also, in justice, that their

---

[86] Ricks, *Essays in Appreciation*, 305.   [87] Yeats, *Mythologies*, 350–1.

insistence on the plain facts does not always coexist with a respect for facts that may be at variance with their arguments: one recent attack on T. S. Eliot, which concludes that 'like a true politician [he] never apologizes and he never explains' still prints a misattribution as a crucial part of its evidence, labelling this 'Wrong' in a footnote, without apologizing, explaining, or taking stock of the damage done to the facts of the case.[88] In reading Yeats, the poetry's complex relations with facts, whether these are facts of the poet's private life or of the life of his times, are always critically relevant. Acknowledging this, and acknowledging the difficulty of understanding these relations with the necessary fullness, it is vital to add that the poetry itself is another fact in the matter, and that it too demands respect. To seek out and evaluate Yeats's uses for remorse is, in this sense, to take the measure of remorse *in* Yeats's poetry as well as *for* his poetry; this is to insist on form as something other than accidental or narrowly functional in literature and in literary meaning. In taking the measure of remorse, Yeats's poetry enacts what Geoffrey Hill calls 'that "return upon the self" which may be defined as the transformation of mere reflex into an "act of attention", a "disinterested concentration of purpose" upon one's own preconceived notions, prejudices, self-contradictions and errors'.[89] Such attention (an attention to form in its truest sense) is part of a fundamental respect for the facts, and finally it is bound up with that honesty about the facts of which Yeats was time and again capable. It was this capacity in Yeats to which T. S. Eliot responded when he wrote of the poet's 'exceptional honesty and courage' and praised 'the honesty with oneself expressed in the poetry' in its 'revelation of what a man really is and remains'.[90]

Yeats's remorse should not be confused with his regret, or his sense of guilt with regard to things done or left undone in his private and public lives. Rather, Yeats's imagination settles on remorse, and is able to act upon it, as part of the attempt to 'hold in a single thought reality

---

[88] Tom Paulin, 'T. S. Eliot and Anti-Semitism', in *Writing to the Moment: Selected Critical Essays 1980–1996* (London: Faber and Faber, 1996), 160. Paulin's laconic 'Wrong' (p. 151) refers to a misattribution of an anonymous review in the *Criterion*; but cf. Paulin's 'Getting it Wrong' later in *Writing to the Moment*: 'The history of criticism is littered with tiny errors, huge *faux pas* and comic misquotations. What critic worth their salt has a clear conscience in this matter?' (p. 311) If Paulin's own conscience is troubled on this particular matter, it still does not lead him to discuss the question of whether the Eliot misattribution is a tiny error or a huge *faux pas*: it may, perhaps, be more in the nature of a comic misquotation.

[89] Geoffrey Hill, *The Lords of Limit: Essays on Literature and Ideas* (London: André Deutsch, 1984), 155.

[90] T. S. Eliot, 'Yeats' (1940), *On Poetry and Poets* (London: Faber and Faber, 1957), 257.

and justice'. The poet's returns upon himself, and the returns so insistently attempted by the dead upon the living, are themes which Yeats
does not regard as separate, and together they constitute the underlying
facts of, and conditions for his writing. The notion of 'the dead living in
their memories' remains more than Yeats's eccentricity, however dis-
tinctively Yeatsian its expression; and in this sense, at least, the poet's
Irish reception is especially alert to the specific dimensions of his
continuing importance. Yeats's dealings with remorse are in tune with
the kinds of honesty Eliot and others praised, for they do not allow
emotion—whether it is regret, pain, humiliation, grief, or simple frus-
tration—to overcome the proper freedom of poetic action. To take
remorse as the measure of integrity is to understand the facts of art, and
the facts of life, in altogether too plain a manner. For in serious terms,
remorse is never enough: it has been said (against Eliot) that 'Remorse
without atonement has its own equilibrium; introspection and the
private acknowledgement of error do not always lead to amends being
made.'[91] More simply, Geoffrey Hill has classed remorse among 'impure
motives' for writing, when he postulates that 'a man may continue to
write and to publish in a vain and self-defeating effort to appease his
own sense of empirical guilt', and adds that 'It is ludicrous, of course.'[92]
When such as Yeats casts out remorse, these facts continue to matter;
and the poetry's reality goes on answering to, and answering for, its
sense of justice.

[91] Anthony Julius, *T. S. Eliot, Anti-Semitism, and Literary Form* (Cambridge: Cambridge
University Press, 1995), 177.
[92] Hill, *The Lords of Limit*, 7.

CHAPTER 3

Yeats's Poetic Structures

At the end of 'Coole Park, 1929', W. B. Yeats commends his patroness to a posterity more enduring than that of her house:[1]

> Here, traveller, scholar, poet, take your stand
> When all those rooms and passages are gone,
> When nettles wave upon a shapeless mound
> And saplings root among the broken stone,
> And dedicate—eyes bent upon the ground,
> Back turned upon the brightness of the sun
> And all the sensuality of the shade—
> A moment's memory to that laurelled head.

'Here' is not, at this point of the poem, exactly here and now, for the poem is written, and published first, at a time when both the house and Lady Gregory are still standing. The voice which begins Yeats's poem seems to be speaking in (and immediately of) the present: 'I meditate upon a swallow's flight | Upon an aged woman and her house'. Yet the final stanza is pitched into a future in which the house is pulled down and the woman dead, so that 'Here' must be 'Here' at some time other than the 1929 which Yeats incorporates, unusually, into his poem's title. There is, then, something of a paradox in this last stanza, though it is a paradox which, typically for Yeats, is a condition of the poetry's power rather than any self-undermining contradiction in its fabric. The 'traveller, scholar, poet' of the future, who are the 'scholars and . . . poets after us' of the first stanza, are addressed and commanded from a site which accommodates ruin and in which ruin is both a condition and a proof of the voice's power of endurance. This site, this projective 'Here', is a place the poem makes, and which the stanza builds, and builds upon.

[1] W. B. Yeats, *The Variorum Edition of the Poems of W. B. Yeats*, ed. Peter Allt and Russell K. Alspatch (London: Macmillan, 1956), 489.

The poem's last command, to 'dedicate...A moment's memory to that laurelled head', is placed and timed very carefully by Yeats in relation to the construction of this final stanza. As the second impera-tive in the pair 'take your stand...and dedicate', it sits at the midpoint of the stanza's eight lines, as though to mark a formal division into two symmetrical units of four lines each. However, the verb 'dedicate' is no sooner spoken than its object is suspended in Yeats's syntax, in the three-line interruption of 'eyes bent upon the ground, | Back turned upon the brightness of the sun | And all the sensuality of the shade': 'dedicate' then, but 'dedicate' what, and to whom? The delayed object of the dedication is revealed in the last line as 'A moment's memory', but there has been a certain design implicit in the waiting here, for the lines of 'interruption' have served in some ways to define the poem's image of its reader, and at the same time that reader's image of himself, as a figure who shuns the visible world in favour of 'memory'. In terms of the stanza's shape, the interruption introduces a marked asymmetry, while the mounting delay as one end-stopped line is followed by another, then 'a third, makes all the more audible the poetry's rhetorical structure. If the first four lines seem to contemplate the reversion of architecture back to nature, the final four lines take pains to avoid the overly 'natural', whether in surroundings or in tone of address. The future reader is commanded to 'take your stand', but the site of this, the 'Here', is a willed, constructed environment and the stanza itself is a type of what Yeats had called in an earlier poem the place 'Where we wrought that shall break the teeth of Time'.[2]

It is perhaps a familiar observation that Yeats makes play out of the relation between poems and places, and poems *as* places, so that (for example) Big Houses are celebrated in poems with big stanzas. And the architectural aspect of Yeats's poetry is, indeed, noted by many of his critics as one of the distinguishing features of his middle and late style. Nevertheless, the strangeness of the ending to 'Coole Park, 1929' is seldom registered; the poem's architecture is more often taken for granted than examined, as when Harold Bloom writes that its 'impres-sive meaning is that...things did not fall apart, because Lady Gregory maintained the ceremony of innocence'.[3] The oddness of this becomes apparent when we remember that the poem speaks finally to a situation

---

[2] 'The New Faces', ibid. 435.
[3] Harold Bloom, *Yeats* (New York: Oxford University Press, 1970), 381.

in which Coole Park *has* fallen apart. Jahan Ramazani is more alert to Yeats's paradoxical dynamics when he compares it to 'The Municipal Gallery Revisited':[4]

'Coole Park 1929' resembles the Gallery elegy in seeming to defer to a commemorated structure; but it also substitutes its own poetic 'rooms and passages' for the house. Double in meaning, the deictic *here* again points to both the poem and the physical dwelling, while alerting us to their differences.... Against the coming shapelessness, Yeats sets his poem's exquisitely sculpted stanzas in *ottava rima*.

The interesting question which might follow from this reading is that of how far the ruin is a necessary condition of Yeats's specifically poetic structure, so that poems do not imitate the forms of building and order, but rather replace these forms with their own ideal and rhetorical shapes. Do Yeats's poetic structures, in other words, require, or even create, the 'shapelessness' integral to their meaning? How much has to fall apart for the poetic centre to hold?

Asking questions like these puts an immediate metaphorical strain on the vocabulary of poetic structure. In part, this is owing to Yeats's own prior emphases on the relation between building the lofty rhyme and the rise and fall of ancestral houses; in part, too, it is a result of the prevailing habit of seeing ideological sermons in the stones of poetic constructions. One recent study, for example, speaks of how 'Yeats's Anglo-Irish nationality...deliberately and elaborately exposes itself as a construction', and notes how 'the original vitality of the house also contains an original impulse towards crisis and disintegration'.[5] But the theoretical import of the metaphor here is false to its literal source: houses don't (or shouldn't) have impulses towards disintegration, and the views of a property surveyor on the matter might properly command more confidence than those of a literary critic. Nevertheless, such metaphorical observations may turn in other, more fruitful directions, and we could consider the extent to which 'impulses...towards disintegration' are indeed present in the 'houses' of Yeats's poetic constructions. The appearance of symmetrical division in the final stanza of 'Coole Park, 1929', for example, and the arrangement for asymmetry

[4] Jahan Ramazani, *Yeats and the Poetry of Death: Elegy, Self-Elegy, and the Sublime* (New Haven: Yale University Press, 1990), 51.

[5] Marjorie Howes, *Yeats's Nations: Gender, Class, and Irishness* (Cambridge: Cambridge University Press, 1996), 116, 122.

which Yeats in fact makes there, might provide such an enquiry with a serviceable starting-point. More generally, it is possible to ask how far Yeats's larger poetic structures are built with disintegration in mind, so to speak; in this sense, the contrapuntal effects of syntactic order and stanzaic rhyme schemes might take on a particular significance. Again, any disintegrative impulse here is part of a drive towards some more enduring structure.

The ways in which Yeats's poems envisage or anticipate ruin are partly imitated in those poems' forms, but partly too they are undermined or questioned by the ways in which the forms cohere to provide a site on which the reader can be instructed to 'take your stand'. Even the poet's own house, Thoor Ballylee, is marked in the poetry as a place bound for ultimate ruin, whose life in letters will be more enduring than its existence in stone. The earliest versions of the lines 'To be carved on a stone at Thoor Ballylee' seem to hope for material preservation of what the poet and his wife have restored:[6]

> They call a curse
> On him who alters for the worse
> From fashion or a vulgar mind
> What Rafferty built & Scott designed.

But the poem's final version no longer feels the need of any such insurance policies, and moves directly from building to ruin as an inevitability:[7]

> I, the poet William Yeats,
> With old mill boards and sea-green slates,
> And smithy work from the Gort forge,
> Restored this tower for my wife George;
> And may these characters remain
> When all is ruin once again.

'These characters': *these* is the word proper to an inscription, but of course the finished poem is something *as well as* an inscription. The characters that remain in a posterity beyond the Tower's material future are the characters of the printed poem, and their endurance is made

---

[6] The lines are quoted here as transcribed in Michael Robartes and the Dancer*: Manuscript Materials*, ed. Thomas Parkinson with Anne Brennan (Ithaca, NY: Cornell University Press, 1994), 200.
[7] Yeats, *Variorum Poems*, 406.

possible by the poem's continuing life in memory. The life in form, then, of Yeats's lines is something over and above the lifetime of the material form of whose foundation—and ruination—the poem speaks. It is necessary here to brave the dangers of organicist critical metaphor, since Yeats's poetry is especially attuned to the ways in which a poem's life in memory is dependent upon its ability to create a life in form. The poet operates often by manipulating parallels between the notion of memory—of historical and personal versions of the past, and of posterities and perpetuities—and the workings in poetic structure in readers' memory—in the returns and anticipations of rhyme, in the suspensions and resolutions of syntax, and in the larger recurrence of poems and parts of poems as the sounds of any reader's poetic knowledge. Perhaps such manipulation, or at least such an awareness, is no more than a commonplace among poets; yet it is more awkwardly approached, in the main, by critics whose agendas have difficulty in accommodating poetic form as something other than a mere formality.

The Tower's provision for ruin becomes a major resource for some of Yeats's most ambitious poems of the 1920s, and here the doubling of perspective—of memory as history, and memory as posterity—takes on particular importance. The fourth poem in the sequence 'Meditations in Time of Civil War', 'My Descendants', perhaps elaborates the 'curse' which Yeats had edited out of early versions of the Ballylee inscription:[8]

> And what if my descendants lose the flower
> Through natural declension of the soul,
> Through too much business with the passing hour,
> Through too much play, or marriage with a fool?
> May this laborious stair and this stark tower
> Become a roofless ruin that the owl
> May build in the cracked masonry and cry
> Her desolation to the desolate sky.

This brings the Tower into alignment with the sequence's other 'Ancestral houses', as a site of 'desolation' which the poetry itself looks forward to inhabiting. Again, the deictic '*this* laborious stair and *this* stark tower' emphasizes the palpability of a context for the speaking voice, while at the same time the poem's rhetorical direction is set for the material ruin of that context. At the end of 'My Descendants', Yeats writes in a register close once more to that of the inscription:[9]

---

[8] Ibid. 422–3.   [9] Ibid. 423.

> And know whatever flourish and decline
> These stones remain their monument and mine.

'*These*' stones may be the stones as restored in the present; they may be equally well the stones in a state of future ruin or disrepair. As in 'Coole Park, 1929', the voice concludes the poem by speaking in its present tense and to the different present tense of posterity at the same time. Of course, 'These stones' is working also according to the convention which means that actual stones need not be produced and put on display in order for the poem to be read; once again, the insistent metaphorical identification of poetic with material structure underpins Yeats's rhetoric. And in fact Yeats is, in some senses, engaged here in recycling the 'stones' of his poem: the final couplet's 'whatever flourish and decline' compresses a pattern of growth and decay established in the opening stanza, but it is also a kind of formal recapitulation of key sounds, since 'flourish and decline' ghosts the 'nourish' and 'mind' of the first lines:[10]

> Having inherited a vigorous mind
> From my old fathers, I must nourish dreams
> And leave a woman and a man behind
> As vigorous of mind . . .

The poem's final couplet, then, comes very close to rhyming with its opening line. In a work much occupied with cycles, and with coming full circle ('The Primum Mobile that fashioned us | Has made the very owls in circles move'), such returns seem appropriate. Helen Vendler has noted with regard to 'My Descendants' that 'The models of history to which Yeats has recourse—a tragic model of rise and fall; a catastrophic model of repeated fall; and a comic model of the eternal return—are not of themselves new', adding that 'What is new is how they are made convincing in stanzas that act them out.'[11] The observation is an acute one; yet the mimetic implications of acting out the various models of history proposed here need careful consideration in the context of Yeats's developing interest in the punning relation between architectural and poetic structures.

In his critical writings, Seamus Heaney has responded interestingly to the felt physicality of Yeats's forms, and has explored convincingly

---

[10] Yeats, *Variorum Poems*, 422.
[11] Helen Vendler, 'Yeats and *Ottava Rima*', in Warwick Gould (ed.), *Yeats Annual 11* (London: Macmillan, 1995), 35–6.

ways in which 'Yeats . . . created a fortified space within the rooms of many powerfully vaulted stanzas'. Heaney pushes this awareness to a point beyond that of a mimetic acting out of themes, however, and he sees the pervasiveness of decay as part of the meaning of Yeats's architecture: 'The tower', Heaney writes, 'may be crumbling into a destructive future, but that very crumbling is part of an inexorable reality which the mind must accept as truth.'[12] The Yeatsian vocabulary Heaney adopts here is in line with the accuracy of his perception, and is in some ways more useful than the metaphorical treatment of the 'themes' of structure and ruin attempted by many critics. Michael North's remark for example, that in Yeats's poetry 'ruin is both the problem to be solved and an indispensable part of the solution' is absorbed in an argument which too quickly forgets the specifics of poetic 'ruin' in its anxiety to read the 'problem' as one primarily political in its nature and meaning.[13] Heaney goes much deeper than this by following Yeats's logic into politically unforthcoming areas of writing, where the authorial will functions with seeming arbitrariness, and where building and destroying are complementary acts. Heaney mentions 'two simple, important points':[14]

. . . that the poetic imagination in its strongest manifestation imposes its vision upon a place rather than accepts a vision from it; and that this visionary imposition is never exempt from the imagination's antithetical ability to subvert its own creation. In other words, once the place has been brought into written existence, it is inevitable that it will be unwritten.

Both these points are important to any consideration of Yeats's later writing and its self-consciousness about the structures which poetry builds. Heaney's sense of the 'fortified space' in Yeatsian architecture, and its 'crumbling' condition, gives a compellingly sharp focus to the relation between writing and 'unwriting' in the later Yeats. The observations help consolidate earlier critical assessments of the ways in which the late Yeats turns upon his own achievement. Denis Donoghue, to take one instance, had recourse to architectural metaphors in discussion of *Last Poems*, when he wrote of how 'The idiom of a lifetime was now in danger of collapse' for a Yeats who 'put these poems together to keep

---

[12] Seamus Heaney, *The Place of Writing* (Atlanta, Ga.: Scholars Press, 1989), 29–30.
[13] Michael North, *The Political Aesthetic of Yeats, Eliot, and Pound* (Cambridge: Cambridge University Press, 1991), 54.
[14] Heaney, *The Place of Writing*, 20.

himself from falling apart'.[15] Heaney's contention that 'once the place
has been brought into written existence, it is inevitable that it will be
unwritten' develops and illuminates Donoghue's argument that 'Yeats
comes within an ace, in these last poems, of repudiating the whole
structure he has made: having made it, he can think of nothing to do but
pull it down.' However, Donoghue's register of puzzlement is less
convincing than Heaney's alertness to what seems inevitable consequence.

There are, of course, a number of different kinds of poetic structure
involved in such discussions, and Yeats's later career results in different
kinds, and scales, of building and destroying, writing and unwriting. If
the particular structure of the individual poem is at one end of the scale,
then the huge structure of the life's work, the personally constructed
canon, is at the other as 'something intended, complete'. These different
kinds of construction may be related in intimate ways. In order to see
this, it is helpful to shift the focus of attention from Thoor Ballylee and
the 1920s to Coole Park and the 1930s, and from Yeats's sense of his life
as rooted in a fortified keep to a slightly later, more peripatetic and in
some ways conventionally situated retirement of Riversdale and its
'Acre of grass'.

Yeats stayed a great deal at Coole Park during Lady Gregory's illness
in 1931 and early 1932. When Lady Gregory died, on 22 May 1932, the
poet was in Dublin on theatre business, and he arrived at Coole on the
morning after her death. Back in Dublin a week or so later, he wrote to
Olivia Skakespear, first (briefly) about Lady Gregory ('She was her
indomitable self to the last but of that I will not write, or not now'),
then about his new domestic plans:[16]

We have taken a little house at Rathfarnham just outside Dublin. It has the most
beautiful gardens I have seen round a small house, and all well stocked. I shall
step out from my study into the front garden—but as I write the words I know
that I am heartbroken for Coole and its great woods.

Yeats's intention not to write, 'or not now', about Coole Park and Lady
Gregory cannot really be fulfilled in the letter, and Yeats moves on to

---

[15] Denis Donoghue, *Yeats* (Glasgow: Fontana, 1971), 127.
[16] Letter dated 31 May [1932], in *The Letters of W. B. Yeats*, ed. Allan Wade (London: Rupert
Hart-Davis, 1954), 795–6. The truth (or otherwise) of the admission that 'I cannot spell tonight'
(see following extract)is made impossible to assess by Wade's decision to regularize Yeats's
spellings. The ongoing project of the new Oxford University Press edition of the *Letters*, which
adheres to the poet's original spellings, remains as yet many volumes short of 1932.

recall an incident from the Monday morning on which he found himself at Coole, just too late for the death of his old friend:

A queer Dublin sculptor dressed like a workman and in filthy clothes, a man who lives in a kind of slum and has slum children, came the day after Lady Gregory's death 'to pay his respects.' He walked from room to room and then stood where hang the mezzotints and engravings of those under or with whom (I cannot spell to-night—that word looks wrong) the Gregorys have served, Fox, Burke and so on, and after standing silent said 'All the nobility of earth.' I felt he did not mean it for that room alone but for lost tradition. How much of my own verse has not been but the repetition of those words.

It is a complicated anecdote, and Yeats's preoccupations here are beginning to shift in relation to one another. The realization of loss with Lady Gregory's death (a death Yeats had expected for some time, and which seems already anticipated in the elegiac notes of 'Coole Park, 1929' or 'Coole Park and Ballylee, 1931') becomes a kind of stocktaking, carried out 'from room to room' of the big house by an artist from the slums. What is more, this stocktaking is itself a complicated mixture of loss and gain, for images symbolic of an Anglo-Irish political past are gathered as parts of 'lost tradition', while the lament for that loss, 'All the nobility of earth', becomes the burden of Yeats's own poetic work, assessed finally in another act of weary stocktaking. The rooms of Coole Park and the poems of W. B. Yeats are brought into an elegiac conjunction, and both seem the richer for their imminent demise.

The tone of this was repeated in Yeats's letters over the coming month. Writing to Mario Rossi on 6 June, Yeats told his correspondent of how Lady Gregory in her last days had been 'indomitable':[17]

On the Wednesday though every movement gave her pain and she had long lived between two rooms on the same floor... she got herself helped downstairs that she might visit all the chief rooms—'saying good bye' the servants thought.... When she died the great house died too.

Again the association of Lady Gregory, the rooms of Coole Park and the act of a last stocktaking or setting in order is made by Yeats, and the end of 'the great house' is a point of elegiac finality. But Yeats's domestic life was, as he had informed Olivia Shakespear, also in the process of making another new start with the move to Riversdale in July. In literary matters, as he told Herbert Grierson on 9 June, Yeats was involved in

---

[17] *Letters*, ed. Wade, p. 796.

finishing off his own kind of stocktaking, in correcting proofs for 'my own new collected edition', though 'three months ago ... my imagination stopped and has showed no sign of moving since'.[18] A letter to Olivia Shakespear at the end of June contemplates the move to Riversdale (then being redecorated by George) alongside the new collected edition; a week later, stationed in the Royal Hotel at Glendalough in preparation for his move, Yeats tells Olivia how 'I hope I shall there [at Riversdale] re-create in some measure the routine that was my life at Coole ... We have a lease for but thirteen years but that will see me out of life.'[19] A letter of 25 July announces Yeats's installation:[20]

My dear Olivia, I am writing in my new study—sometimes I go out of the glass-door into the fruit garden to share the gooseberries with the bullfinches. I can hear the workmen putting in the electric bells; through the window on my left I can see pergolas covered with roses. At first I was unhappy, for everything made me remember the great trees of Coole, my home for nearly forty years, but now that the pictures are up I feel more content. This little creeper-covered farm-house might be in a Calvert woodcut, and what could be more suitable for one's last decade?

The passage makes a suggestive contrast with a poem like 'My House' in *The Tower*; in place of the dramatic starkness of 'An ancient bridge, and a more ancient tower' set in 'An acre of stony ground', there is now a thoroughly bourgeois and suburban house and garden, where men come not as 'Benighted travellers | From markets and from fairs' who have seen the scholar's 'midnight candle glimmering', but to equip the poet with modern gadgets for his front door.[21] Yet here too Coole Park seems to intrude, or to be in some way implicit in the domestic arrangements. Reflecting again on how this will be his *last* house, the one which will 'see [him] out of life', Yeats has found an environment for his last acts of stocktaking.

The letter marks one moment only, and it is not, in fact, an altogether accurate prediction of Yeats's 'last decade' and its settings. Nevertheless, there seems to be recorded here an ambition which might have been taking shape in Yeats's mind over the months of Lady Gregory's final illness and into 1932, of finding a site in which the poet, like his patroness, can take stock of his life's artistic structure, 'from room to room', and find the final form for his achievement. Again, the ambition

[18] *Letters*, ed. Wade, 797.   [19] 8 July [1932], ibid. 799.
[20] Ibid.   [21] Yeats, *Variorum Poems*, 419–20.

was not to find any very precise fulfilment, or even perhaps to remain stable for very long. It is worth bearing in mind that the death of Lady Gregory, and the move to Riversdale, take place during a lull in Yeats's writing of poetry; the achievement which the projected collected edition was to memorialize seemed complete to the Yeats who wrote to Olivia Shakespear to note the continuities and circularities in his own writing from youth to age: 'My first denunciation of old age I made in *The Wanderings of Usheen* (end of part 1) before I was twenty and the same denunciation comes in the last pages of the book.'[22] Unlike Lady Gregory, Yeats was not dead; yet at this point his relation to his last collected edition parallels her relation to her house, and leaves the poet in a situation with something of a posthumous air.

However, the collected edition for which Yeats was reading proofs was not quite the completed structure which such a parallel requires. As Yeats must have suspected, and as Macmillan very probably knew, the project, which was an expensive one to enter upon at a time of severe financial depression, was unlikely to be viable until it was indeed a posthumous publication, to which the author could not add new material or still further revisions. As he read over his proof sheets in 1932, Yeats was in some sense engaged in setting his textual, or canonical house in order; at the same time, he was beginning to write poetry again, and in this respect, a degree of domestic disruption was inevitable. Macmillan, as a publishing company, could make the kinds of provision for this which Yeats, as a poet, quite properly could not do; and yet the extent of Yeats's later unsettling of various 'final forms' of his poetry and thought suggests a reluctance to enter prematurely the realms of the posthumous. It was in October 1932 that Yeats and Macmillan took steps to secure a new *Collected Poems* to replace the much-valued and, until recently, steadily selling book of 1899; by April 1933, Yeats was going along enthusiastically with Macmillan's plan for a browser-friendly arrangement of poems in the new volume: 'I am delighted with your suggestion to put long poems in a section at the end. I wish I had thought of it before.'[23] This was to be—now notoriously—the poet's last word

---

[22] 30 June [1932], ibid. 798.
[23] Letter to Harold Macmillan, 2 Apr. 1933 (British Library Add. MS 55003, fol. 141). As evidence in a complex editorial problem, the interpretation of Yeats's words here is hotly disputed, and detailed (sharply opposing) arguments have been mounted by Richard Finneran and Warwick Gould. For Finneran's readings, see his *Editing Yeats's Poems* (Basingstoke: Macmillan, 1983), *Editing Yeats's Poems: A Reconsideration* (Basingstoke: Macmillan, 1990), and 'Text and Interpretation in the Poems of W. B. Yeats', in George Bornstein (ed.), *Representing*

on the matter, but it is worth taking full account of Yeats's briskness on the subject: this is the tone of a man doing business, and a man moreover who is not going to confuse business with the seriousness of his artistic life; it is also, most interestingly, the tone of someone who has other, and more important, matters to think about. Yeats's 'delight' is also the relief of getting something tiresome out of the way, for the *Collected Poems* (1933) records the poet's past at a time when his artistic future was still coming into being. The two-part division adopted in that volume, between 'Lyrical' and 'Narrative and Dramatic' work may indeed obscure and otherwise damage the ordered fabric of Yeats's poetic canon, as a number of critics have argued. However, it is far from clear that Yeats himself, in 1933, felt inclined to worry about such damage. Partly, this may be a result of his knowledge that arrangements remained in hand (on however long-term a scale) for an eventual *Collected Works*; yet partly also this may be owing to the poet's increasing willingness to pull down the structures he had constructed, to rearrange and reconfigure them, or to let them fall into other hands, and in so doing to have the creative space in which to reinvent himself yet again.

The move to Riversdale can be seen, in this light of such things, as one aspect only of Yeats's ambitions for his 'last decade'; another, and equally important, side of his activities during these last years was to be his unsettledness, his cultural and geographical eclecticism, which facilitated in part the 'unwriting' of his work. By 1936, the suburban quiet of Rathfarnham could be both evoked and renounced in 'An Acre of Grass':[24]

> Picture and book remain,
> An acre of green grass
> For air and exercise,
> Now strength of body goes;
> Midnight, an old house
> Where nothing stirs but a mouse.

Modernist Texts: Editing as Interpretation (Ann Arbor: University of Michigan Press, 1991), 17–47. For Warwick Gould's presentation and interpretation of the evidence (making, in my own view, the more sensible case), see his 'The Definitive Edition: A History of the Final Arrangements of Yeats's Work', in an Appendix to *Yeats's Poems*, ed. A. Norman Jeffares (Basingstoke: Macmillan, 3rd edn., 1996), 706–49, and 'W. B. Yeats and the Resurrection of the Author', *The Library: A Quarterly Journal of Bibliography*, 16/2 (1994), 101–34.

[24] Yeats, *Variorum Poems*, 575.

> My temptation is quiet.
> Here at life's end
> Neither loose imagination,
> Nor the mill of the mind
> Consuming its rag and bone,
> Can make the truth known.

The poem begins with a domestic stocktaking, similar (though drastically reduced in its circumstances) to Lady Gregory's 'saying good bye' to the rooms of Coole Park. However, the stillness here is the stillness of 'temptation', the choice of silence which the house represents being presented as the quiet of work completed, leaving only the mechanical 'mill of the mind' to go through the motions until the end. The revolt against this 'temptation' which the second half of the poem represents is expressed as a prayer, but this is a prayer in part for the ability to begin building again:

> Grant me an old man's frenzy,
> Myself must I remake
> Till I am Timon and Lear
> Or that William Blake
> Who beat upon the wall
> Till Truth obeyed his call; ...

The remaking here keeps its traces of structural work, and destruction: not only is Blake made to 'beat upon the wall' (to secure it, or to bring it down?), but Timon and Lear are both summoned to the poet's side, perhaps also as tragic dwellers or architects—Lear who is driven out of doors into Poor Tom's hovel, and Timon who, in lines Yeats quoted, 'hath made his everlasting mansion | Upon the beached verge of the salt flood'.[25] The paradox in Shakespeare's lines, where the 'flood' seems to make a mansion anything but 'everlasting', is in key with Yeats's celebration of tragic joy, but it is also close to the poet's peoccupations with houses that fall and are to be built again.

Fine poem though it is, there is something slightly ramshackle about the structure of 'An Acre of Grass', by comparison at least with Yeats's earlier poems celebrating, or in memory of, big houses. The lines are

---

[25] *Timon of Athens* V. ii. 100–1. One of Yeats's allusions to these lines comes in 'Poetry and Tradition' (1907), where 'Timon of Athens contemplates his own end, and orders his tomb by the beached verge of the salt flood' (*Essays and Introductions* (London: Macmillan, 1961), 255): the poet's transformation of 'mansion' to 'tomb' here perhaps inadvertently conflates Timon with Browning's tomb-ordering Bishop.

shorter, and the stanzas are loosely constructed now (the first and third lines do not rhyme), while the poet seems to take few pains over syntactic patterns or rhetorical trajectories (the grammatical status of the last stanza's governing 'A mind Michael Angelo knew...' is not clear: the mind could be the object of 'Grant me...', or simply be, as the punctuation suggests, a further instance in the list of Timon, Lear, and Blake, another thing that 'I am'). In recognizing that such elements of the poem's style do not very perceptibly reduce its artistic success, and in fact seem to be a condition of the success, one feature of Yeats's late manner comes into view. It is not just that Yeats chooses to leave poems a little 'unfinished', but that his late work tends generally to loosen rather than tighten up the metrical and stanzaic structures which he had already brought to perfection. Sometimes, it is true, this can present itself with visual prominence, as in the one stanza of 'The Municipal Gallery Revisited' which falls a line short of the *ottava rima* form, or the first stanza of 'Parnell's Funeral' which (though without the accompanying textual note) does the same. More generally, Yeats's poetry in the years after 1932 inhabits a great many different metrical structures, from the grand and spacious stanzas of poems like 'The Statues' or 'The Gyres' to the ballad forms, often with idiosyncratic mutations, of many pieces in *New Poems* (1938). This degree of variety, with its promiscuous mixing of high and low architecture, distinguishes what was to prove Yeats's final poetic idiom.

The 'danger of collapse' in such an idiom, to return to Denis Donoghue's phrase, is more in the nature of an effect which the poet engineers in the poems. Certainly, there are some poems in which the change in structure coincides with an almost parodic relation to previous writings. In 'The Curse of Cromwell', for example, the final stanza revisits Yeats's characteristic interest in the Big House:[26]

> I came on a great house in the middle of the night,
> Its open lighted doorway and its windows all alight,
> And all my friends were there and made me welcome too;
> But I woke in an old ruin that the winds howled through;
> And when I pay attention I must out and walk
> Among the dogs and horses that understand my talk.
> > *O what of that, O what of that,*
> > *What is there left to say?*

[26] Yeats, *Variorum Poems*, 580.

If this is glancing ahead to *Purgatory*, it is also glancing back at Coole Park and other ancestral houses in Yeats's work. With 'And all my friends were there', Yeats comes close to reducing one of his own late preoccupations to bathos. To set these lines against the poet's various celebrations of Thoor Ballylee is also to understand the degree to which Yeats's altered formal structure is a way of shifting perspective as well as register, with the rhythm of the ballad singer exposing the structures of aggrandizement to the most radical of questioning. The refrain, in this as in other late poems, brings into play a very different kind of repetition—and, by that token, of memory inside the poem—from the returns and changes of the rhymes in Yeats's grand stanzas. Here, the refrain is the return of the thing that simply refuses to go away, the question that repeats and repeats because it cannot be answered.

Such inbuilt instability is not, of course, the same thing as 'collapse', and 'The Curse of Cromwell', like many others among the later poems, has its own kinds of integrity and cohesion. What is more, the poem's relation to earlier themes is not *just* a parodic one, and the question of its refrain does not anticipate the answer 'Nothing': while there may indeed be no more to say of *that*—or no more to say of it in that way—there is still more to be said beyond this point of retrospect. The poem 'What Then?' might be read in just this sense also, with its refrain functioning as much as a spur as a doom-laden tolling of the bell. It is important that Yeats follows that poem's last '*What then?*' with 'Beautiful Lofty Things', a return to the autobiographical first-person voice in defiant celebration of a theme, and of friends, celebrated before. The change, however, lies again in the alteration of form; unlike earlier poems such as 'All Souls' Night', or later ones such as 'The Municipal Gallery Revisited', 'Beautiful Lofty Things' is not disposed into stanzas, but allows its twelve long lines to be mostly unrhymed: while the last line sounds triumphantly its 'train/again' rhyme, previous lines include the threefold 'tables', 'table', 'table' endings, which an earlier Yeats would very likely have been careful to avoid. The variation on established practices continues when Yeats follows this poem with 'A Crazed Girl', a fourteen-line piece, divided as a sonnet, with a rhyme scheme which is both irregular and incomplete. The celebration here of Margot Ruddock 'improvising her music' seeks to give the effect of improvisations of its own.

There are, therefore, ways of answering questions like '*What is there left to say?*' and '*What then?*' if such questions are understood in relation to the evolving arrangements of Yeats's new work in the 1930s. If the questions are turned on Yeats's earlier work, their subversiveness is still far from complete, for Yeats's relation to poetic form had been for many years (and had perhaps always been) one that pushed and altered the usual effects of patterns of metrical arrangement. There is no period of continued metrical regularity or orthodoxy in Yeats's career. Even the *ottava rima* in which so many of the major poems of Yeats's maturity are written is hardly an inert mould, and here Helen Vendler's observations have a particular critical value. Explaining how Yeats treated the stanza as 'a vehicle he could not resist distorting', Vendler touches on the seeming opposites which Yeats's forms characteristically conjoin:[27]

In his hands, its stately Renaissance measure—which Shelley in large part preserved—can remain ceremonious, musical and harmoniously proportioned ... Or, it can be 'rewritten', structurally, semantically and rhymingly, into a modern, nervous, colloquial and cacophonous version of itself.

The terms here give the opportunity for a different, and perhaps a more valuable, angle of critical approach on Yeats's 'impulse towards ... destruction', one in which 'Modernity ... seems always to be bursting through traditional form, until we realise that a new traditional form ... has been added, almost before we realised it, to the register of available dwelling-places for the poet's work.' It may be that Vendler overstates the case a little, but any slight exaggeration can be reconciled without much difficulty to Yeats's own later attitudes to the uses of form as a means of 'bursting through' artistic blocks and dead ends.

Bearing this in mind, the question of Yeats's intimacy with ruin, and its importance in his feeling for poetic structure, keeps its centrality. The late poetry revisits Yeats's established preoccupations in many ways, but one of these is in its sharpening of the perception that solidity and precariousness can coexist, and that the memory in which poetry deals is not exempt from such paradoxes. 'Lapis Lazuli' incorporates these ideas into its long perspectives:[28]

> No handiwork of Callimachus,
> Who handled marble as if it were bronze,
> Made draperies that seemed to rise
> When sea-wind swept the corner, stands;
> His long lamp-chimney shaped like the stem

---

[27] Vendler, 'Yeats and *Ottava Rima*', 43.   [28] Yeats, *Variorum Poems*, 565.

Of a slender palm, stood but a day;
All things fall and are built again,
And those that build them again are gay.

The cycle here, of falling and building, gives compressed expression to Yeats's most fundamental experiences of the creating of form in poetry. It is noteworthy that his example, in the sculpture of Callimachus, puts to work the poet's own powers of construction in a particularly testing way. The lines describing the sculptor's most daring works are placed in a kind of interval, as the reader waits for the delayed verb. The eventual arrival of 'stands', as a word rhythmically set apart from the rest of its end-stopped line, creates a phantom meaning: although the syntax spells out unambiguously the message that 'No handiwork . . . stands', the line allows the ghost of an assertion to materialize, as though something *does* 'stand' here. The lines have a doubleness of effect in keeping with 'Lapis Lazuli''s buoyant determination to multiply perspectives and replace solidity with a risky precariousness of structure, its transitions made, as Jon Stallworthy has put it, 'without a word of explanation; simply with the space between paragraphs'.[29] The nature of Yeats's rhyme words in these lines is also important to the effect achieved, for the fragility of the connections in sound between 'Callimachus' and 'rise', 'bronze' and 'stands', is an important factor in the reader's growing feeling here *for* fragility. When rhymes like these are sounded, the relation between rhyme and memory is made to seem perhaps less 'natural', and more willed; at any rate, that relationship certainly becomes more self-conscious. Again, the genesis of this technique belongs much earlier in Yeats's writing career, but by now it has become a crucial resource in the construction of looser metrical fabrics, where a degree of precariousness is required. The rhymes in question here were in fact jotted down together in Yeats's drafts for the poem, suggesting that it was exactly this effect which he wanted to clarify and concentrate in the process of composition.

Yeats's poetry challenges our critical resources in many ways, but in the matter of its existence in poetic form, his work seems often to pose insuperable problems for current modes of critical thinking and expression. In this sense, Yeats is in fact a more extreme example of a case which includes most major poets; it is only his degree of self-consciousness

---

[29] Jon Stallworthy, *Vision and Revision in Yeats's* Last Poems (Oxford: Clarendon Press, 1969), 52.

on the subject which makes him particularly visible. Yeats chooses very frequently to think about form in terms of metaphors which are themselves points of growth in his writing and thought, and which have complex sources in his own life. The critical reflex, on the other hand, is to interpret poetic form as something that is already a metaphor, and can thus have various kinds of interpretative meaning attached to it, in accord with a given framework of ideas. But such models are static ones, and remain profoundly false to the ways in which poetry works. Poetic form can be a metaphor only in a secondary sense: in poems, form is the pressing reality according to which metaphors and meaning must make their way. In Yeats, the tensions implicit here are both inscribed and accommodated in especially complex ways. The full implications of Heaney's insight, that 'once the place has been brought into written existence, it is inevitable that it will be unwritten', go beyond the case of Yeats alone; but they answer particularly closely to his poetry, its forms and their meanings, their falling and their building again.

In his protracted leave-taking of Coole Park, Yeats laid the foundations for his own 'final decade'. The degrees of reversal which the poet achieved in his later years present critics with problematic issues—of the nature and worth of the late writings, of the biographical continuities and discontinuities involved, and even of the difficulties in understanding the writer's textual decisions and final intentions. However, the poetry of this leave-taking points towards a conception of poetic endeavour as something complicit with destruction, where no dwelling place can be permanent:[30]

> A spot whereon the founders lived and died
> Seemed once more dear than life; ancestral trees,
> Or gardens rich in memory glorified
> Marriages, alliances and families,
> And every bride's ambition satisfied.
> Where fashion or mere fantasy decrees
> We shift about—all that great glory spent—
> Like some poor Arab tribesman and his tent.

Even within the stately frame of its *ottava rima*, a stanza like this works to unsettle the repose of 'died', 'glorified', 'satisfied' by disposing those rhymes where they must hand on to other sounds in the line of succession; but 'trees' and 'families' are syntactically hampered in extending

---

[30] Yeats, *Variorum Poems*, 491.

that line unbroken, for 'satisfied' has been so completely self-enacting that it has closed the period. Instead, the final couplet is ushered in by 'decrees', and the humiliating potential of necessity is proved in the final rhyme, of 'spent' and 'tent'. Like Crazy Jane, for whom 'Love has pitched his mansion in | The place of excrement', such rhymes put to proof the understanding that 'Nothing can be sole or whole | That has not been rent'.[31] The kind of architecture Yeats creates here is one which comprehends its own falling apart. Where does this leave Yeats? As an answer to such a question, or as a starting-point in the long process of understanding it, we would do well to remember the complexity of the most complex word in 'Coole Park, 1929': 'Here'.

[31] Ibid. 513.

CHAPTER 4

Three Critics: T. S. Eliot, Seamus Heaney, Geoffrey Hill

> I am always interested in hearing what a poet has to say about the
> nature of poetry, though I do not take it too seriously. As objective
> statements his definitions are never accurate, never complete and
> always one-sided. Not one would stand up under a rigorous
> analysis. In unkind moments one is almost tempted to think that
> all they are really saying is: 'Read me. Don't read the other fellows.'
>
> W. H. Auden, 'Making, Knowing, and Judging' (1956)[1]

I *T. S. Eliot's embarrassment*

T. S. Eliot lived to experience the fullest extent of his own critical
authority, and, to judge from the evidence of his later essays and
addresses, he became increasingly bemused by the weight which his
own opinions had come to carry. The young Eliot, the reviewer and
essayist who dealt lethal blows to the culture of English belles-lettres,
and whose show of erudition was, in its own way, as fearsome as the
sting of his intellect and the finality of his judgements, went on to be
seen as the ancestor of an altogether less dangerous school of (largely
academic) criticism in the United States and Britain, many of whose
members adopted his literary enthusiasms and dislikes, along with a
few motifs of interpretation held to be his ideas. The author of *The
Sacred Wood* (1920) is indeed, from some angles, recognizable as the
begetter of New Criticism; but from other points of view, he is an
altogether different creature, one whose reflexes and reactions are
honed to protect and promote the kind of art in which his own interests
were vested.

---

[1] W. H. Auden, *The Dyer's Hand and Other Essays* (London: Faber and Faber, 1953), 52.

Eliot was not, of course, a New Critic; he was, again of course, a poet-critic. But perhaps we should not let this pass as a matter of course: as a term, 'poet-critic' looks more clear than it is, and not just in the case of Eliot himself. There is a roll of poet-critics from before the twentieth century which gives the term a formidable weight: very selectively, this would include Sidney, Dryden, Johnson, Wordsworth, Coleridge, and Arnold. The effect of a list like this is to incline us towards a relatively passive acceptance of the notion of the poet-critic, and the kind of critical authority this poet-criticism might possess. But in a literary culture, on both sides of the Atlantic, where there are very nearly as many practising poet-critics as there are poets, this kind of acceptance is not always helpful. A very late retrospective from Eliot is relevant here:[2]

I am, I admit, much more interested in what other poets have written about poetry than what critics who are not poets have said about it . . . But the nearest we get to pure literary criticism is the criticism of artists writing about their own art . . . In other types of criticism, the historian, the philosopher, the moralist, the sociologist, the grammarian may play a large part; but in so far as literary criticism is purely literary, I believe that the criticism of artists writing about their own art is of greater intensity, and carries more authority, though the area of the artist's competence may be much narrower.

The ascription of purity of motive here to artists writing about their own art suggests an innocence that is scarcely credible in a man who had been a professional editor and publisher for over forty years. Assuming Eliot to be indulging himself in the charitableness of age, we might still wonder about the precise bearing of his observation that poets' criticism 'carries more authority' on account of its supposed purity. In context, it is possible that Eliot is speaking with a strictly personal emphasis: the authority, in this case, is an authority over the writer alone, and does not necessarily carry beyond his own likes and dislikes. Yet the issue of poets' more general authority as critics is inescapable here, and indeed Eliot's lecture takes his own case as a test-case in the wider problem of how critics are to be understood in relation to their times and their callings.

'To Criticize the Critic' takes a sceptical view of the long-term worth of some of Eliot's own most widely circulated ideas, such as the 'objective correlative' or the 'dissociation of sensibility'. Hearing terms like these in the context of their use and overuse by mid-century literary

---

[2] T. S. Eliot, 'To Criticize the Critic', *To Criticize the Critic and Other Writings* (London: Faber and Faber, 1965), 25–6.

critics, Eliot chooses to see them as things that 'may soon go out of
fashion completely', and reads them as 'conceptual symbols for emotional preferences'.[3] Perhaps the professional, or academic, currency of
such phrases is something Eliot wishes to distinguish from a more
substantial and further-reaching critical authority, one which locates
itself in artistic practice and tradition rather than formal disciplines of
study. Here, as elsewhere in later Eliot, there is an apparent relaxation
into candour, as the much-honoured and heavily studied poet, critic,
and cultural commentator politely ventures to ask his academic audience what all the fuss was about.

The same note is struck by Eliot in 1955, in 'The Frontiers of
Criticism', when a degree of frankness comes in to spoil the academics'
fun. 'I have been somewhat bewildered,' Eliot tells his audience, 'to find,
from time to time, that I am regarded as one of the ancestors of modern
criticism, if too old to be a modern critic myself.' However, Eliot does
go on to outline what he thinks of as his own critical contribution, again
with candour:[4]

The best of my *literary* criticism—apart from a few notorious phrases which
have had a truly embarrassing success in the world—consists of essays on poets
and poetic dramatists who had influenced me. It is a by-product of my private
poetry-workshop; or a prolongation of the thinking that went into my own
verse. In retrospect, I see that I wrote best about poets whose work had
influenced my own, and with whose poetry I had become thoroughly familiar,
long before I desired to write about them, or had found the occasion to do so.
My criticism has this in common with that of Ezra Pound, that its merits and its
limitations can be fully appreciated only when it is considered in relation to the
poetry I have written myself.

There are two things to notice about the effect of this: first, Eliot's
recourse to autobiographical retrospect manages to convey modesty
without any obtrusive self-deprecation (and here, his admission of
'embarrassment' about famous soundbites fits well with a reader's likely
impatience with critical jargon—what we are hearing, we feel, is a
reasonable reaction, and blessedly *not* professional rigmarole); second,
these admissions do not disown the authority of their own judgements,
and Eliot does not announce or imply either that his criticism is

    [3] T. S. Eliot, 'To Criticize the Critic', *To Criticize the Critic and Other Writings* (London: Faber
and Faber, 1965), 19.
    [4] T. S. Eliot, *On Poetry and Poets* (London: Faber and Faber, 1957), 106.

unsound or that it is not worth taking seriously. All of this adds up to a perhaps surprisingly complex tone, as the poet-critic assesses his own position authoritatively (the 'I' here is still the 'I' of an evaluating critic, not just the first person of memory or anecdote), and effects the conjunction of himself with Ezra Pound as subjects for study, and for the assessment of 'merits and limitations'.

In 1942, Eliot had begun his lecture 'The Music of Poetry' with the observation that 'The poet, when he talks or writes about poetry, has peculiar qualifications and peculiar limitations', and spelled out these simultaneous advantages and disadvantages with reference to himself:[5]

> I can never re-read any of my own prose writings without acute embarrassment: I shirk the task, and consequently may not take account of all the assertions to which I have at one time or another committed myself; I may often repeat what I have said before, and I may often contradict myself. But I believe that the critical writings of poets, of which in the past there have been some very distinguished examples, owe a great deal of their interest to the fact that the poet, at the back of his mind, if not as his ostensible purpose, is always trying to defend the kind of poetry he is writing, or to formulate the kind that he wants to write. ... What he writes about poetry, in short, must be assessed in relation to the poetry he writes.

This confession of embarrassment is, like later confessions, part of a collaboration with the audience, a sharing of discomfort in the cause of honesty. In the same year, the poet went still further in the inspection of his own faked credentials, now the matter for red faces all round, speaking of how 'In my earlier years I obtained, partly by subtlety, partly be effrontery, and partly by accident, a reputation amongst the credulous for learning and scholarship, of which (having no further use for it) I have since tried to disembarrass myself.'[6] In paying his audiences the compliment of not considering them credulous, Eliot is able to share with them the interest of observing a poet's mind at its critical work, engaged in defending its particular patch and feeling its way towards the poetry. Left at this stage, the critical display, like the critical interest in the display, would be bland and impressionistic, and open itself to the risk of embarrassing exposure.

Yet there are always 'limitations', and in 'The Frontiers of Criticism' we soon hear more about these 'limitations'. In using the word first in

---

[5] Ibid. 26.

[6] T. S. Eliot, 'The Classics and the Man of Letters', *To Criticize the Critic*, 145.

relation to Ezra Pound as well as to himself, Eliot knowingly risks an apparent understatement: any audience in 1955, and especially an American audience, knew of failures of judgement in Pound beside which a word like 'limitations' pales. Many might be forgiven for overlooking his 'merits'. Of course, Eliot is speaking carefully about '*literary*' judgements only, and any raising of hackles with 'limitations' could therefore seem out of place; yet, 'limitations' still allows us to hear, if only for a moment, the sound of hollow inadequacy in Eliot's vocabulary. The case for its amounting to a deliberate, and deliberated, infelicity is strengthened by considering Eliot's choice to stand together in public, as it were, with his old friend and collaborator, only a short time after the Bollingen Prize controversy of 1948. Very quickly, Eliot picks up on limitation again, this time to fix on the limits of the competence allowable to poets in their critical views:[7]

This kind of criticism of poetry by a poet, or what I have called workshop criticism, has one obvious limitation. What has no relation to the poet's own work, or what is antipathetic to him, is outside of his competence. Another limitation of workshop criticism is that the critic's judgement may be unsound outside of his own art.

With Pound's name still ringing in the audience's ears, Eliot tries to put in place what we might think of as a statute of critical limitations, which sets strict bounds to the fields of a writer's 'competence'. (And 'competence' is not without its ironies, for Pound, notoriously, had not been deemed competent to stand trial for his wartime treasons.) Now 'limitation' is functioning as a kind of critical *cordon sanitaire* around the area of the poet-critic's judgements; but again, 'limitation' cuts two ways, since if poets' competence does not travel beyond their workshops, other critics' competence should not try to intrude on those places and the mysteries contained there.

The measure of authority enjoyed by Eliot's poet-critic is being seen in 'The Frontiers of Criticism' as the delimitation of competences—that of the poet himself, and that of the critic who is not the poet. There is surely some element of, if not provocation, at least daring in the bringing forward of Pound in this context; and Eliot's admissions of 'limitation' in his own academic, New Critical credentials are balanced by his implicit deprecation of the academic milieu in which phrases by

[7] Eliot, *On Poetry and Poets*, 107.

which he is now embarrassed have assumed an unquestioned currency. And that 'truly embarrassing success in the world' is a phrase which, before it is printed, is uttered in front of an audience of 46,000 in a Minnesota sports stadium; arguably, the poet-critic (Eliot, but *any* poet-critic) is here in another potentially embarrassing situation, and an audience's feeling for his susceptibility to embarrassment is therefore something to be implicitly solicited. Success, on this scale and in a context like this, is a truly embarrassing business for all concerned. The more we consider Eliot's phrase and its context, the more Jamesian become its tonal complexities.

All of this might be described as the rhetorical working of candour; but we should not on that account simply dismiss Eliot's frankness, nor shallowly distrust his motives. It soon becomes clear that Eliot is not putting forward the argument that poetry enjoys a special realm of unaccountability as discourse, where it is immune to any questions which the intellect informed by religious, political, or scientific beliefs and knowledge might pose. And Eliot's own candour in matters of politics and religion is not irrelevant in this context; especially in the later critical work, the voice is seldom one of *covert* political or religious intent; it tends to come clean about such things. In 1947, this had been a dominant feature of Eliot's lecture on Milton (itself supplementing and to some degree revising his 1936 essay on the poet), in which he made plain his 'antipathy towards Milton the man', an antipathy with political as well as historical resonances. Eliot's frankness goes beyond this admission, by forcing his audience to consider how the admission itself, properly thought through, reflects upon *them* as well as the poet-critic:[8]

The fact is simply that the Civil War of the seventeenth century, in which Milton is a symbolic figure, has never been concluded. The Civil War is not ended: I question whether any serious civil war ever does end. Throughout that period English society was so convulsed and divided that the effects are still felt. . . . No other English poet, not Wordsworth, or Shelley, lived through or took sides in such momentous events as did Milton; of no other poet is it so difficult to consider the poetry simply as poetry, without our theological and political dispositions, conscious and unconscious, inherited or acquired, making an unlawful entry.

Eliot carries off a wonderfully strong rhetorical manoeuvre here: first comes admission of the poet-critic's own prejudice, which inclines an

[8] Eliot, 'Milton II' (1947), *On Poetry and Poets*, 148.

audience to a slightly complaisant sympathy for anyone willing to admit to a prejudice; then comes the shock of the sentences quoted above, in which history teaches a startling lesson, one that undermines the complacency of the audience in its present, only apparently peaceful, situation. The manoeuvre is not uncommon in Eliot's prose, where the procedural noise of a slightly ponderous and over-correct English accustoms the reader to its tone, then a surprise is suddenly sprung: it is the equivalent in critical writing to what Eliot identified (in Middleton's drama) as the 'mixture of tedious discourse and sudden reality'.[9] The remarks on civil war carry force in both of the contexts in which they were uttered, for Eliot delivered his lecture in New York as well as London, and an American audience was if anything more likely than an English one to be made uncomfortable by the idea that 'any serious civil war' never really comes to an end. Then Eliot produces again, this time in a context fraught with difficulty, the apparent common sense of the critic's duty 'to consider the poetry simply as poetry'. By now, this aim sounds like the hope to lead a life free from sin: an impossibility in absolute terms, but no less necessary and laudable for that. The 'unlawful entry' of 'dispositions', then, is not to be a matter for surprise; but Eliot puts his audience in the position which, he claims, the poet-critic himself must occupy, guarding the artistic property against one's own illicit incursions.

Earlier in the lecture, Eliot ventures explicitly upon the nature of a poet's criticism. He distinguishes between the 'scholar' and the 'practitioner' of poetry, assigning to the academic concerns such as 'the world in which that author lived, the temper of his age, his intellectual formation, the books which he had read, and the influences which had moulded him'. For the working poet, on the other hand, a rather different agenda applies:[10]

The practitioner is concerned less with the author than with the poem; and with the poem in relation to his own age. He asks: Of what *use* is the poetry of this poet to poets writing today? Is it, or can it become, a living force in English poetry still unwritten?

These questions are, as a matter of fact, exactly the questions Eliot had been asking about Milton in 1936, and which the 1947 lecture will

---

[9] T. S. Eliot, 'Thomas Middleton' (1927), *Selected Essays* (London: Faber and Faber, 1951), 162.
[10] Eliot, 'Milton II', 147.

reformulate and attempt to answer. The idea that 'the scholar's interest is in the permanent, the practitioner's in the immediate'[11] makes an effective antithesis out of two kinds of interest which can never, as both of Eliot's Milton essays prove, be quite so securely sealed off from one another as this suggests. The author who stings his contemporary audience with the observation that civil wars do not truly come to an end is something other than a 'practitioner' in the sense employed here; and the lecturer who appraises and adapts Johnson on Miltonic blank verse to conclude that 'We cannot, in literature, any more than in the rest of life, live in a perpetual state of revolution'[12] is something a little different from a 'scholar'.

In part, Eliot's second major engagement with Milton is an exercise in the candour which was more and more to characterize his later critical writing. The scholar/practitioner antithesis, coming at the beginning of his lecture, is made to seem increasingly ideal rather than practical as the lecture progresses; questions of good and bad influence are treated with caution, and Eliot is careful to remind his audience of his (and their) limitations in answering such questions: 'As for the remote future,' he writes, 'what can we affirm about the poetry that will be written then, except that we should probably be unable to understand or to enjoy it, and that therefore we can hold no opinion as to what "good" and "bad" influences will *mean* in that future?'[13] So, it is only with 'the immediate future' that an answer to the question of influence can concern itself, and even here Eliot is more careful to disqualify blanket observations than to make them: caution is the recommended attitude in the critic, and modesty is its equivalent in the poet. Again, Eliot must encounter his own critical authority with the show of surprise, and he returns to the 'dissociation of sensibility' as 'one of the two or three phrases of my coinage—like "objective correlative"—which have had a success in the world astonishing to their author'.[14] The modesty is winning, though Eliot manages at the same time to allow the subtle implication that it is the world, and not necessarily the author, which is culpably accountable for these phrases' 'success'.

The vestiges of an earlier style are discernible in the 1936 piece, with its calculated intemperance on Milton's failings, and its refusal to put up even a show of resistance to the 'unlawful entry' of political and theological opinion. On *Paradise Lost* and Milton's narrative of the

---

[11] Ibid.   [12] Ibid. 160.   [13] Ibid. 152.   [14] Ibid.

Fall, for example, Eliot finds a register of entertaining (but shallow) disdain: 'So far as I perceive anything,' he writes (in the context of an argument that makes a point of the stylistic consequences of Milton's blindness) 'it is a glimpse of a theology that I find in large part repellent, expressed through a mythology which would have better been left in the Book of *Genesis*, upon which Milton has not improved.'[15] The blind leads the half-blind, then; but the criticism here is being directed by the wit—a clearly political kind of wit—to which it is secondary. Eliot is upfront, also, on the matter of poets and their criticism, asserting unapologetically that 'of what I have to say I consider that the only jury of judgment is that of the ablest poetical practitioners of my own time'.[16] When Eliot convicts Milton of embodying in his work 'a division . . . between the philosopher or theologian and the poet', he is impelled to see much of the poetry as something which cannot be fully itself: 'I feel that this is not serious poetry, not poetry fully occupied about its business, but rather a solemn game.'[17]

There is not the merest suspicion of self-doubt in Eliot's authoritative critical tone; and perhaps this in fact continues to be the case in the later criticism, which puts self-deprecation in the place where self-doubt ought to be. We need to remember that the self-deprecation of the later Eliot is anything but a way of lessening or qualifying the authority which his criticism sets out to exercise. On the contrary, it provides a firm support for that authority in a culture of irony, modesty, and scepticism about high claims for poetry, and of increasing regulation of literary activity along academic lines. From the beginning, Eliot believes that the authority of a poet writing about his own art is a potent thing, and much of the earlier criticism voices his confidence in this authority with unembarrassed and unembarrassable directness.

The earlier text which lies behind 'The Frontiers of Criticism' is Eliot's 1923 essay 'The Function of Criticism'. The Arnoldian title is meant as a provocation, and this piece is powered by an unmisgiving, vitriolic energy as it hounds the inheritors of Arnold's tradition, the followers of 'the Inner Voice'—most prominent among these, John Middleton Murry. The ferocity of Eliot's attack issues in moments of potent ridicule:[18]

The inner voice, in fact, sounds remarkably like an old principle which has been formulated by an elder critic in the now familiar phrase of 'doing as one likes'.

---

[15] T. S. Eliot, 'Milton I' (1936), *On Poetry and Poets*, 144.   [16] Ibid. 139.
[17] Ibid. 144.   [18] Eliot, *Selected Essays*, 27.

The possessors of the inner voice ride ten to a compartment to a football match at Swansea, listening to the inner voice, which breathes the eternal message of vanity, fear, and lust.

The intensity and unexpectedness of this vignette do, perhaps, show the hand of the poet, and have a remotely Augustan feel. Of course, all of this is unfair to Murry; but Eliot's purpose in the essay has the single-mindedness of the poet, rather than the open-mindedness of the critic, as its driving force.[19] What Eliot takes seriously is the poet's ability to think critically, an ability which is proved in the poetry itself, and not acquired in some separate sphere. Since he writes good poems, a good poet is necessarily a good critic in his poetry. Eliot reflects archly on 'the use of the terms "critical" and "creative" by one whose place, on the whole, is with the weaker brethren':[20]

Matthew Arnold distinguishes far too bluntly, it seems to me, between the two activities: he overlooks the capital importance of criticism in the work of creation itself. Probably, indeed, the larger part of the labour of an author in composing his work is critical labour; the labour of sifting, combining, constructing, expunging, correcting, testing: this frightful toil is as much critical as creative. I maintain even that the criticism employed by a trained and skilled writer on his own work is the most vital, the highest kind of criticism; and (as I think I have said before) that some creative writers are superior to others solely because their critical faculty is superior.

This may be an *ars poetica* for Eliot, and it is arguably one which has validity in more general terms. It is certainly, however, a polemical statement of position, and flies deliberately in the face of attempts (which Eliot at that time would have identified with a 'Romantic' rather than 'Classic' temperament) to keep creativity and intelligence in separate compartments.

At this point, Eliot is obliged to assert the authority of his position. The suspicion that creativity might not be confined to poets, and may inhere in critical writing in and for itself, is one which Eliot's argument cannot countenance. There is no other way than to maintain a superior authority:[21]

[19] For an excellent account of the relations between the two writers, see David Goldie, *A Critical Difference: T. S. Eliot and John Middleton Murry in English Literary Criticism, 1919–1928* (Oxford: Clarendon Press, 1998).

[20] Eliot, *Selected Essays*, 29–30.

[21] Ibid. 30–1.

But this affirmation recoils upon us. If so large a part of creation is really criticism, is not a large part of what is called 'critical writing' really creative? If so, is there not creative criticism in the ordinary sense? The answer seems to be, that there is no equation. I have assumed as axiomatic that a creation, a work of art, is autotelic; and that criticism, by definition, is *about* something other than itself. Hence you cannot fuse creation with criticism as you can fuse criticism with creation. The critical activity finds its highest, its true fulfilment in a kind of union with creation in the labour of the artist.

Reading this, it becomes easier to see how Eliot would go on to find in the literary criticism of later decades an embarrassing or astonishing propensity to take his own critical phrases as literal rather than 'symbolic' things. It is easier, too, to understand Eliot's more general reservations about the 'unlawful entry' of one kind of criticism into the discussion of art, and his suspicions here begin to appear protective, rather than merely self-asserting manoeuvres.

The assumption that a particular work of art is autotelic—that is, that it has its end in itself, and not in any project beyond its own completion—is not an assumption which the Arnoldian tradition can tolerate. On the surface, at least, it seems to have affinities with what is often taken as the characteristic New Critical approach to poems: the belief that a poem can be analysed rigorously in terms of its own language and structure so as to reveal the full compass of its meaning. As many subsequent writers have pointed out, this is a critical tenet which is itself very far from being autotelic, and its protective effects operate in ways remote from the artistic protectiveness which Eliot sees in art. Here, Eliot's careful distinction between art and criticism, and his refusal to countenance an artistic licence for critical activity, is already dissenting from the New Critical dogma in its severer forms. This becomes more explicit: 'If in literary criticism, we place all the emphasis upon *understanding*, we are in danger of slipping from understanding to mere explanation.'[22] However, no simple alternative of historical criticism is being proposed here, and Eliot sets limits to the possibility, and the usefulness, of this kind of understanding also:[23]

Such knowledge ... has a value of its own, as history; but for the appreciation of the poetry, it can only lead us to the door: we must find our own way in. For the purpose of acquiring such knowledge ... is not primarily that we should be able to project ourselves into a remote period, that we should be able to think and

[22] T. S. Eliot, 'The Frontiers of Criticism', *On Poetry and Poets*, 117.   [23] Ibid.

feel, when reading the poetry, as a contemporary of the poet might have thought and felt, though such experience has its own value; it is rather to divest ourselves of the limitations of our own age, and the poet, whose work we are reading, of the limitations of *his* age, in order to get the direct experience, the immediate contact with his poetry.

Historical knowledge, then, is finally incidental in poetry; and the conditions of the present, as well as the past, are limitations to be seen past in the understanding of poetry. What Eliot is doing here is cutting away the positions where the critic might usually seem to have the advantage over the poet: 'the direct experience', in this argument, in fact gives us a better vantage-point than either the exegetical procedures of 'explanation' or the historical researches of scholarship.

Eliot was no fool, and we should not expect this 'direct experience' to be a naive concept. Indeed, he had written long before (in 1933) of how 'Criticism, of course, never does find out what poetry is, in the sense of arriving at an adequate definition . . . Nor can criticism ever arrive at any final appraisal of poetry', going on to complicate the nature of 'direct experience':[24]

But there are these two theoretical limits of criticism: at one of which we attempt to answer the question 'what is poetry?' and at the other 'is this a good poem?' No theoretic ingenuity will suffice to answer the second question, because no theory can amount to much which is not founded upon a direct experience of good poetry; but on the other hand our direct experience of poetry involves a good deal of generalising activity.

'Direct experience', looked at closely enough, is a puzzle: like the creation of poetry itself, it is an impure activity, which involves criticism in its very performance. In its essentials, this anticipates a number of the objections which were eventually made to New Critical practice; and we should remember that, although Eliot is one of the greatest critical masters of quotation, he is not, any more than Coleridge or Arnold, committed on the whole to sustained and dense close reading in his essays. Of course, quotation is the most critically potent means of giving the 'direct experience' of an author under discussion, and it offers Eliot (especially perhaps in his earlier essays on Elizabethan and Jacobean dramatists) a way of reapproaching an experience of particular passages and lines that are demonstrably influential on his own creative work:

[24] T. S. Eliot, *The Use of Poetry and the Use of Criticism: Studies in the Relation of Criticism to Poetry in England* (London: Faber and Faber, 1933; 2nd edn. 1964), 16.

here, Eliot's quotations are certainly the furniture of the workshop. Close reading, as we understand and practise it, engages with 'direct experience', finding ways in which to describe the working resources of the language in action, but does not (if it has any sense) offer itself either as a substitute for the 'direct experience' or as its comprehensive explanation. Eliot's acknowledgement of the 'generalising activity' that is necessarily in, or behind, our 'direct experience' has a part to play in his understanding of 'tradition' in literature as well as of criticism; but it is also a way of ensuring, by making a careful distinction, that we remain aware of the difference between 'poetry' and 'theory'. Again, the fact that an absolute distinction is not possible in this world, and in the language of this world, is no disproof of the distinction itself.

A great deal of Eliot's critical writing concerns itself with our propensity to confuse one thing with another: 'direct experience' with 'generalising activity', poetry with beliefs, or history with understanding. It does not assume that such confusions are necessarily foolish or wrong-headed: on the contrary, Eliot is increasingly at pains to show how far he is himself liable to take one thing for another. If the more candid later critical style admits to embarrassment, that is the embarrassment of being subject to the kind of misinterpretation for which one is oneself, in some degree, responsible. The earlier criticism is more likely to give us a feeling *for* embarrassment: not just for Eliot's victims and straw-men, the Murrys and Arnolds, but for the fundamental error of taking one thing for another, and its exposure under the critical gaze. For Eliot, the proof of a poet-critic's authority is that he offers no definition of poetry, and that poetry is so real to him, so much and so bewilderingly a 'direct experience', that he is able to see it intensely and immediately for what it is not—not history, not philosophy, not politics. One more negative needs to be added to the list, for Eliot's absorption in and eventual commitment to religious beliefs, their debate and expression in the past and in his own time, never brought him to the point of identifying poetic with religious meaning. The authority of the poet-critic is not, for Eliot, some parallel to the priest's function, any more than it is a career path whose heights look across to the successful politician or pundit at the top of their professions. The poet-critic's authority does not answer the calls from any such eminences, or necessarily look up to them. In contexts like these, moreover, its insistence on the recognition of distinctions and limitations is unusual, and its capacity for, and cultivation of embarrassment is unique.

II *Seamus Heaney's redress*

Discussing W. B. Yeats's forthright editorial interventions in Oscar Wilde's *The Ballad of Reading Gaol* (where 38 of the poem's original 109 stanzas were done away with), Seamus Heaney describes that energetic editor of the 1936 *Oxford Book of Modern Verse* as 'an authoritative public poet, a Nobel Prize winner, "the finished man among his enemies"'.[25] In the context of a lecture on Wilde, this description of Yeats is little more than an aside; but time and good fortune have given an extra dimension to Heaney's remarks. The three aspects of this assessment—Yeats is accorded public authority, international recognition, and unassailable self-sufficiency—reflect sides of Heaney's own artistic character and reputation which the award to him of the Nobel Prize for Literature in 1995 could only consolidate. The Prize added lustre to Heaney's (already Yeatsian) finish, and in as much as it set a seal on the particular character of the poet's ambitions and (so far as this can be judged) the nature of his success, the Nobel Prize was indeed fitting recognition for the breadth and intensity of his talents. In another sense, of course, the Nobel Prize must be a matter of mere 'finish', the highest veneer of literary (and extra-literary) currency and esteem; in this respect, as Yeats was well aware, 'the finished man' in poetry has to remain something other than a man who is finished, and whose voice responds mainly to its own public resonances. Heaney's understanding of the plight of the 'authoritative public poet', which had been developing in both his prose and his poetry for a long time, was more likely to be regularly tested after the Nobel award, and his ability to interpret and make use of this strongly Yeatsian dilemma became itself more likely to be seen as central to his artistic success.

In the speech with which he accepted the Nobel Prize, and which he subsequently printed as a coda to his quasi-collected poems, *Opened Ground* (1998), Heaney offers an *ars poetica* that tries to find terms for the yoking of inward working reflection and outwardly crafted projection in the poetic voice—a voice which he locates emphatically in Yeats, his predecessor on the Stockholm platform. 'Crediting Poetry', like some of Yeats's own prose, functions in ways that suggest the prose-poem, with its dominant images recurring at artful intervals, and with subtle turns of combination and significance. Heaney puts together a haunting and poignant sequence of memories (the childhood house, voices from

---

[25] Seamus Heaney, *The Redress of Poetry: Oxford Lectures* (London: Faber and Faber, 1995), 89.

the kitchen and from the wireless) and points of more public history (wartime, the Northern Irish Troubles, sectarian violence): these motifs come together in a celebration of Yeats's poetry of civil war, and in particular 'The Stare's Nest by my Window'. In his praise of this poem, Heaney gives his own description of what poetry should be:[26]

I have heard this poem repeated often, in whole and in part, by people in Ireland over the past twenty-five years, and no wonder, for it is as tender-minded towards life itself as St Kevin was and as tough-minded about what happens in and to life as Homer. It knows that the massacre will happen again on the roadside, that the workers in the minibus are going to be lined up and shot down just after quitting time; but it also credits as a reality the squeeze of the hand, the actuality of sympathy and protectiveness between living creatures. It satisfies the contradictory needs which consciousness experiences at times of extreme crisis, the need on the one hand for a truth-telling that will be hard and retributive, and on the other hand the need not to harden the mind to the point where it denies its own yearnings for sweetness and trust. It is a proof that poetry can be equal to *and* true at the same time, an example of that completely adequate poetry which the Russian woman sought from Anna Akhmatova and which William Wordsworth produced at a corresponding moment of historical crisis and personal dismay almost exactly two hundred years ago.

There is an internal economy at work here—an economy of images and instances within 'Crediting Poetry'—which both illustrates and puts in process an argument about poetry's economy when it is 'completely adequate'. At an especially public moment of reflection, Heaney finds himself in an inescapable dialogue with his Irish predecessor, and he makes this dialogue one between not just poet and poet, or public man and public man, but between poem and poem: it is not only Yeats's 'Stare's Nest by my Window' which is absorbed into the critical argument here, but also Heaney's own 'St Kevin and the Blackbird'.[27] The *ars poetica* has been understood, in the process, as something whose meaning is invested in the poetry behind it; rather than a theory whose applicability is general (and therefore, notionally at least, impersonal), this is a testimony whose validity is guaranteed by the quality of the creative work to which it alludes.

The issue of authority has always dogged Heaney's critical thinking, just as it has haunted much of his poetry: the authority of poetry itself,

---

[26] Seamus Heaney, *Opened Ground: Poems 1966–1996* (London: Faber and Faber, 1998), 464.
[27] Ibid. 410.

and the authority possessed by the writer of poetry, are twin themes in a great deal of his work, and they are explored with particular subtlety and elegance in the best of his critical writing. *The Government of the Tongue* both worried over and made large claims for the integrity and authority of poets, asserting what Heaney called 'the jurisdiction of achieved form'.[28] In *The Redress of Poetry*, which collects ten of Heaney's lectures as Professor of Poetry at Oxford, the strength of poetry itself is to the fore, and its power of 'redress' (rather than the somewhat forbidding notion of 'jurisdiction') in the world of chance and contingency is celebrated with Heaney's distinctive warmth and eloquence. But this is undoubtedly celebration rather than analysis; each lecture seems planned as a tribute to someone or something, a poet's hour in the warm sun of Heaney's admiring attention. In literary criticism, as in much else, it is prudent not to take celebration alone as the measure of achievement; sooner or later, we need to be sure of what exactly we are celebrating, why we are doing so, and what we are doing when we celebrate. However, issues like these seem distinctly out of place in the particular sub-genre of criticism which is occupied by lectures like Heaney's: raising them feels like—and perhaps *is*—a breach of etiquette. It would be hard to deny that Heaney's performance during his tenure of the Oxford Chair was anything less than brilliant, or that it was a job for which he was anything other than 'completely adequate': *The Redress of Poetry* gives more than a glimpse of the charm, grace, and carefully judged gravity with which the poet handled his acts of praise, and Heaney's display of personal authority is both beguiling and seductive. On the other hand, the issue of poetry's power of 'redress' in the world beyond the theatre of critical cherishing is, as Heaney formulates it at any rate, much too important to rest on the 'authority' of a single poet. For better or worse, the problems here are 'public' ones, and Heaney's critical engagement with them is in the nature of 'public' speech. As the poet told Seamus Deane as long ago as 1977, 'If you live as an author your reward is authority':[29] in discussing poetry's power of 'redress', the older Heaney inevitably subjects this authority to some very severe critical tests—so much so, that it is possible to wonder whether it is as much a liability as a 'reward'.

[28] Seamus Heaney, *The Government of the Tongue: The 1986 T. S. Eliot Memorial Lectures and Other Critical Writings* (London: Faber and Faber, 1988), 92.
[29] Seamus Heaney, interviewed by Seamus Deane, *The Crane Bag*, 1 (1977), repr. in *The Crane Bag Book of Irish Studies* (Dublin, 1983), 72.

The contextual circumstances of *The Redress of Poetry* seem to describe exactly the difficulties as well as the opportunities involved in Heaney's poetic (and critical) authority. When the poet began his tenure of the Oxford Chair in 1989, he was already a figure of major significance for literary worlds on both sides of the Atlantic, a 50-year-old smiling public man whose Irish (and, beyond that, Yeatsian) affiliations were widely known, and bound up with the weight of his critical authority. Even in 1989, a cynic might say, the Nobel Prize was as good as won: at any rate, it was in no sense a remote possibility then, and Heaney's Oxford appearances were those of a major literary star. Given this, the massiveness of Heaney's theme in his inaugural lecture (and in the lectures that followed), its fundamentalist insistence upon the actual worth of poetic art in a flawed and perpetually disappointing world, was both courageous and, to a certain extent, expected. Inaugural lectures, even in Oxford, are all too often exercises in the higher platitude—or rather, it is part of their specifically *public* nature and significance that this should be the case— and they are not the occasions for professions of bafflement, for struggles with recalcitrant detail, or enactments of earnest puzzlement or confusion: the Professor seldom rises (intentionally at least) to argue against his or her own competence to speak. In such situations, Professors lecture not just from a position of eminence, but *on account of* that very eminence, and giving an account of it; for good or ill, an inaugural lecture puts on display a 'finished man' (or woman), among friends as well as enemies. For the Oxford Professor of Poetry, serving his five-year term usually after all the publicity of a contested election, every lecture can bring with it the pressures and expectations of the inaugural.

In Heaney's case, the opening lecture on 'The Redress of Poetry' asks some of the big questions which the poet was elected in order to ask, but which he was not especially expected to answer. Defining 'redress', Heaney speaks of 'tilting the scales of reality towards some transcendent equilibrium', and continues:[30]

And in the activity of poetry too, there is a tendency to place a counter-reality in the scales—a reality which may be only imagined but which nevertheless has weight because it is imagined within the gravitational pull of the actual and can therefore hold its own and balance out against the historical situation. This redressing effect of poetry comes from its being a glimpsed alternative, a revelation of potential that is denied or constantly threatened by circumstances.

[30] Heaney, *The Redress of Poetry*, 3–4.

And sometimes, of course, it happens that such a revelation, once enshrined in the poem, remains as a standard for the poet, so that he or she must then submit to the strain of bearing witness in his or her own life to the plane of consciousness established in the poem.

These statements have their own 'situation'—a complex one, combining Heaney's particular moment of authoritative speech in Oxford with the more general context of his poetic career and the preoccupations of his poems—which marks them out as in keeping with their occasion. That is to say, Heaney is attuned here to the particular kind of attention which his statements will receive, and tacitly acknowledges that he is himself, as an artist, part of the subject in hand. In some of his earlier prose writings, Heaney allowed this awareness to become more explicit, and to generate a densely metaphorical register of literary discussion, one which seemed (sometimes too obviously) a kind of ruminative extension of his poems. An advantage of this was the relative ease with which Heaney was able to sidestep the harder critical questions which his essays raised: the 'creative' side of his criticism could always, as it were, cover eloquently and winningly for any 'theoretical' failings. The language of 'The Redress of Poetry' here is still in some ways safely metaphorical, but it is also insistent—with its 'transcendent', 'revelation', and 'bearing witness'—on a dimension of poetic value for which critical language alone is seldom adequate. If all this is largely expected from Heaney, his pursuit of the theme beyond the expected point is more courageous, and the lecture goes on to locate 'redress' in poems themselves, rather than in what (metaphorically or otherwise) we choose to say *about* poetry:[31]

The movement is from delight to wisdom and not vice versa. The felicity of a cadence, the chain reaction of a rhyme, the pleasuring of an etymology, such things can proceed happily and as it were autistically, in an area of mental operations cordoned off by and from the critical sense.... It is only right that this should be the case. Poetry cannot afford to lose its fundamentally self-delighting inventiveness, its joy in being a process of language as well as a representation of things in the world. To put it in W. B. Yeats's terms, the will must not usurp the work of the imagination.

In directing his attention to 'an area of mental operations cordoned off by and from the critical sense', Heaney finds himself speaking

[31] Ibid. 5.

literally about poetry, while keeping Yeats at his elbow. For a moment, the poet's authority separates itself from the constraints of 'critical sense', and begins to threaten some of the things which that 'critical sense' serves to promote (including 'a late-twentieth-century context of politically approved themes', as Heaney puts it);[32] the Professor of Poetry is then able to insist on the 'imperative' facing poets, 'to redress poetry *as* poetry, to set it up as its own category, an eminence established and a pressure exercised by distinctly linguistic means'.[33] The conditions of Heaney's own 'eminence', from which he speaks, are not irrelevant to the force of these observations, and are being very gently questioned: the Professor of Poetry, we are reminded, will be a Professor of 'poetry *as* poetry'.

In many academic domains of 'the critical sense', of course, the idea of engaging with 'poetry *as* poetry' is regarded as, at best, an under-informed absurdity. Similarly, Heaney's sly formulation of 'an area of mental operations cordoned off by and from the critical sense' is calculated to put that 'sense' firmly in its place. In terms of the implied polemic, it is easy to agree with Heaney's emphasis; indeed, *The Redress of Poetry* includes, as a volume, more first-rate close observation of poetry, and intelligent and suggestive views of individual poetic achievements, than the modish mediocrity of the bulk of academic literary criticism manages in the average year. Nevertheless, the weight of emphasis which *The Redress of Poetry* places on poetry as 'a process of language' means that Heaney's criticism brings along with it many assumptions and implications that repay questioning, especially those which shed some light on the nature, as Heaney sees it, of the language of poetry and the possibility of its answerable relation to the quotidian environment in which it is read as well as written.

To claim that there is such a thing as poetic language, and that it is capable of effecting change in a world outside discourse, may well seem like striding blithely into a theoretical minefield. Although in fact he is completely right to make these claims, Heaney's success in this respect is partly a consequence of his ability to ignore the explosions: and in any case, post-structuralist mines (a few of which are still lying about in most departments of English) have a way of failing to detonate comprehensibly. In dissenting from the dogmas of contemporary literary theory, Heaney states simply and gracefully some elementary points, and his

---

[32] Heaney, *The Redress of Poetry*, 5.   [33] Ibid.

authority as a poet seems to guarantee safe passage: it is as though (to borrow one of his own favoured myths) Heaney the critic is protected by the Golden Bough of his own poetry. Thus, in politely rejecting the belief that poetry is, like all writing, classifiable as 'discourse', Heaney insists upon 'pleasure'; while accepting that literary history, like all history, has built-in biases and injustices, he is not willing to take the self-approving outrage at such things as a substitute for literary experience. As he puts it in his lecture on Marlowe:[34]

But even so, it still seems an abdication of literary responsibility to be swayed by these desperately overdue correctives to a point where imaginative literature is read simply and solely as a function of an oppressive discourse, or as a reprehensible masking. When it comes to poetic composition, one has to allow for the presence, even for the pre-eminence, of what Wordsworth called 'the grand elementary principle of pleasure', and that pleasure comes from the doing-in-language of certain things.

This is valuable and necessary, and its finely judged simplicity makes Heaney's statement extremely effective: rather than appearing to be a metaphorical meditation on what makes his own writing tick, this is the authoritative criticism of an important poet, correcting the failed perceptions of much contemporary argument about literary experience (themselves, arguably, results of the failure or inability to have a literary experience in the first place). 'The doing-in-language of certain things' is, essentially, Heaney's theme in *The Redress of Poetry*, and all of the lectures operate on the assumption that certain things are better worth doing than others. Here, the willingness to examine poetic language and procedure in and for themselves enables Heaney to tackle more successfully the problem of what, as readers, we ask poetry to achieve. In defining the element of 'redress' which poetry offers, Heaney maintains that 'the creative spirit remains positively recalcitrant in the face of the negative evidence', and this recalcitrance, along with a dogged bias towards the 'positive', is located in the fabric and structure of poetry itself:[35]

This reminding, this work of immunity building, is effected by intrinsically artistic means, for it is obvious that poetry's answer to the world is given not only in terms of the content of its statements. It is given even perhaps more emphatically in terms of metre and syntax, of tone and musical trueness; and it is given also by its need to go emotionally and artistically 'above the brim', beyond the established norms.

[34] Ibid. 24.   [35] Ibid. 15

Writing like this earths Heaney's habitual transcendentalism to a definite source in the 'intrinsically artistic means' of poems. The power of poetic language, then, is understood to be the source of whatever power we decide to attribute to poetry, and Heaney sets the stakes dauntingly high in seeing literature's capacity for 'redress' in such universal, and un-apologetically transcendental terms.

If Heaney is right to make such claims for the integrity and power of poetic language, then the strength of his critical grasp on 'the doing-in-language of certain things' is a matter of some importance. It is not enough (and not, perhaps, even possible) to be right only *in theory* about these things. Here, it is necessary to ask questions about the poet's masterly self-consciousness, the sense of hearing himself, or of hearing himself being overheard, which is an inescapable condition of the lectures. Occasionally, this element of self-consciousness obtrudes unduly, as when Heaney sees John Clare rather too firmly in his own image, remarking on how he 'inspires one to trust that poetry can break through the glissando of post-modernism and get stuck in the mud of real imaginative haulage work'.[36] Besides the infelicitous 'stuck in the mud', this expression of trust is bogged down by its own confusion about what is 'real' and what is metaphorical: haulage workers will not have their tasks performed for them by John Clare, however grateful 'imaginative' (or imaginary) hauliers may be to him. Of course, Heaney is speaking primarily about ambitions of his own in sentences like these, but he is guilty, nevertheless, of a certain 'glissando' between the literal and the metaphorical which makes 'the doing-in-language' of criticism more difficult. Something similar happens when Heaney chooses George Herbert as an example of 'redress', seeing 'in the clear element of Herbert's poetry a true paradigm of the shape of things, psychologic-ally, politically, metaphorically and, if one wants to proceed that far, metaphysically'.[37] Comprehensive as this sounds, Heaney in fact avoids considering the sense of this poetry as *literally* 'a true paradigm of the shape of things'—and this mattered to Herbert a good deal. Thus, when Heaney imagines Herbert's mind 'as it moves across the frontier of writing, out of homiletics and apologetics into poetry, upon the im-pulses and reflexes of awakened language',[38] he cordons off poetic language from the 'impulses' and 'reflexes' which, on the other side of the 'frontier', count for more than Heaney's purposes will allow. The

---

[36] Heaney, *The Redress of Poetry*, 82.   [37] Ibid. 10.   [38] Ibid.

subsequent definition of poetry as 'an upright, resistant, and self-bracing entity within the general flux and flex of language'[39] praises an upright-ness in Herbert which that poet could not acknowledge without refer-ence to the 'impulses and reflexes' of those very 'homiletics and apologetics' from which Heaney tries to separate him; the critic's enthusiasm here is too visibly conditioned by a kind of retrospective romanticism in which poetic language is made to operate within com-paratively narrow limits. If Heaney's instincts about the power of poetic language are sound, his sense of the specific dimensions of such language can seem at times constrained by the pressing purposes of his own art.

The language of poetry, as Heaney sees it, can achieve something which sets it apart from the language of quotidian expression and exchange; he is more reticent, however, about the fact that such lan-guage is made of the same stuff as the words of poetry, that its dynamics influence poetic language, and that poetry is constantly open to infec-tion from the linguistic element in which it has its meaning. The flip-side of transcendence, as it were, is present perpetually in the language in which that transcendence is attempted (and in which it may seem to be achieved). Even when a poet's language is most his own, it is not his alone: adept as he is at celebrating poetic victories, Heaney forgets that no poetic victory can ever be complete. When he describes 'lyric purity of the purest sort', Heaney observes how in poetic form 'Suddenly the thing chanced upon comes forth as the thing predestined: the unfore-seen appears as the inevitable.'[40] This is a wonderfully clear observation, but at the same time as it celebrates the imaginative potential of the felicitous, it reveals the significance of chance in poetic expression, and suggests that it is on the level of chance that the poet has his or her dealings with 'the inevitable'. It is a pity that Heaney does not pursue this particular paradox further, for it would lead him to a more direct confrontation with the problems at the heart of a critical concept like 'poetic language': poetry may well be the 'doing-in-language of certain things', but how far is the poet the sole agent in this process? The warm humanity—and transcendent humanism—with which Heaney under-stands the 'redress' offered by poetry are threatened by the impersonal-ity of the mechanisms (and even the medium) which make the 'unforeseen' into the 'inevitable'.

[39] Ibid. 15.   [40] Ibid. 108.

In the lecture which is at the heart of *The Redress of Poetry*, 'Joy or Night: Last Things in the Poetry of W. B. Yeats and Philip Larkin', Heaney faces head-on the challenges to a transcendent view of poetry's capacities, allowing Larkin to exemplify the 'negative evidence' (in a meticulous and subtle reading of his late, bleak 'Aubade'), while the work of Yeats stands for the incurably 'recalcitrant' imagination. Here, the ageing Larkin, whose 'vision got arrested into a fixed stare at the inexorability of his own physical extinction', is presented as a poet to whom 'human wisdom' seemed 'a matter of operating within the mortal limits, and of quelling any false hope of transcending or outfacing the inevitable'.[41] For Yeats, on the other hand, 'all flourish and theatrical challenge', such despairing accommodation is out of the question, and Heaney is forthright in his endorsement of the Yeatsian recalcitrance, and effective in asking 'whether [Larkin's] famous rejection of Yeats's more romantic stance has not been too long and too readily approved of'.[42] Again, the 'negative evidence' is faced down by the processes of poetry itself:[43]

Still, when a poem rhymes, when a form generates itself, when a metre provokes consciousness into new postures, it is already on the side of life. When a rhyme surprises and extends the fixed relations between words, that in itself protests against necessity. When language does more than enough, as it does in all achieved poetry, it opts for the condition of overlife, and rebels at limit.

Spurred on by this aesthetic *credo*, Heaney is able to face up to the paradox of 'the inevitable' in poetry, claiming that 'the best it can do is to give us an experience that is like foreknowledge of certain things which we already seem to be remembering'.[44] It is unclear whether this particular evidence, for all the brilliance with which Heaney sets it out, is finally 'positive' or 'negative' in character. By framing a contest between Larkin and Yeats, however, Heaney is hardly providing for an even match; a few glancing remarks on Beckett, which occur in this context, suggest that Heaney has not quite taken the measure of the more formidable 'negative evidence' about literary language:[45]

Indeed, Beckett is a very clear example of a writer who is Larkin's equal in not flinching from the ultimate bleakness of things, but who then goes on to do

---

[41] Heaney, *The Redress of Poetry*, 147.   [42] Ibid.   [43] Ibid. 158.
[44] Ibid. 159.   [45] Ibid.

something positive with the bleakness. For it is not the apparent pessimism of Beckett's world-view that constitutes his poetic genius: his excellence resides in his working-out a routine in the playhouse of his art which is both true to the depressing goings-on in the house of actuality and—more important—a transformation of them.

For once, Heaney's judgement here seems askew, and the determination to root out the 'positive' leads him towards a blandly euphemistic transformation of Beckett into the required 'world-view'. How such a concept would survive in the rigorous and unsparingly ironic medium of Beckett's language, along with concepts like 'overlife', and phrases like 'more than enough' or 'do something positive', may be imagined readily enough. It is one thing to use Yeats to put Larkin's achievement in its proper perspective (and Heaney does this very well); it is quite another to test a romantic view of poetic language against the questions posed by Beckett's writing. In this sense, although Heaney is exceptionally strong when he imagines the poetic consequences of inhabiting an artistic Thoor Ballylee, it is Beckett who waits for him at another dark tower, and who presents a more serious challenge to his ideas of language and poetry.

It would be a poor critic who confused the authority of a piece of literature with its reputation; as Heaney's criticism shows very well, literary significance is not an abstract affair: poems *do* things, and good poems do more than anything the critical summaries of their effects can hope to account for. And in Heaney's own case, it has been necessary for some time to make the distinction between his poetic authority and his contemporary reputation, something which his status as a Nobel Prize-winner has rendered even more needful. To say this is not to begrudge Heaney his public success: in terms of 'public' significance alone, he is an outstandingly good ambassador for poetry, and is able to speak to a large audience with the kind of sense, excitement, and artistic integrity long eschewed by the academic literary industry. The public 'finish', in other words, is far from unattractive, and seems in many ways something for which to be grateful.

Even in Heaney's poetry, however, the distinction between the sources of authority and the satisfactions of reputation—or between the poet hearing himself, and hearing himself being heard—is liable to break down. In his criticism, this blurring of a line puts him squarely in the position occupied so uncomfortably by the later Eliot; unlike Eliot,

Heaney seems at ease there, and relies on his own good intentions to save the situation. Finally—that is to say, beyond the occasion of a lecture, or even of the publication of another book whose warm reception is a foregone conclusion—this is not enough. Authority is something quite distant from popularity, or even well-judged or timed agreeableness; as Heaney seems to know, it resides instead in the intellectual strength of poetic language, and those dealings with the world of confusion, complication, and hostility in which that language has its real and unavoidable element. Here, however, the discourse of pleasantry and complaisance is inevitably ill at ease. To risk discomfort in these terms, to suggest that language is perhaps indifferent (or worse) to our best intentions when we use it, and that poetry registers this indifference as a chill at its heart, is to risk everything. Yet this is what Yeats risks, and indeed what Heaney praises him for risking. In the context of eloquent professorial celebrations and affirmations, and all the talk of transcendence and humanity, we might remember that Yeats—both before and after his Nobel Prize—was a much-hated figure. In some quarters, he still is. For all that, Yeats could still announce in his poetry that 'I thirst for accusation'.[46] The 'finished man' was, after all, 'the finished man among his enemies'.[47]

III   *Geoffrey Hill's defence*

In the 1930s, poets were given to writing manifestos, or even to having them written on their collective behalf. By the 1990s, the manifesto as such was long out of fashion, and had been replaced by the more classical (and less insistent) form of the *ars poetica*. Testaments of the poet-critics, from both sides of the Atlantic, would together make up a huge volume of writing from the 1970s to the end of the century. When asked to say a few words, the average poet falls back on his *ars poetica*. The difficulty with this, from the point of view of a poet-critic, is that it puts testimony in a place where some degree of prescriptive force may be thought to inhere; writing on the art of poetry generally defends poetry, and recommends it, in terms that will be applied to more than just the individual poet who is doing the writing. There are hazards in

---

[46] W. B. Yeats, 'Parnell's Funeral', *The Variorum Edition of the Poems of W. B. Yeats*, ed. Peter Allt and Russell K. Alspatch (London: Macmillan, 1956), 542.

[47] W. B. Yeats, 'A Dialogue of Self and Soul', *Variorum Poems*, 479.

this, just as there are dangers in the appetite for it amongst contemporary audiences. One defence of the Defence as a modern genre might be that it makes available the full personality of the poet, the man or woman behind the art, and therefore contributes in the end to art's accessibility and human approachableness. But from other angles, this can be more of a condemnation than a defence.

Geoffrey Hill's critical oeuvre does not tend towards the testamentary or the self-pondering; nor does it, in the more obvious ways, set out to define and discuss the arts of poetry with a legislative intent. Yet this should not be taken to imply that Hill's critical work is without implications for the art and reading of poetry as currently practised; on the contrary, it may well be that some of this work amounts to the most serious, deeply reasoned, and far-reaching material on the meaning and conditions of poetry of the twentieth century. By and large, Hill's essays choose to stand or fall according to their hold on their particular subjects; they are not simply a poet's reflections on those subjects, but substantial engagements with them, whose worth is independent of any interest in the fact of their authorship. In this respect, Hill is perhaps the antithesis of the poet-critic, as that term is often understood, in that he is both a real poet and a true critic, at a time when both categories are underpopulated.

Even so, Hill's critical work has its bearing on contemporary poetry other than his own, and needs to be more widely taken into account. Two essays by Hill in particular, 'Poetry as "Menace" and "Atonement"' (1977), and 'Our Word is Our Bond' (1983) are of major importance, and between them make up a powerful formulation of the difficulties and opportunities in, about, and bearing on the language of poetry. They also give claims for the strength of that language substance and weight. Calling the latter essay Hill's 'great enquiry', and 'nothing less than a Defence of Poetry for our age', Christopher Ricks relishes 'a uniquely formidable encounter of a poet's exactions with a philosopher's slighting of the poet's enterprise'.[48] Whether or not Ricks writes 'our time' with an ironic awareness of the commonness— and common coerciveness—of that phrase, it is true that the essay concerns itself with a situation we have truly in common, and it speaks to that condition with a more than personal authority.

If authoritative criticism can exist, there is no reason why it should not be written by a poet; the fact of the poet's authorship is no guarantee

---

[48] Christopher Ricks, *Essays in Appreciation* (Oxford: Clarendon Press, 1996), 261.

of the authority, however, and Hill does not make the mistake of assuming as much. 'Poetry as "Menace" and "Atonement"' is amongst other things a professional document, for it is Hill's inaugural lecture as Professor at the University of Leeds. Hill is careful to qualify the extent to which this is a poet's lecture, acknowledging that 'I have been drawn towards my present theme by way of the technical and metaphysical problems which I have encountered as a practitioner of verse', but also making it clear that 'I shrink from any implication of special pleading' and 'disdain the "confessional mode" as currently practised'.[49] What Hill goes on to say about language clearly derives from the understanding of language in his own poetry; at the same time, it sets an agenda for any consideration of literary language in relation to ideas of artistic ambition and achievement. Hill begins by directing attention to the common ground which poetry shares with its criticism, that of language itself, and brings forward an arresting image for the struggle (if it is that) between language's poetic effort and direction and its inescapable conditions, with their tendency to misdirection:[50]

Language, the element in which a poet works, is also the medium through which judgments upon his work are made. That commonplace image, founded upon the unfinished statues of Michelangelo, 'mighty figures straining to free themselves from the imprisoning marble', has never struck me as being an ideal image for sculpture itself; it seems more to embody the nature and condition of those arts which are composed of words. The arts which use language are the most impure of arts, though I do not deny that those who speak of 'pure poetry' are attempting, however inadequately, to record the impact of a real effect.

Hill's distinction between effect and essence is crucial, and his insistence on impurity in poetic language keeps that distinction in mind. As he continues, this sense of the tension between the effort and the medium is addressed more directly:

The poet will occasionally, in the act of writing a poem, experience a sense of pure fulfilment which might too easily and too subjectively be misconstrued as the attainment of objective perfection. It seems less fanciful to maintain that, however much a poem is shaped and finished, it remains to some extent within the 'imprisoning marble' of a quotidian shapelessness and imperfection. At the same time I would claim the utmost significance for matters of technique and

---

[49] Geoffrey Hill, *The Lords of Limit: Essays on Literature and Ideas* (London: André Deutsch, 1984), 1.
[50] Ibid. 2.

I take no cynical view of those moments in which the inertia of language, which is also the coercive force of language, seems to have been overcome.

Hill does not short-change the experience of writing a poem, nor deny to the rest of us some sense of the reality of that experience. At the same time, he does not mistake euphoria for judgement. 'The inertia of language' is not really something a reader wants to be reminded about, any more than a poet might wish to succumb to it; but Hill's writing here does not flinch from this dark, and apparently unhelpful, aspect of language's common currency.

It may appear that the academic in Hill pours cold water on the artist, and that talk of language's 'inertia' amounts to little more than a cracking of the critical whip at moments when the poetic impulse looks too frisky. This may even, on a more general level, be a not uncommon interpretation of Hill's practice. Yet it misses the point entirely, by allowing the difficulty of the insight to be shrugged off by appeal to a mistaken belief in poets' power over language. As a critic *and* as a poet, Hill insists on the reality of 'the inertia of language'. It is easy to find instances of language obviously at a standstill, or dragging thought towards thoughtlessness: cliché, simple rhetoric, and diminished, unreflective vocabulary are the staple of many levels of written and spoken communication, from politics to daily intercourse. These things are not unknown in even the most widely praised works of contemporary literature. This applies also to the criticism of such literature; in the promotion of contemporary poetry, for example, 'dynamic' is a word with an inertia all of its own. But Hill does not mean this, or not primarily this: he does not contend that a certain quantity of effort, or quality of original force, can free a poet's language from the 'imprisoning marble'; he insists, rather, on poetry's ability to understand the nature of its imprisonment.

Perhaps for this reason, the language of Hill's critical writing is often not his own: it belongs to an extraordinarily eclectic range of cited texts, 'literary' and other, from which the critic quotes, and which he places in complex and subtle patterns of relation and juxtaposition. While the ability to quote to effect is the best test of any critic, the density of Hill's (meticulously accurate) webs of quotation is still remarkable. There is a certain forensic effect to this, as Hill characteristically goes about the minute searching of particular phrases, words, and cadences; for the reader—however assiduous—there may also be a sense of bombardment, as Hill launches wave after wave of new texts into and around his subject. No ordinarily alert and intelligent reader can read an essay by Hill without feeling his or her own inattentiveness, and deficiencies in both knowledge and acuity, with regard to language; the precision and deliberated pitch of Hill's own critical writing results in a not altogether welcome feeling of hypersensitivity for his readers. Suavity, urbanity, and comfortable terms of address are not notable features of Hill's prose style. But that this should be a matter for complaint (as it has been) tells us much about the priorities of Hill's less convinced readers, and more about the virtues held more commonly to be necessary in contemporary critical discourse. While a Hill essay is certainly difficult, it is not (unlike the almost limitless acreage of publications claiming to be 'critical theory') difficult for difficulty's sake, or difficult to no end: what the essay addresses *is* difficult, and Hill's work—like the reader's—puts things in a clearer light.

'Inertia' is not a pleasure to contemplate, and language's compounding of inadequacies with felicities is not exactly good news. For this reason, Hill's criticism does not look remotely like the standard work of a poet-critic: it is affirmative, but not in the more usual sense, for what it affirms is the predicament (not just artistic) in which artists find themselves, rather than some triumph of art over hardship, or song over suffering. Hill does not set out to praise poetry, to recommend or endorse it. The contemporary *ars poetica* is often little more than this, a 'poetic' staging of praise and hyperbole, with the personal assurance of the art's redemptive power: 'I have tried it, and found it works.' Of course, for Hill, poetic language functions only by comprehending its possible, inherent, or inevitable scope for malfunction.

For many, it is preferable either to ignore such liabilities, or to invest in a transcendental idea of art which sees poetic language as fixing on a horizon beyond these worldly failings. In 'Poetry as "Menace" and "Atonement"', Hill quotes Eliot, who speaks of 'feeling we can only detect, so to speak, out of the corner of the eye, and can never completely focus... At such moments, we touch the border of those feelings which only music can express.'[51] Hill treats this coolly:[52]

As Eliot well knew, however, a poet must also turn back, with whatever weariness, disgust, love barely distinguishable from hate, to confront 'the indefinite extent' of language itself and seek his 'focus' there. In certain contexts the expansive, outward gesture towards the condition of music is a helpless gesture of surrender, oddly analogous to that stylish aesthetic of despair, that desire for the ultimate integrity of silence, to which so much eloquence has been so frequently and so indefatigably devoted.

There is an important accuracy to the reference here to Eliot's 'expansive, outward gesture', which captures the essence of his critical stance, especially in the later work, while also reminding the reader of the poet's actual strengths of intensive, inward contemplation in language—more visible, on the whole, in his poetry than in his critical prose. For Hill, too, it is the intensive energies of thinking about language, energies which drive words back on themselves, impact upon words the meanings they avoid, or seek to suppress, and the contexts they do not solicit, or admit with too uncritical a selectiveness, that characterize poetic composition, and are answered in critical work. Hill is aware that Eliot's 'outward gesture' to music can vindicate other kinds of expansiveness, including the 'principles of Christian penitence and humility which were . . . the disciplines of conscience within which Eliot and Auden increasingly worked'. But here again, Hill insists on the distinction between life and language, personality and art:[53]

One is left with the awkward observation that the acceptance of a principle of penitential humility in the conduct of life does not necessarily inhibit a readiness to accept the status of 'maestro' conferred by a supportive, yet coercive public. It's worse than awkward, it's damned awkward; it cannot but be seen as a churlish refusal to concede honour where honour is due. I would reply that it is not a matter of *ad hominem* rebuke but a suggestion that fashionable adulation of the 'maestro' when there is so little recognition of the 'fabbro', 'homo faber', is one aspect of what C. K. Stead mordantly but not unfairly calls the 'struggle between poets and "poetry-lovers"', except that the very word 'struggle' suggests purpose and engagement.

There is a wry comedy in Hill's observations, which he knows are observations on himself, as 'worse than awkward . . . damned awkward', and the necessarily 'churlish' face such criticism wears in the world of Stead's 'poetry-lovers'; and there is a dark wit, also, in moving from Pound's 'il miglior fabbro' for Eliot to the poet as 'homo faber', when Faber and Faber are Auden's, as well as Eliot's, publishing house. But the jokes are made possible by the very thing Hill is talking about, and which he contends artists as well as critics take too little into account:

[53] Ibid. 10.

language's tendency to let down the more exalted intentions of its users, and to be—like a contemporary public—coercive in its supportiveness. Any humility that thinks it can get the better of words is not an *artistic* humility.

There is another side to this particular coin. Hill's criticism (and, latterly, his poetry) lays itself open to accusations of 'arrogance', partly because of its own unrelentingness in matters of analysis and language; partly, too, because it does not commend or celebrate those areas of humility which count for so much in 'fashionable adulation' of poetry's realism, human wisdom, and self-deprecation. Oddly, then, Hill finds himself defending the idea of the poet—in ways that recall Sidney and the Renaissance—against the dominion of extra-poetic criteria. It is in this sense that 'Our Word is Our Bond' is indeed the *ars poetica* praised by Ricks. The essay itself is a meditation on the philosopher J. L. Austin, and in particular his *How to Do Things with Words*; it is also, and pointedly, about how to do things with poetry, and how poetry does things. Hill's encounter with Austin eventually becomes an encounter with the forces of social and conventional reasonableness that try to set limits to the difficulties of language. Running through this is a recollection of Sidney's 'as for the poet, he nothing affirmeth, and therefore never lieth', which Hill regards with some caution: in so far as Austin's philosophy takes this literally, Hill is able to show the deficiencies of the seriousness which the philosopher attributes to language other than poetic language. It is language used 'in the course, for example, of making a joke or writing a poem' which Austin regards as 'not seriously meant and we shall not be able to say that we seriously performed the act concerned':[54] Hill sees the irony here, both in Sidney's (possibly strategic) affinities, and (more startlingly) in the fate of Ezra Pound, and his living out of the connections between speech as 'poetic' act, and as an act with judicial consequences. In Hill's essay, the figure of the poet must emerge as someone mired in the complexity of language's relations with both affirmation and seriousness, as well as with imaginative will; as someone in a fix, who is not triumphing over language, but battling a path within language.

Again, the oddness of such a portrait is taken into account by Hill: 'those for whom writing is like "bearing a part in the conversation" must regard with incomprehension those for whom it is "blindness" and "perplexity" and . . . those for whom "composition" is a struggle with

[54] J. L. Austin, *Philosophical Papers* (Oxford: Clarendon Press, 1961), 227–8.

dark and disputed matter will inevitably dismiss as mere worldliness the
ability to push on pragmatically with the matter in hand'.[55] Incomprehension, Hill maintains, is the true condition of most literary relations
between language and the world (which includes language). What the
poet offers, in Hill's Defence, is an exemplary and unique alertness to
this incomprehension, and to the misapprehension with which his
language contends. The essay approaches Hopkins, among others,
with this in mind; but it is on a more negative instance, that of Pound,
that Hill's argument comes most fully into focus. Here, the catastrophic
collapse into incomprehension and misapprehension betrays Pound's
failure to apply the knowledge in his best poetry to his knowledge of
what he supposed his writing to be. Hill is no simple apologist for
Pound:[56]

The moral offence of his cruel and vulgar anti-semitism does not call into
question the integrity of his struggle; neither does the integrity of the struggle
absolve him of responsibility for the vulgar cruelty. The essential culpability of
his wartime broadcasts was not their eruption into 'that stupid suburban
prejudice', as he self-indulgently called it, but their 'insufficient desperation',
as Richard Reid has acutely observed. The more important word here is
'insufficient'. 'Saeva indignatio' is no guarantee of verdictive accuracy, or even
of perception; and it is lack of attention, or 'care', which brings Pound to the
point of 'signing on the dotted line' for the rulers of the darkness of this
world—not in spite of, but through, the mundane struggle, the 'being bound'
to push on with the matter in hand, no matter what . . .

There is no innocence in Hill's defence of poetry, and he spares Pound
nothing here. But all of this has distinct consequences for the question
of the poet's role in relation to language's inertia, and the forces that
know how to exploit such inertia. The apparent appeal of a determination 'to push on with the matter in hand, no matter what' is the
attraction of writing verse which knows too quickly what it doesn't
mean by a word, or knows too well what its poet is known for being, or
for doing; and which knows and cares too little for language's history
and currency, its past and future that are both pressures on its present
use. 'The matter in hand' is also—whether we want it or not—'dark and
disputed matter'.

 As a poet-critic, Hill presents an unusual case. He is, if not unique, at
least extremely unusual, in not using criticism as a means of making

---

[55] Hill, *The Lords of Limit*, 145.   [56] Ibid. 154–5.

himself available, and attractive, as an intellectual personality. Yet Hill's
criticism comes closer than others' to defining in contemporary terms
the task of anyone trying to write poetry without self-flattery or self-
indulgence, in a world where language is more and more an instrument
of forces beyond, and even hostile to, poetry itself. One such force is
our own high view of ourselves, and our wish for others to share that
view; another is the consequent conviction that the force of personality
can make words do what we want them to do. In 'Poetry as "Menace"
and "Atonement"', Hill acknowledges the attractiveness of the prevalent view of poetry, and insists on the need to temper this:[57]

> However much and however rightly we protest against the vanity of supposing it
> to be merely the 'spontaneous overflow of powerful feelings', poetic utterance is
> nonetheless an utterance of the self, the self demanding to be loved, demanding
> love in the form of recognition and 'absolution'. The poet is perhaps the first to
> be dismayed by such a discovery and to seek the conversion of his 'daemon' to a
> belief in altruistic responsibility. But this dismay is as nothing compared to the
> shocking encounter with 'empirical guilt', not as a manageable hypothesis, but as
> irredeemable error in the very substance and texture of his craft and pride.

It is true that this notion of 'irredeemable error' is essential to an
understanding of Geoffrey Hill's poetry; but that is very far from
being the end of the matter, as much contemporary criticism would
like to make it. The knowledge of 'error' in the heart of things, and at the
heart of language, is the starting-point for an art of poetry which cannot
expect to accord very well with pursuing 'the matter in hand', with the
business of self-promotion, or of poetry's celebrity endorsement. In this
respect, the true poet-critic will not be a popular, or even a much-liked,
figure; he will say unacceptable things, and be both awkward and
damned for it; he will expect no redress in poetry for the wrongs in
the world; and his incapacity for embarrassment will make him a shame.
However, even these things can be consistent with what Hill calls a
poet's 'vocation': 'that of necessarily bearing his peculiar unnecessary
shame in a world growing ever more shameless'.[58]

---

[57] Hill, *The Lords of Limit*, 17.   [58] Ibid. 17–18.

CHAPTER 5

One of Us:
Eliot, Auden, and Four Quartets

I

There is a famous footnote in I. A. Richards's short book of 1926, *Science and Poetry*, which accompanies remarks on a 'necessary reorganization of our lives':[1]

> To those familiar with Mr. Eliot's *The Waste Land*, my indebtedness to it at this point will be evident. He seems to me by this poem, to have performed two considerable services for this generation. He has given a perfect emotive description of a state of mind which is probably inevitable for a while to all meditative people. Secondly, by effecting a complete severance between his poetry and *all* beliefs, and this without any weakening of the poetry, he has realised what might otherwise have remained largely a speculative possibility, and has shown the way to the only solution of these difficulties. 'In the destructive element immerse. That is the way.'

The footnote's critical currency began early; in the 1930s, the terms here were often debated and recycled, while critics of Eliot's poem, then and later, found the 'complete severance' motif enormously serviceable.[2] But the most interesting reactions came from T. S. Eliot himself. In January 1927, Eliot wrote of how 'I cannot see that poetry can ever be separated from something which I should call belief,' even though 'The majority of people live below the level of belief or doubt.'[3] By March of

---

[1] I. A. Richards, *Science and Poetry* (London: Kegan, Paul, French, Frubner, 1926), 64.
[2] See Samuel Hynes, *The Auden Generation: Literature and Politics in England in the 1930s* (London: Bodley Head, 1976), 28–9; Valentine Cunningham, *British Writers of the Thirties* (Oxford: Clarendon Press, 1988), ch. 3, 'Destructive Elements'; Peter McDonald, 'Believing in the Thirties', in Keith Williams and Steven Matthews (eds.), *Rewriting the Thirties: Modernism and After* (Harlow: Longman, 1997), 71–90.
[3] T. S. Eliot, 'A Note on Poetry and Belief', *The Enemy. A Review of Art and Literature*, 1 (Jan. 1927), 16–17.

the same year, this had sharpened into 'Poetry "is capable of saving us," [Richards] says; it is like saying that the wall-paper will save us when the walls have crumbled.'[4] By 1934, Eliot was able to provide a far-reaching footnote of his own to this long-continuing difference with Richards. In *The Use of Poetry and the Use of Criticism*, the flat observation that 'We cannot, of course, refute the statement "poetry is capable of saving us" without knowing which one of the multiple definitions of salvation Mr. Richards has in mind' is accompanied by a shrewd piece of practical criticism: 'There is of course,' Eliot points out, 'a locution in which we say of someone "he is not one of *us*": it is possible that the "us" of Mr. Richards's statement represents an equally limited and select number.'[5]

How seriously meant is Eliot's exercise here of his acuteness of hearing, his alertness to possible tones? It is overwhelmingly likely that Richards does not actually mean 'capable of saving *us*' in the sense being proposed; but this does not quite answer the question, for Eliot is making his own sly statement about a statement, raising the possibility that the first-person plural as employed by Richards incorporates—necessarily in contexts like this—an element of appeal to the 'limited and select number'. And if that is so, if Richards's attempt to voice some very broadly conceived redemptive interpretation of poetry is also, in the terms of its very articulation, an exercise in you-and-me-togetherism, then Eliot allows us to contemplate an interesting (and frustrating) irony. Poetry's redemptive mission might, in this reading, be simply poetry's preaching to the converted. We are reading about ourselves: a heartening experience, perhaps, but not necessarily a redemptive one.

This is not an irony peculiar to 1926, nor indeed to Eliot and his own notions of poetry, mission, and redemption at that time. It is a truism to say that poetry's prestige as an element in literary culture declined in Britain through the twentieth century. However one chooses to present this, it is usually the prelude to an attempted solution to the supposed problem: things have been bad and getting worse, but now, at last,

---

[4] T. S. Eliot, *The Dial* (Mar. 1927), 243.

[5] T. S. Eliot, *The Use of Poetry and the Use of Criticism: Studies in the Relation of Criticism to Poetry in England* (London: Faber and Faber, 1933), 130–1. For a detailed discussion of the Eliot–Richards debate on 'belief', see John Constable, 'I. A. Richards, T. S. Eliot, and the Poetry of Belief', *Essays in Criticism*, 40/3 (July 1990), 222–43: this draws upon Richards's notes and correspondence in Magdalene College, Cambridge, to illustrate the progress of a disagreement in which the two men appear to have remained for years locked in earnest incomprehension of each other's arguments.

something can be done. At this point, something incontrovertibly 'new' is generally brought forward, whether a poet, a group of poets, or a full-scale movement. In the 1930s, when Richards's views were of great moment, there was also a new generation to meet his prescription for ways of 'saving us', with its full complement of anthologies and magazines for the necessary work of promotion; at the more talented end, in fact, this generation had as its publishing house Eliot's Faber and Faber. For all that, poetry did not, in the event, save either the day or its own position, and all but two of the most celebrated British poets of the 1930s who appeared in the pages of Geoffrey Grigson's *New Verse*, or in anthologies with titles like *New Signatures* or *New Country*, are by now either in, or well on their way to, critical obscurity. Contemporaries would have been amazed to hear this of Stephen Spender, or of Cecil Day Lewis, but even these once-weighty presences seem presently insubstantial beside Auden and MacNeice. One might make similar observations about subsequent new generations in poetry: whether 'the Movement' of the 1950s, or the 'New Gen' writers promoted in Britain in the early 1990s. Not to have survived a burst of promotion is not necessarily to be lacking in talent or achievement; 'forgotten' poets can very often be shown to have written good poems. And, just as often, both immediate and more distant posterity can get things wrong. But a commitment to the redemptive view of poetry translates all too easily into a conviction that the poet will be saved for posterity by merit—his own merit, which he (or his readers) identify with the merit of his poetry.

Posterity is lusted after by immature artists; and dull critics are its pimps. Yet the posterity of any contemporary art is both inscrutable and indifferent. We know nothing about it, but we can safely assume that posterity will not be predisposed to like us, or indeed want to know about us at all. How many eighteenth-century poets does even the enthusiastic reader of twentieth-century poetry read often, and know well? How many twentieth-century poets will committed poetry readers return to in three centuries' time? But this isn't some doom-laden and doleful saw; still less is it a way of saying that contemporary art simply isn't up to much. Rather, it is the necessary common sense which makes the creation of new art possible. In fact, the creative obstruction lies with the reflex recourse to posterity as a spurious certificate of poetic road-worthiness for the poets one likes, or indeed for the poetry one likes writing. Here, again, is another turn on the hope that 'Poetry is capable of saving us'.

If posterity is one dream of Eliot's 'limited and select number', it is not one on which he is looking kindly, and his engagement with Richards more generally makes it clear that such hopes for salvation (whether artistic, political, or psychological) derive from a now stranded and helpless Arnoldian tradition. Nevertheless, it was perhaps bad news for Eliot that this tradition was still gasping as late as 1926, and is worse news for us, since it looks even now from some angles as if a version of the tradition is still going strong. As poetry becomes more and more a part of an arts consumer-culture, and is not only expected to reflect the experiences and opinions of its time and place, but actively sets out to do so as one of the necessary conditions for its success, so it aspires increasingly towards what Richards called 'a perfect emotive description of a state of mind'. In much late twentieth-century poetry, this mind was in the first place the author's, and a range of autobiographical motifs and details (though perhaps in the end a comparatively narrow one) was commonly adduced by readers as both a mark of original creative authenticity and a more or less direct reflection of the things that had most resonance—or even relevance—in the contemporary cultural context. Richards's development of his remarks, in the notion of a poetry severed from all beliefs, seems perhaps slightly odd in the context of 1926; but it may make more sense once we think of the poetry of the mid-century and afterwards. As Eliot suspected, the idea does little for a critical understanding of *The Waste Land* (and little, also, for much of the literature later classed as Modernist), but it gives a more promising degree of purchase to readings of later poetry in Britain, in which 'beliefs', in Richards's sense, are often things that have been outgrown or left behind, as embarrassments for the ironic, observant, and self-observing voice.

It is hard to imagine a positive account of many successful volumes of contemporary poetry—Heaney's *The Spirit Level* or Hughes's *Birthday Letters*, to take two British examples from the 1990s—which makes a point of praising the way in which 'The intensity of [the poet's] own emotional experience hardly appears'. On the contrary, it is much more likely that such books will be esteemed for their 'perfect emotive description[s] of a state of mind'. The first phrase, in fact, is Eliot's, speaking about an arresting quality of the earlier Yeats; nor does Eliot accept that 'emotional experience' is something which the later Yeats simply expresses. Remembering his own prominent use of 'impersonality' as a critical term, Eliot goes on to make an important distinction:[6]

There are two forms of impersonality: that which is natural to the mere skilful craftsman, and that which is more and more achieved by the maturing artist. The first is that of what I have called 'the anthology piece'... The second impersonality is that of the poet who, out of intense and personal experience, is able to express a general truth; retaining all the particularity of his experience, to make of it a general symbol.

This is a very long way from 'a perfect emotive description of a state of mind', and its bold use of the concept of 'a general truth' tellingly redirects the hope that 'poetry is capable of saving us'. Eliot writes here about the seriousness of and in poetry, to which 'intense and personal experience' may bring the maturing poet; his remarks take it for granted that 'a general truth' is both possible and desirable as the end of this seriousness. In this kind of impersonality, the poetry is more important than the 'us' whom it may (or may not) be capable of 'saving'.

Eliot's objections to Richards on the relation between poetry and belief were developments of his objections to Matthew Arnold and his heirs. At heart, in Eliot's view of the matter, Richards and those impressed by him are susceptible to ideas of poetry that severed art from the most fundamental issues of considered belief, and which were then liable to see belief itself as something for which art could be a safe substitute. Poetry, in this Arnoldian tradition, became its own ultimate good; beliefs—whether political, religious, or other—became embarrassing impurities, fit only to be washed away. At his sharpest, Eliot could make this embarrassment hurt:[7]

For Arnold the best poetry supersedes both religion and philosophy.... The most generalised form of my own view is simply this: that nothing in this world or the next is a substitute for anything else; and if you find that you must do without something, such as religious faith or philosophic belief, then you must just do without it. I can persuade myself, I find, that some of the things that I can hope to get are better worth having than some of the things I cannot get; or I may hope to alter myself so as to want different things; but I cannot persuade myself that it is the same desires that are satisfied, or that I have in effect the same thing under a different name.

[6] T. S. Eliot, 'Yeats', in *On Poetry and Poets* (London: Faber and Faber, 1957), 255.
[7] Eliot, *The Use of Poetry and the Use of Criticism*, 113–14.

This is discomforting writing: Eliot's insistence that one thing is not another thing, and his bluntness in refusing to soften the blow of doing without belief, carry the implicit commitment to poetry as something which is itself and never something else. In the dialogue with Richards, this commitment is absolute and unsparing in the application. At the same time, as Eliot knows, to make this commitment plain and palpable (as he does, here and elsewhere) is to present many readers with an embarrassing set of choices and demands. One acceptable kind of seriousness, about 'us' and our contemporary situation, about our conception of the world and of each other, and about poetry's capacity to fulfil our needs to share and discuss these concerns, is replaced by another kind, in which poetry's integrity is independent of these concerns—and unaccountable to them.

The subversiveness of Eliot's position is commonly underrated, and sometimes discounted altogether. One reason for this is that, on the question of poetry and different kinds of seriousness, Eliot seems so comprehensively to have lost the argument. By now, it is not only poetry, but all kinds of artistic and cultural production and consumption that are uncritically held to be capable of 'saving us', and those kinds of thought and belief which Eliot attempted to save *from* poetry's appropriation are often eager to accommodate themselves to poetry. Seriousness of the kind Eliot intends is now, in fact, an embarrassing gaucheness for most kinds of contemporary literature. In Britain, poetry is in fact more 'high profile' than it has been for decades—in terms, that is, of media visibility and promotional energy. But the dogma on which the activities of organizations like the Poetry Society rely is that poetry is an undeniable good: like exercise or a sensible diet, poetry will do something for you, once you learn to cherish it, and to value the poets who make it. It would be tedious to list all the occasions on which adjectives like 'exciting', 'challenging', 'ground-breaking', and 'modern' are approvingly employed in the promotion of contemporary poetry; but such terms are the effective currency, and suggest how inflated a value is assigned to much contemporary writing. If we accept that poetry should be promoted, we should not be surprised that the language used to promote it is crude, nor that it moves in the opposite direction to the language of criticism. But sooner or later, we will find ourselves wondering about what exactly is being promoted here: is it poetry, or the values attaching to the promotional language? Eliot's remarks on Arnold have a sharp relevance: 'he was so conscious of what, for him, poetry was *for*, that he could not altogether see it for what it is'.[8]

To know and value poetry for what it is, and not for what it is *for*, is never going to be a winning attitude. Likewise, suggesting that the promotion of poetry is not self-evidently a good thing is a position, in present circumstances, of risk and vulnerability. And, it might be added, Eliot's own position is hardly as far beyond the pale of twentieth-century critical habit and expectation as all that: he is, after all, quintessentially 'establishment' in terms of mid-century literary power structures, and centrally placed, by almost any reckoning, in the narrative of poetry's progress through that century. Yet Eliot's insistence on the seriousness of poetry in and for itself, and not necessarily in and for some other thing, is indeed an embarrassment in the world of poetry celebration and mutually awarded prizes, where poetry, like other art, does the decent thing by whatever contemporary orthodoxies of thought or belief call the shots. Eliot was indeed, in the middle decades of the century, very much an 'establishment' figure in Britain; yet by the end of the 1990s, it had become possible to condemn Eliot's writing on the grounds of its supposed unacceptability in terms of shared cultural values. More generally, Eliot's kind of authority, and the degree to which he promoted the idea of authority in matters of knowledge and culture, had become problematic in the world of those academic and literary elites who run the machinery of taste. The problem with Eliot, in this reading, is that he is so completely incapable, not just of saving us, but even of being one of us.

Tom Paulin's review of an important, but partial and over-rhetorical book on Eliot by Anthony Julius, subsequently reprinted in a collection of Paulin's prose, is a significant and depressing document in the history of Eliot's critical reception in Britain. Claiming that 'Julius's study is only the beginning of a long process of revisionist criticism which should diminish the overwhelming, stifling cultural authority which Eliot's oeuvre has acquired', Paulin assembles an assortment of politically unacceptable positions to add to Eliot's (supposedly proven) anti-Semitism. Thus, 'His misogyny is closely connected to his hatred of Jews', while the roots of the whole thing go to bizarre depths: 'a certain strain of conservative discourse tends to identify Judaism with Unitarianism and with other forms of Puritanism'. How could anyone take

---

[8] Eliot, *The Use of Poetry and the Use of Criticism*, 118.

seriously such a disreputable figure as this, and for so long? Paulin
concedes that 'his work seems endlessly subtle and intelligent, many
of his cadences are perfect, but'—and here enters the impressionistic
evidence which carries its own self-validating emotive sincerity—'but
there is a malignity in it which is terrifying'.[9] This may be poetry, in other
words, but it is capable of damning us.

The specifics of Julius's charges against Eliot are complicated and
contentious; certainly, Eliot put into print phrases and remarks about
Jews which are in themselves shameful, and which cannot (and should
not) be blotted from the record. But beyond these specifics, Julius (and,
in his wake, Paulin) accuse Eliot of (to use Richards's phrase) giving 'a
perfect emotive description of a state of mind'. In fact, given what they
and many readers believe poetry to be, Eliot could not do anything
other than this, simply because this is what poetry always does. The
'state of mind' which is anti-Semitic invades and infects the poetry: not
only is the anti-Semitism in the poetry, the poetry is in the anti-Semitism. We should not be surprised, then, to find guilty men like Eliot
trying to downplay poetry's involvement with beliefs. Paulin quotes
Eliot in 1928: 'And certainly poetry is not the inculcation of morals,
or the direction of politics; and no more is it religion or an equivalent of
religion, except by some monstrous abuse of words.'[10] This is, of course,
in line with other things said by Eliot in response to Richards, or in
relation to Arnold; for Paulin, it does not protect the seriousness of
poetry, but fatally undermines it. Seizing on Eliot's 'no more', Paulin
detects the sound of inauthenticity:[11]

In Eliot's sentence it functions on one level as an intensifier—a weightier
version of 'nor'—on another it means 'no longer'. There's just the faintest *ou-
boum* sound to this, because Eliot is signalling almost invisibly that something is
absolutely finished now. Poetry is not sacral or ethical or civic, it's just a higher
form of limerick. We're close to Bentham's equation—quantity of pleasure
being equal—of poetry to pushpin.

Eliot's 'no more' does not mean 'no longer': Eliot never believed that
poetry was, in anything but the most remote and unrecoverable of pasts,
'religion or an equivalent of religion'. In 1928, what 'is absolutely
finished now', as far as Eliot is concerned, is the Victorian hope that

---

[9] Tom Paulin, 'T. S. Eliot and Anti-Semitism', *Writing to the Moment: Selected Critical Essays
1980–1996* (London: Faber and Faber, 1996), 160.
[10] T. S. Eliot, 1928 Preface to *The Sacred Wood*, quoted in Paulin, *Writing to the Moment*, 156.
[11] Ibid. 156.

poetry might be a serviceable stand-in for religion. As Paulin apes
Julius's forensic techniques, pushing on to the supposedly logical consequences of the alleged ideas, he descends into bathos: the 'higher form
of limerick', and the invocation of Bentham as a kind of Philistine
bogeyman, too obviously lose all contact with any position one could
plausibly ascribe to Eliot. All the same, it is interesting that Paulin finds
himself accusing Eliot of being unserious about poetry: felicities of
cadence apart, Eliot's a fake, and the proof of his poetic fraudulence
is in the unwholesomeness of his attitudes.

Behind Paulin's essay is the appeal to a consensus about what serious
poetry is: it is sacral, ethical, civic. It feels good, of course, to agree about
this—for one thing, it makes thinking about the sacral, the ethical, or the
civic a good deal less trouble, since we can refer these difficult and
demanding things back to the world of poetry. But a consensus can be
mistaken, vain, and self-serving; and it might be worth the certainty of
apparent embarrassment to point out that poetry is no more sacral or
ethical than it is legal or mathematical: we do not frame deeds of trust in
verse, or work out how to keep an aeroplane in the air by means of
heroic couplets. Paulin inherits and appeals to a consensus for which
Eliot was always, sooner or later, going to look unacceptable. The
wonder is that his 'stifling authority' endured so long.

From the mid-century onwards, British criticism and poetry were
indeed much taken up with Eliot. Just as media-establishment critics like
Paulin misread Eliot in the 1990s, so the first admirers of *Four Quartets*
fuelled a misreading that put in place Eliot's 'authority'. Both phases of
misreading, however, relied on the hope that 'Poetry is capable of saving
us'; neither noticed, or took seriously enough, Eliot's own emphatic
dissent from this hope.

II

One reader who was more than approximately attuned to Eliot's
subversive scepticism was W. H. Auden. That this should be so is
especially interesting, for Auden felt early in his career the influence
both of I. A. Richards himself, and (more acutely) of psychological
theory. At the time of his greatest British success, in the 1930s,
Auden found himself in some respects a more appropriate object of
Richards's 'poetry is capable of saving us' than Eliot: the enthusiasm
with which books like *Poems* (1930), *The Orators* (1932), or *Look, Stranger!*

(1936) were received was an enthusiasm for the poetry of command and engagement, which seemed to contain 'beliefs' by the bucketload, and to have at its centre (however cryptically encoded) a message of potential social, psychological, and political salvation. The warmest admirers of the 1930s Auden felt themselves to be in a select club, where the poet was one of 'us'; in his later writing, Auden tried to speak to a somewhat different constituency. If all this was certainly a matter of change in substance for Auden's poetry, it was also, and crucially, the occasion for a change in tone.

It is in the tone of the post-1930s Auden that his engagement with Eliot is most acute and telling. How far this tone has been influential, in terms of style, is a moot point; but its influence in terms of artistic orientation and intent have been considerable, supplementing and even—arguably—coming to replace the powerful influence of Eliot himself on the question of art's seriousness, and poetry's role. In 'The Sea and the Mirror' (begun in 1942 and published in 1944), Auden composed what he was himself later disposed to think of as his major poem, a sustained and elaborate meta-dramatic meditation on art's seriousness in the world. Like Eliot's *Four Quartets*, this can be thought of as a wartime production; and Auden had the advantage of reading the *Quartets* in writing his poem (all but *Little Gidding* had been published when Auden started work in August 1942; and *Little Gidding* was in print by October of that year). While 'The Sea and the Mirror' is obviously a work whose explicit literary relations are with Shakespeare and *The Tempest*, its sensitivities of tone and subject are sharpened by Eliot, and in particular the Eliot of *Four Quartets*.

Auden's figure of Prospero is, on one level, a self-portrait, and Prospero's dismissal of Ariel is undoubtedly in part a reflection of particular incidents in Auden's relationship with his younger lover, Chester Kallmann. Of course, this is not the whole story, and both Prospero and Ariel are required by Auden to carry a number of other strata of significance: Prospero, for example, can also be Shakespeare, or the artist in general, or a particular aspect of the artistic temperament; he may even be the side of art that dislikes art, and wants to give it up for more serious pursuits. Allegorical possibilities proliferate, perhaps not entirely to the poem's advantage. However, Prospero communicates in a very distinctive tone of voice:[12]

---

[12] W. H. Auden, *Collected Poems*, ed. Edward Mendelson (London: Faber and Faber, 1991), 405.

Now, Ariel, I am that I am, your late and lonely master,
    Who knows now what magic is:—the power to enchant
That comes from disillusion. What the books can teach one
    Is that most desires end up in stinking ponds,
But we have only to learn to sit still and give no orders,
    To make you offer us your echo and your mirror;
We have only to believe you, then you dare not lie;
    To ask for nothing, and at once from your calm eyes,
With their lucid proof of apprehension and disorder,
    All we are not stares back at what we are.

There can be no mistaking the style here, which is Eliot's: 'What the books can teach one' catches in its cadence, and in its use of the line-break, exactly Eliot's tone in *East Coker* V ('And what there is to conquer | By strength and submission...'),[13] while 'we have only to learn to sit still' echoes *Ash-Wednesday* VI ('Teach us to care and not to care | Teach us to sit still'),[14] and 'All we are not stares back at what we are' adapts the 'And where you are is where you are not' motif from the end of *East Coker* III.[15] Beyond these particulars of echo or allusion, it is Prospero's verbal world which is so markedly Eliotic, rather than Shakespearian, in its tone.

What is the point of this? As far as 'The Sea and the Mirror''s allegorical and philosophical bearings are concerned, it may well be that the presence of Eliot is a largely unnecessary and unhelpful distraction. Perhaps Auden is a stylistic magpie, and there is no more to be said. But the relation between tone and meaning in this section of the poem ('Prospero to Ariel') is a good deal more interesting than Auden's evolving argument, and makes the matter of Eliot's presence an import-ant one. Prospero, who speaks in Auden's approximation or adaptation of classical elegiacs, is engaged in finding the eloquence for a farewell to eloquence, a wordy and rhetorically self-aware style of elaboration which indicates—with whatever degree of sorrow—the ultimate inad-equacy and inauthenticity of words for the higher purposes of the spirit. Auden plays extended variations on several of Eliot's motifs and ex-pressions, and this has the effect of further elaborating manners already somewhat ornate. Where *East Coker* II announces 'Do not let me hear | Of the wisdom of old men, but rather of their folly, | Their fear of fear and frenzy...',[16] Auden's Prospero gives his own, more detailed,

---

[13] T. S. Eliot, *Complete Poems and Plays* (London: Faber and Faber, 1969), 182.
[14] Ibid. 98.   [15] Ibid. 181.   [16] Ibid. 179.

notion of 'the long looked forward to, | Long hoped for calm, the autumnal serenity | And the wisdom of age':[17]

> When I am safely home, oceans away in Milan, and
> Realise once and for all I shall never see you again,
> Over there, maybe, it won't seem quite so dreadful
> Not to be interesting any more, but an old man
> Just like other old men, with eyes that water
> Easily in the wind, and a head that nods in the sunshine,
> Forgetful, maladroit, a little grubby,
> And to like it.

There is perhaps more than a hint of Eliot's 'Gerontion' here too, but the major element in the background for Auden's Prospero is the *East Coker* challenge to 'the wisdom of old men'. Auden takes Eliot's bare (and sharp) outline, and makes it both more particular and less powerful:

> When the servants settle me into a chair
> In some well-sheltered corner of the garden,
> And arrange my muffler and rugs, shall I ever be able
> To stop myself from telling them what I am doing,—
> Sailing alone, out over seventy thousand fathoms—?
> Yet if I speak, I shall sink without a sound
> Into unmeaning abysses.

Prospero here imagines being self-constrained to silence in his old age; in this, he is no longer (in Eliot's phrase, also in *East Coker* II) 'risking enchantment'—enchanting others or himself, the two amounting possibly to the same thing. What Prospero must renounce is the very eloquence he is exercising; the price to be paid is the loss of entertainment value in (or out of) life:

> Can I learn to suffer
> Without saying something ironic or funny
> On suffering? I never suspected the way of truth
> Was a way of silence where affectionate chat
> Is but a robbers' ambush and even good music
> In shocking taste; and you, of course, never told me.

Prospero is reacting here to propositions which seem to resemble those of *East Coker*:[18]

---

[17] Auden, *Collected Poems*, 409.   [18] Eliot, *Complete Poems and Plays*, 181.

        In order to arrive there,
    To arrive where you are, to get from where you are not,
        You must go by a way wherein there is no ecstasy.
    In order to arrive at what you do not know
        You must go by a way which is the way of ignorance.
    In order to possess what you do not possess
        You must go by the way of dispossession.
    In order to arrive at what you are not
        You must go through the way in which you are not.

Again, what Eliot renders abstract and formulaic in this litany of reversal, Auden's Prospero makes both personal and imaginable; the need to
stop saying 'something ironic or funny' about the serious business of
suffering leads to the 'way of truth' being necessarily 'the way of silence'.

When Auden picked up the tone of parts of *East Coker* for his
Prospero, he was proving himself an acute reader of Eliot's later
manner. At the same time, he transforms what he hears in Eliot: inward,
meditative poetry becomes now quasi-dramatic, demonstrative poetry.
Whether or not such a transformation entails a certain coarsening, it
certainly makes more visible the consequences of artistic renunciation.
For Eliot, in whose poem 'The poetry does not matter',[19] art is not
enough—though not *simply* so; for Prospero, art will simply have to go,
and life's serious task will mean 'getting to know | The difference
between moonshine and daylight'. Actually, the effect of reading 'Prospero to Ariel' alongside parts of *Four Quartets* is to make Eliot's voice
more closely akin to that of a stagey and slightly camp old man, whose
show of humility remains incorrigibly histrionic. Of course, this is a
mistaken way to approach what Eliot is trying to do, and finally an
unrewarding angle from which to assess his poetry. But Auden's exaggeration of Eliot's voice is in the service of an artistic ambition every bit
as high and serious as *Four Quartets*, and one which dwells as much on
art's insufficiency as on its potential. And most tellingly, Auden recognizes that poetry's attitude to the seriousness of its burden, and the
limitations of its capacities, is a matter of voice.

Auden's critics have always been aware of his various disapprovals,
and in particular his disapproval of an art that takes itself too seriously as
either the centre of its own universe or the vehicle for saving formulae.
Nevertheless, only a few of his admirers are willing to confront explicitly

---

[19] Ibid. 179.

some of Auden's more emphatic dismissals of artistic pretension. Lucy McDiarmid encounters her subject's anti-aesthetic tendencies most fully and rewardingly, making them the heart of a study of Auden's poetic apologetics; she calls 'The Sea and the Mirror' as a whole 'a discussion of the spiritual fraudulence of aesthetic effects', and maintains that every later Auden poem 'assumes that all poems, itself not excluded, are silly and trivial, examples of "incorrigible staginess" that need to be apologized for and forgiven'.[20] This tone, which McDiarmid calls one of 'Deference, apology, self-deprecation',[21] is perhaps best understood as a development of Prospero's infatuation with the later Eliot; where 'The Sea and the Mirror' is more complex and subtle than its Prospero on this subject, a good deal of the later Auden is more bluntly dismissive of art's purpose.

In 1947, Auden concluded a series of lectures on Shakespeare with a warning against over-seriousness, and a commendation of his subject's apparent disregard for posterity (a matter only of concern in 'the early minor sonnets'):[22]

There is a continual process of simplification in Shakespeare's plays. What is he up to? He is holding the mirror up to nature. In the early minor sonnets he talks about his works outlasting time. But increasingly he suggests, as Theseus does in *A Midsummer Night's Dream*, that 'The best in this kind are but shadows', that art is rather a bore. He spends his life at it, but he doesn't think it's very important. . . . I find Shakespeare particularly appealing in his attitude towards his work. There's something a little irritating in the determination of the very greatest artists, like Dante, Joyce, Milton, to create masterpieces and to think themselves important. To be able to devote one's life to art without forgetting that art is frivolous is a tremendous achievement of personal character. Shakespeare never takes himself too seriously. When art takes itself too seriously, it tries to do more than it can.

As reported here, Auden's voice is busy simplifying even as it commends simplicity, and there is a note of briskness along with envy in the ascription to Shakespeare of the view that 'art is rather a bore'. As so often in Auden, the language and its tone are in the register of good and bad behaviour, and literary conduct is part of a comedy of manners in

[20] Lucy McDiarmid, *Auden's Apologies for Poetry* (Princeton: Princeton University Press, 1990), 16.

[21] Ibid. 120.

[22] W. H. Auden, *Lectures on Shakespeare*, reconstructed and edited by Arthur Kirsch (London: Faber and Faber, 2000), 319.

which the wrong beliefs are *faux pas*, and high pretensions signs of ill-breeding. The figure who takes himself too seriously is, of course, a comic figure, and Auden suggests here that the best way for an artist to avoid falling into this role, to avoid becoming Malvolio, is to hold fast to a belief in the ultimate unseriousness of art, its essentially 'frivolous' nature.

Such a tone is by no means uncommon in Auden's poetry as well as in his prose. What is most interesting about it, perhaps, is the relation in which it stands to the writing's sense of authority. Self-deprecation is always complex; here, it serves as a means of bonding with a readership, reassuring and confirming them in certain kinds of expectation and predisposition. Far from disabling any sense of authority, Auden's manner of self-deprecation makes the authority all the stronger: in its tonal insistence on literary discourse as comedy, it enters a world of rules and axioms that will exclude and possibly ridicule those who fail to get the joke. Not taking poetry too seriously becomes, in much of the later Auden, what poetry is all about.

What happens to the seriousness in this process is simple, for it goes somewhere else, into the realm of the sacred, where art has no proper or secure place. In one of his attempts to present this, Auden tried to re-inhabit Coleridge's distinction between Primary and Secondary Imagination, making the Primary something the 'only concern' of which 'is with sacred beings and sacred events', and whose realm 'is without freedom, sense of time or humour'. The Secondary Imagination, on the other hand, inhabits a more gregarious and possibly garrulous place:[23]

To the Primary Imagination a sacred being is that which it is. To the Secondary Imagination a beautiful form is as it ought to be, an ugly form as it ought not to be.... It does not worship the beautiful; it approves of it and can give reasons for its approval. The Secondary Imagination has, one might say, a bourgeois nature. It approves of regularity, of spatial symmetry and temporal repetition, of law and order: it disapproves of loose ends, irrelevance and mess.

This kind of imagination sounds a little like a poet using regular forms; but it also sounds a little like a children's nanny, or a nagging school-teacher. That Auden is in fact describing a way of regarding art, rather than a way of making it, becomes even clearer when he observes that

[23] W. H. Auden, 'Making, Knowing and Judging', *The Dyer's Hand and Other Essays* (London: Faber and Faber, 1953), 56–7.

'the Secondary Imagination is social and craves agreement with other minds'. If this is so, then tone of address is crucial; it is everything—or rather, it is all that is left.

In 'The Truest Poetry is the Most Feigning' (1954), Auden fits into rhyming couplets the kind of instruction which his prose sometimes offers to an imaginary poetic apprentice. The form suits the didactic mode, but the unmisgiving nature of Auden's instruction is all in the service of a deprecation, rather than a recommendation, of poetry's capacity to tell the truth. Poetry's hyperbolic metaphors for the loved one are considered ('From such ingenious fibs are poems born'), and the would-be poet is told not to confuse these with the true state of things:[24]

> Then, should she leave you for some other guy,
> Or ruin you with debts, or go and die,
> No metaphor, remember, can express
> A real historical unhappiness;
> Your tears have value if they make us gay;
> *O Happy Grief!* is all sad verse can say.

To call the tone of 'or go and die' callous would, of course, be to fail to get the joke, or to misunderstand the tonal rules Auden plays by in the poem; yet 'A real historical unhappiness' is soon trying very hard to state the cold, sober fact of the matter: its tone is flat, not ironic, and Auden would be appalled if we read it as an Americanism that renders its idea comic (this unhappiness is real historical). By the next line, however, his serious moment both past and still serious, Auden is off into a cheaply Yeatsian flourish, too coarse to carry off anything like parody. The whole poem gives instructions in the impersonality of art, even when art feels most personal to its maker, and extends to matters of politics as well as love. The tone is brisk, the verse florid, and the effect of the whole baroque: flaunted artificiality fits a poem about artificiality, but the problem with Auden's performance is the extent to which it exercises a coercive strength on the audience which, rather than craving agreement with other minds, assumes that it would be (at least) silly of those minds to do anything but agree. The conclusion swells with the certainty of approval:

> For given Man, by birth, by education,
> Imago Dei who forgot his station,

---

[24] Auden, *Collected Poems*, 620–1.

The self-made creature who himself unmakes,
The only creature ever made who fakes,
With no more nature in his loving smile
Than in his theories of a natural style,
What but tall tales, the luck of verbal playing,
Can trick his lying nature into saying
That love, or truth in any serious sense,
Like orthodoxy, is a reticence?

'Reticence', we might remark, has not been much in evidence in Auden's poem; but this is not quite an irony which is lost on the author, for it is not poetry, but 'love, or truth in any serious sense' which has an essentially reticent character. Poetry is all these things are not; the faking possible uniquely to man is involved with 'the luck of verbal playing' which poetry (unlike 'serious' things) amounts to.

Auden's poem has been read as an 'explicit farewell' to 'the notion of truths and essences', which 'argues in favour of the inevitable entanglement of human beings in the constructions and discourses that shape their existence as well as their understandings of themselves'.[25] But this humanely postmodern interpretation seems astray: it misses the poem's tone almost entirely, by taking its dismissal of seriousness for an embrace of plurality. For Auden, the serious is still what matters; and poetry—like other artistic responses to life—is finally an unserious business. As Rainer Emig goes on to consider, the 'explicit farewell' Auden has in mind is one that renders poetry fundamentally inauthentic:[26]

The plurality, flexibility, and openness of poetry enables it exactly to be inauthentic when it chooses to be—as a response to the particular pressures surrounding it. Its ambiguities and obscurities, however, also enable its reader to take up the position he or she chooses.

This makes inauthenticity into a kind of stylistic option. Perhaps Emig is closer to the truth of the matter than might first appear, for although the breadth and variety of Auden's stylistic palette are not really the same thing as a postmodern openness and indeterminacy, his more fundamental deprecation of seriousness in poetry enables 'ludic' interpretation and practice. For Lucy McDiarmid, 'The Truest Poetry is the Most Feigning' also denies poetry's equivalence with 'love, or truth in any serious sense', since 'The notion of inauthenticity is built into poetry.'

[25] Rainer Emig, *W. H. Auden: Towards a Postmodern Poetics* (Basingstoke: Palgrave, 2000), 210.
[26] Ibid. 210.

McDiarmid understands how centrally related the poem's own tone is to
what it has to say about poetry's tone, comparing it with the end of
Caliban's speech in 'The Sea and the Mirror':[27]

And so just as Caliban can only indicate the failure of his own performance and
the inadequacy of his words, just as the Stage Manager identifies ripeness with
silence, so Auden here can only suggest that what is genuine is not expressed
...And the poem has to end on that note. The frivolity and insignificance of
poetry have been amply demonstrated; having introduced the possibility of a
'serious' love, Auden can do no more than acknowledge its existence somewhere off the page.

Wisely, McDiarmid does not claim this as a liberation into postmodern
play. What is interesting, though, is the shrewd observation that, in
matters of poetry and inauthenticity, it takes two to tango: inauthenticity, McDiarmid writes, 'forms, however unconsciously, a fundamental
part of any reasonably sophisticated reader's expectation'.[28] At a certain
level, this may be common sense; but Auden's poem is operating
somewhere beyond that level, and asks for an uncommon degree of
unserious expectation from his reader. 'This', McDiarmid adds, 'is what
Eliot meant when he wrote that "Poetry is not an expression of
emotion; poetry is an escape from emotion." '[29] But it is far from
what Eliot meant, either in 'Tradition and the Individual Talent' or
later, by 'impersonality', and Auden's notion of poetry as a less serious,
less binding thing than truth or love is in fact a very long way from
Eliot's concern to see poetry for itself and not as something else.

   Auden's belief in tone as the ground on which poet and reader can
meet in a common agreement to understand poetry's inauthenticity, and
enjoy its frivolity in relation to a seriousness that lies off the page, is not
merely an effect or affectation made for the sake of poems like 'The
Truest Poetry is the Most Feigning'. With a straighter face, and in a verse
form and level of diction we associate with his most assured and
authoritative manner, Auden makes much the same point in his 1955
'Homage to Clio'. This poem is moving, where the other is witty; yet the
reservation of seriousness for the world beyond poems is in each case a
dogmatic certainty. The Muse of history is addressed, but remains silent
throughout, while the poet's voice works to reconcile itself to this

---

[27] McDiarmid, *Auden's Apologies for Poetry*, 41.   [28] Ibid. 40.
[29] Ibid. misquoting T. S. Eliot, 'Tradition and the Individual Talent', *Selected Essays* (London:
Faber and Faber, 1951), 21.

silence, and to understand where that leaves the poetic voice itself, in a
world where history seems again and again to demand some response.
Clio is 'Muse of the unique | Historical fact, defending with silence |
Some world of your beholding, a silence | No explosion can conquer';
Auden has as his task the comprehension of this silence, this unrespon-
siveness, in a Muse whose area of concern seems so immediate. However, the poem's progress is towards a point where Clio's silence can be
met and measured up to by the poet's reticence—something which is
against the grain, and therefore difficult, but still essential. In the
concluding lines, Auden prays to Clio to 'forgive our noises | And
teach us our recollections':[30]

> to throw away
> The tiniest fault of someone we love
> Is out of the question, says Aphrodite,
> Who should know, yet one had known people
>
> Who have done just that. Approachable as you seem,
> I dare not ask you if you bless the poets,
> For you do not look as if you ever read them,
> Nor can I see a reason why you should.

Auden's readers (who are, after all, necessarily engaged in reading at
least one of the poets) are made to feel on the same side as Auden here,
looking on with a sense of their own limitations as the serious business
of suffering—like the serious business of love—goes on and on beyond
the page and outside the poetic voice. One critical reader of Auden has
identified a 'louche playfulness' here,[31] but this is probably to play up
too eagerly to the poet's sharing of resignation. Even so, the poignancy
of the last line is partly a matter of tone, its recognition falling in with a
reader's need for reassurance that there are limits to a poem's demands.
All this is a prayer for and about reticence; like much of Auden's later
work, it appeals to a consensus about what is seriously the case: paradoxically, this consensus is an agreement that poetry—'noise'—is irrelevant
to the serious concerns of a suffering world.

   Paradox and the paradoxical are themselves terms that are often
covers for critical slippage: one person's paradox is another's illogic or
contradiction. And Auden, or more precisely Auden's tone, seems to
appeal to our propensity as readers for paradox; a poem, for example,

---

[30] Auden, *Collected Poems*, 612–13.
[31] Stan Smith, *W. H. Auden* (Oxford: Blackwell, 1985), 172.

which memorably and beautifully speaks of its limitations, and powerfully makes apparent its degree of powerlessness, is at some level
banking on our liking for paradox, and our acceptance that clarity in
statement and assertion, or in analysis and argument, may be neither
possible nor desirable. It is in this respect that Auden's post-war writing
meets the taste of readers impressed by limitation and (though this term
may seem odd for Auden) modesty, offering them a fully expansive kind
of poetry which does not challenge the common sense of the world in
which, like its readers, it works to make its way.

One of the early and decisive signs of Auden's reorientation of his
poetry comes at the conclusion to 'At the Grave of Henry James', a
much-revised poem written in 1941. Like 'Homage to Clio', this is a
prayer (though a Christian's prayer, and therefore to a figure in whose
prayer-answering power the poet cannot actually believe) which finally
stakes everything on its tone:[32]

> All will be judged. Master of nuance and scruple,
> Pray for me and for all writers, living or dead:
>   Because there are many whose works
> Are in better taste than their lives, because there is no end
> To the vanity of our calling, make intercession
>   For the treason of all clerks.

Here again is a form of address which is, and yet is not, entirely serious.
Like Prospero dismissing Ariel, the poet's voice in these lines is con-
sciously putting on a show, for which James is only the ostensible
audience (Henry James isn't really listening, nor is he a saint from
whom the faithful can request intercession; Auden knows this, the
real audience knows this: and as far as the poem is concerned, it really
doesn't matter). The poet's equivalent of Prospero's camp staginess is a
degree of apparently candid self-exposure, and here the hint of remorsefulness in comparing work with life is dropped very carefully, but
in terms of what is (or isn't) in good taste. The prominently American
final rhyme is a reminder of the overstepping of limits by a class of
intellectuals prone to overrate their own importance, and the self-
chastisement implicit here is not, perhaps, entirely without a hint of
self-congratulation. Auden's phrase, 'because there is no end | To the
vanity of our calling' concentrates the difficulties of register which

---

[32] Auden, *Collected Poems*, 312.

the poem's tone might be trying to level out, since it starts to break down once we ask how vain a statement it might actually be. Is this self-deprecation or self-aggrandizement? Given that the voice has been addressing James as 'Master of nuance and scruple', we should be listening hard for the nuances of 'vanity', and be alert to the 'scruple' involved in Auden's use of the word.

'Vanity' is, of course, very much at issue here; its relation to self-consciousness is clear enough, but its links with apparent self-deprecation are just as real—even if they are not, for Auden, quite so problematic. From one point of view, it might appear that Auden is accepting, on behalf of 'all writers living or dead', the charge of 'vanity': it is 'the vanity of our calling', something not to be avoided because of the very nature of that calling. So, what we have here is a kind of collective or generic self-deprecation. But it is not, perhaps, all that grave a matter, for a 'calling' is not something which one can finally resist or for which, in the end, a called individual can be held responsible: the vanity is in the calling. In personal terms, moreover, this is a calling to inauthenticity: works have the 'taste' that lives may lack, and 'there is no end', even in the end of the poem itself, to the continuing 'vanity' of the artist. Again, Auden's tone is perfectly attuned to this, since the prayer is couched in terms that render it something other than a *real* prayer (there is no fringe religious community, even in the USA, that prays to Henry James).

Obviously, the questioning of poetry's worth, and eventually the taking for granted of poetry's limited worth in moral, ethical, and religious terms, is at the heart of Auden's developing sense of himself as an artist, and it lies behind his finest as well as his more mannered or routine productions. Although this kind of doubt may at times become little more than a tic in Auden's style, it is also, and more importantly, essential to his poetic ambitions and achievements, even the highest and best of these. However, the degree to which all this is invested in tone in Auden's verse, and to which tone itself is understood as the ground on which a poet's and his audience's doubts about poetry's seriousness can meet, collude, and agree, suggests something of the significance which Auden's characteristic stance might carry for post-war culture in Britain. To value irony and paradox, to deprecate an art that takes itself too seriously, and to acknowledge poetry's final unsatisfactoriness in relation to 'truth', turns subversive scepticism into conformable limitation.

III

Auden's reference to 'the vanity of our calling' bears comparison with the use of 'humility' near the end of *East Coker* II:[33]

> Do not let me hear
> Of the wisdom of old men, but rather of their folly,
> Their fear of fear and frenzy, their fear of possession,
> Of belonging to another, or to others, or to God.
> The only wisdom we can hope to achieve
> Is the wisdom of humility. Humility is endless.

'Because there is no end | To the vanity of our calling' is likely to be indebted to Eliot (Auden published his poem in England in June 1941, and probably composed it in the spring of that year; *East Coker* was published in September 1940, and had appeared in the Easter *New English Weekly*). Eliot's lines also make an impact upon Auden's Prospero, but although Auden undoubtedly hears them loudly in 'The Sea and the Mirror' and 'At the grave of Henry James', the more general relation between Eliot's passage and Auden's exercises in poetry and tone, authenticity and inauthenticity, is just as pressing a matter. Some of Eliot's words here are important through the whole of what was to become *Four Quartets*: 'wisdom', 'folly', and 'humility' between them sum up many of the concerns at the heart of the work. These words are, just as obviously, related in significant ways to Auden's spectrum of seriousness in and about poetry. And for two of the words at least, both Eliot and Auden are indebted to another source, in the work of Yeats.

In trying to gauge the importance of Auden and of *Four Quartets*, in relation to questions of poetry's seriousness and authority, Yeats remains a constant presence both in and behind issues of tone, authenticity, and limitation. Auden's reactions to Yeats's death in 1939 include his enduringly influential elegy, 'In Memory of W. B. Yeats', and at a deeper level the legacy of the older poet worries at and perhaps in some ways undermines Auden's artistic projects for the rest of his life. But it is T. S. Eliot whose work embodies the most influential refiguring and redirection of Yeats, and in particular the Eliot of *Four Quartets*, who makes much of the later Yeats's 'revelation of all that a man is and remains'.[34] The 'humility' which *East Coker* commends is Eliot's

---

[33] Eliot, *Collected Poems and Plays*, 179. [34] Eliot, 'Yeats', *On Poetry and Poets*, 257.

addition to, or reconciliation of, the two terms crucial to late Yeats, 'wisdom' and 'folly'. How far this 'humility' includes the deprecation of poetry is an important question, and one with obvious significance for Auden. Indeed, one way of putting it was given to Eliot by Auden in his elegy—'For poetry makes nothing happen'—and reformulated within a year or so (again in *East Coker* II) as 'The poetry does not matter'.[35] Between them, Eliot and Auden taught a British post-war audience how to read Yeatsian 'wisdom' and 'folly' in terms of a necessary 'humility' quite alien to the Irish poet himself. In the short term, the effect of this was to secure Eliot's pre-eminence as a modern poet; and in the longer term, it was to secure the authority of 'humility' as poetry's distinguishing characteristic. By the time that Eliot was himself under attack for his beliefs and political positions, 'humility' had gone further, so that poetry not only was to know its place, but literary success often depended on accepting this, and playing along.

It is extremely doubtful whether any contemporary poet would wish to have her or his work associated with 'wisdom'. The very word carries with it a hint of battiness, or what Auden identified as the 'Southern Californian' element in Yeats. Eliot's alternative, 'humility', is also, perhaps, pitched a little oddly for contemporary tastes: its religious overtones are in most quarters scarcely acceptable, and it undoubtedly gets in the way of busy promotion or self-promotion. But 'humility is endless' is also more complicated and far-reaching a line than it might appear at first: in the context of Eliot's lifelong meditation on limitation and demarcation, on the things, including poetry, that are themselves and not some other thing, humility's 'endless' range extends towards the discourses and concerns that affect the reader of the poem. 'We', Eliot's first-person plural, is employed often in *Four Quartets* as a part of the poetry's pattern of tonal relationship with the reader; like any inclusive address, it fails without the impression of frankness or even candour in the speaker. 'Humility' rings hollow unless it is that of the poet as well as that being recommended to an audience. The difference between this and Auden's first-person plural in 'At the Grave of Henry James' is obvious, since there 'the vanity of our calling' is something the reader is called upon to indulge, and not presumed to share.

In a reading of *Four Quartets* in terms of its tone, we need to find the points at which Eliot's poetry stages meetings with its readership, and

---

[35] Eliot, *Collected Poems and Plays*, 179.

folds that readership into a common language. The close of *East Coker*
II is one such point, and it sets the terms for others. It is important not
to underestimate the extent of Eliot's success, in the 1940s and subsequent decades, as a convincing communicator with a large audience.
Four Quartets in particular enjoyed a wartime success that was translated
into a post-war eminence as a classic text, in which Eliot's authority as a
writer found its most concentrated, and most apparently consensual
expression. If we wish to criticize Eliot's tone, or his reliance on tone, in
the *Quartets*, we have to begin by acknowledging how brilliantly that
tone chimed with the wishes of the poet's first readership. Probably the
most extreme contemporary expression of this was the declaration that
'Finally, to understand *Four Quartets* we need to live with them, and even
to live by them,'[36] but a more general acclamation of Eliot as a guide in
dark times was certainly to be heard in the 1940s and 1950s, and even,
sporadically, later on. John Xiros Cooper writes of the poem's 'profound effect on the intelligentsia', pointing out the complexity of the
agenda of *Four Quartets* along with the difficult situation in which it met
with its audience:[37]

> The poem, of course, pursued radical intellectual and aesthetic purposes. It
> needed, for one thing, to openly acknowledge the validity and appropriateness
> of the experience of nihilism in a desolate time. It could not pay lip service to
> feelings of despair and devastation; the poem had to seem to mean them. . . .
> The poem needed to address readers who had been trained, even by Eliot
> himself in his early years, to savour ambiguity, irony and the deliciousness of the
> knowingly obscure, an intelligentsia that could not trust itself any more to
> believe the simple teachings of a naïve faith, especially if that faith were
> expressed in the blunt words of the dogmatist.

This is all relevant to Eliot's first-person plural, and its balancing of 'lip
service' with the need 'to seem to mean' catches well the treacherous
and uneasy territory which the poetry's tone has to negotiate. Cooper
(who examines tellingly the contemporary reception of the *Quartets*, and
its willingness to accept Eliot not only as a poet but also—and perhaps
more importantly—as a modern sage) understands that ambiguity and
irony can never be *merely* matters of style. For Eliot, the tone of poetry is
attuned to a more general climate of caution, in which notions like

---

[36] Raymond Preston, *'Four Quartets' Rehearsed: A Commentary on T. S. Eliot's Cycle of Poems*
(London: Sheed and Ward, 1946), 64.
[37] John Xiros Cooper, *T. S. Eliot and the Ideology of* Four Quartets (Cambridge: Cambridge
University Press, 1995), 114.

'wisdom' have to be couched in terms of 'humility'—irony and ambiguity are among these, for both these traits remind an audience that they are in the select company of the author's realism and disillusion.

Towards the end of his life, Eliot closed a lecture of retrospection with the hope of his having grown into a 'greater wisdom and humility'.[38] The two terms had, of course, been long linked for Eliot, and by this point they seem to be natural partners. The stamp of Yeats on 'wisdom' might appear to be almost erased here, but this was far from the case in *Four Quartets*, where the notion that 'Old men ought to be explorers' (and all that follows from this) could almost be taken for a commentary on Yeats's later life and work. 'I am sure,' Eliot said in 1947, 'that for a poet humility is the most essential virtue',[39] and this humility is something which, in the poetry as well as the prose, forms an essential condition for wisdom. Writing about Goethe in 1955, Eliot found a revealing definition of a writer's wisdom:[40]

For wisdom is communicated on a deeper level than that of logical propositions; all language is inadequate, but probably the language of poetry is the language most capable of communicating wisdom. The wisdom of a great poet is concealed in his work; but in becoming aware of it we become ourselves more wise.

Here is another instance of poetry's capacity for knowing its limits, and the passing on of this capacity, adding up to 'The only wisdom we can hope to achieve'. Of course, Eliot is making a point of 'the language of poetry' being less inadequate than other kinds of language, but we should still notice that wisdom is 'concealed' in the poet's work, as something we become aware of and respond to. 'The language of poetry' as a medium for communication is not quite the same medium as that in which 'logical propositions' are framed and understood; but Eliot's clear implication here, in line with his own poetry and its reception, is that the communication of wisdom is a matter of finding common ground between poet and reader in poetic language, almost a collaborative process.

In the light of this, Eliot's 'we', like his 'you' or 'I', are important tonal indicators, and are implicated in the 'humility' that conditions 'wisdom'.

---

[38] T. S. Eliot, *To Criticize the Critic and Other Writings* (London: Faber and Faber, 1965), 26.
[39] T. S. Eliot, *On Poetry* (Concord, Mass.: Concord Academy, 1947), 9. Quoted in Ronald Schuchard, *Eliot's Dark Angel: Intersections of Life and Art* (New York: Oxford University Press, 1999), 190.
[40] Eliot, *On Poetry and Poets*, 226.

There are points in *Four Quartets* at which the poet's particular, highly individual and idiosyncratic perception of key images is brought together with another, altogether more public, language of abstraction. In section V of *The Dry Salvages*, this results in an especially difficult oscillation between the personal and impersonal:[41]

> For most of us, there is only the unattended
> Moment, the moment in and out of time,
> The distraction fit, lost in a shaft of sunlight,
> The wild thyme unseen, or the winter lightning
> Or the waterfall, or music heard so deeply
> That it is not heard at all, but you are the music
> While the music lasts. These are only hints and guesses,
> Hints followed by guesses; and the rest
> Is prayer, observance, discipline, thought and action.
> The hint half guessed, the gift half understood, is Incarnation.

'For most of us' is nicely judged: in a passage so full of talk of hints, we should be able to get the hint here—'For most of us' is inclusive in its tone, and doesn't intend to say 'For most of us, but not for *you*'. Yet the images that follow are profoundly, even inaccessibly, personal ones; if the reader recognizes them, he does so from his experience of *Four Quartets* (*East Coker*'s 'winter lightning' and 'wild thyme unseen'),[42] but not from life. No reader will be in a position to respond unaffectedly to Eliot's claims ('Yes, of course, *that* waterfall . . .'), but all attentive readers will be able to recognize the personally charged images from the poem itself. And yet, the lines move from 'us' to 'you': 'you are the music | While the music lasts'. How is a reader to respond to this? Anything other than readerly assent seems destructive, but there remains some doubt as to how far Eliot has actually earned this assent; and when 'prayer, observance, discipline, thought and action' enter the picture, the room for interpretation is severely cramped, as though the lyric power of the preceding lines had been suddenly switched off, and replaced with the abstract nouns of a common rule. It is interesting that an earlier draft of these last lines, 'Hints followed by guesses: but our ultimate term | And ultimate gift, is Incarnation', glossed at that stage by Eliot's 'hint unguessed' and 'gift not understood' failed to convince an early reader, when Geoffrey Faber asked the author: 'Isn't this in want of *some* qualification? *You* must guess and understand, or you couldn't say

---

[41] Eliot, *Complete Poetry and Plays*, 190.   [42] Ibid. 180.

it; and you wouldn't claim to be the only percipient, would you?'[43] Eliot's solutions, 'half guessed' and 'half understood', are compromises in tone, where the word 'half' is, in fact, a means of having it both ways: Faber's '*You*' had broken into the original tone, pointing to the first-person voice behind the poetry's use of the second person, and Eliot had to find a way of acknowledging simultaneously his own guess and understanding alongside the less clued-up comprehension of the poem's 'you'.

That Eliot is having it both ways is an uncharitable interpretation, and certainly not in key with the collaborative goodwill that the tone of *Four Quartets* requires for enjoyable or improving reading. And, in more sophisticated terms, this could be seen as a manifestation in the realm of poetic argument of paradox, a form of irony as pervasive as it is comfortable in much post-war poetry. Any reader unresponsive to paradox as a poetic effect will have trouble with *Four Quartets* as a whole. Yet paradox can get out of control: paradox is endless. One critic, writing on the consequences of Eliot's conversion to Christianity, has noted how 'It had the virtue for him, however, of allowing for discipline and purgation as well as spontaneity and unconscious inspiration, and it combined in a curious way authority and humility, pathos and power, asceticism and accessibility.'[44] This is less true of Eliot's conversion in matters of religious belief than it is of his stylistic development in matters of poetic tone. The paradoxical is of particular relevance here, for this tone relies on our being able to read Eliot's 'I' as both 'I' and 'you', his 'you' as also 'I'.

One of the most important uses of the second person in *Four Quartets* is in a direct address which cannot, however paradoxical our inclinations, be taken to refer primarily to *us*. The Dantean encounter of *Little Gidding* II, in which the first-person voice recounts an exchange with a 'familiar compound ghost' in the ruined streets of London after an air-raid, is a part of Eliot's poem which has come to be seen by many as its most important and fascinating passage. It bears weight, also, in the arguments about Eliot's conduct and motivation, and the ways in which these things might be viewed—remorsefully or otherwise—by the older and wiser poet. Indeed, the passage can be seen to have been made necessary as early as the 'wisdom of humility' passage in *East Coker*, the

---

[43] Helen Gardner, *The Composition of* Four Quartets (London: Faber and Faber, 1978), 145.
[44] Cleo McNelly Kearns, *T. S. Eliot and Indic Traditions: A Study in Poetry and Belief* (Cambridge: Cambridge University Press, 1987), 158.

advice of which it seems to put into practice. For many readers, the
stakes are high, and Eliot's staging of accusation or admonishment is
exemplary. Christopher Ricks writes of the passage as one of Eliot's
'acts of redemption', and 'his conclusive enterprise as a poet', quoting
the climactic lines of the ghost:[45]

> And last, the rending pain of re-enactment
> Of all that you have done, and been; the shame
> Of motives late revealed, and the awareness
> Of things ill done and done to others' harm
> Which once you took for exercise of virtue.

For Ricks, the second-person pronoun counts, and counts us all in:
'*You*,' he comments, 'both Eliot, admonished by the ghost, and we,
admonished by Eliot; not you "the *other people*".'[46] If 'you' is 'both
Eliot . . . and we', then the identification between the voice of the poet
and the poet's audience has become near complete. But there remain
questions about the degree to which Eliot actually pulls off the trick
which Ricks so beautifully describes, for in its most important respect
'you' is not in fact 'we': however sensitive we are to Eliot's work, and
however closely we can make our own pulses as readers beat in time to
the poet's, we are not, in the end, T. S. Eliot. We are '*other people*'. If what
Eliot is doing in this passage is of such momentous import for himself
and his life's work (and it may well be so), it is also significantly
personalized: 'you' is T. S. Eliot, and the voice that says 'you' to
T. S. Eliot belongs—in the poet's conception at least—to someone else.

To discuss the ghost's voice is not the same thing as discussing
the ghost's identity. This latter is, of course, 'compound', and many
separate elements are indeed there to be observed.[47] However, the
dominant presence in this identity is the lately-deceased W. B. Yeats, as
Eliot acknowledged and as internal evidence makes clear. The voice,
though, is not Yeats's—nor could it be, for Eliot's success or failure in the
section depends on making the style an English equivalent of Dante, and
not one to be easily associated with any distinctive poet in English. So
Yeats, in effect, finds 'words I never thought to speak | . . . | When I left

[45] Christopher Ricks, *T. S. Eliot and Prejudice* (London: Faber and Faber, 1988), 238–9,
quoting Eliot, *Collected Poems and Plays*, 194–5.
[46] Ricks, *T. S. Eliot and Prejudice*, 239.
[47] One critic counts fifteen distinct poetic presences in the ghost (including that of Eliot
himself). See Sebastian D. G. Knowles, *A Purgatorial Flame: Seven British Writers in the Second
World War* (Philadelphia: University of Pennsylvania Press, 1990), 223–31.

my body on a distant shore',[48] in the address to the author of *Four Quartets* (who is also, as this section ruefully comprehends, the author of much else, not all of it finally creditable). The lesson to be taught here is the lesson Eliot has already taught 'us': 'humility is endless'. This seems hardly to be a Yeatsian theme, and it is certainly not a Yeatsian conclusion. But the situation Eliot imagines for himself is one where Yeats's shade would be at home, for it is the scene of remorseful encounter between the living and the dead, where purgation has fire as its element. The voice that says 'you' must come from somewhere very different to the locales habituated by Eliot. Ronald Schuchard's comments are pertinent:[49]

It is the more ironic that the most discernible voice of the shade is that of Yeats, whom Eliot had criticized severely during his lifetime for his romantic, self-redemptive view of art and reality. But as Yeats's and Dante's shades testify, art provides no protection from sin and error, no possible means of redemption, and all suffer remorse for their intellectual pride.

Schuchard summarizes the message of the encounter as that 'the poet must achieve humility in his art as well as his life'. And poetry, it is clear, is not capable of saving him. It is one thing for a meditative poet to tell his attentive audience that 'the poetry does not matter'; it is quite another for the poet to be told this—told what 'you' must do—by a ghost who, like Hamlet's father, will not count the cost of setting things to rights.

Many of Eliot's critics write of 'purgation' in the *Little Gidding* encounter with reference to Dante's *Purgatorio*—which undoubtedly provided Eliot with many of his own spiritual or religious conceptions of what purgation might involve. Few, though, consider Yeats as another author much occupied by purgation's meaning and possibility. But this major area of Yeats's artistic concentration was far from lost on Eliot himself, and *Little Gidding* II offers plentiful evidence of the painfully different kind of purgation imagined by the dead poet. In his lecture on Yeats (delivered during the protracted composition of this section of the poem) Eliot dwelt on the salutary shock which the poet could deliver, instancing the subject of lust in age in 'The Spur' with its 'revelation of what a man really is and remains'. At the same time, Eliot tempered his praise for Yeats's late play *Purgatory* with reference to 'questions of difference, objection and protest...in the field of doctrine': 'I wish he had not given it this title,' Eliot said, 'because

[48] Eliot, *Collected Poems and Plays*, 194.   [49] Schuchard, *Eliot's Dark Angel*, 190.

I cannot accept a purgatory in which there is no hint, or at least no emphasis upon Purgation.'[50] Certainly, *Purgatory* dramatizes a cycle of spiritual suffering from which there seems to be no point of escape, and ends with the despairing plea 'O God, appease | The misery of the living and the remorse of the dead.' Against this, we can set Eliot's ghost and its reminder of 'the rending pain of re-enactment | Of all that you have done, and been'; it could be summarizing the plot of *Purgatory*, and even its apparently Christian (or at least Dantean) solution to this painful cycle of 're-enactment' relies on our not confusing one kind of purgatorial fire with another:[51]

> From wrong to wrong the exasperated spirit
> Proceeds, unless restored by that refining fire
> Where you must move in measure, like a dancer.

This is not—crucially not—the fire of 'Sailing to Byzantium' or 'Byzantium', but the *Purgatorio*'s fire; 'refining' is the real signpost for this, sending readers to a passage already made familiar through Eliot's quotations of and allusions to it in poetry and prose (most importantly, it appears in Italian in *The Waste Land*). If 'like a dancer' carries a hint of Yeatsian vocabulary alongside its Shakespearian allusion (to *Antony and Cleopatra*, where Octavius 'at Philippi kept | His sword e'en like a dancer),[52] an earlier draft had given more ground to Yeats, speaking of 'that refining fire | Where you must learn to swim, and better nature'.[53] However Dantean Eliot intended 'swim' to be, it is overpowered by 'better nature', a solidly Yeatsian ambition ('Once out of nature I shall never take | My bodily form from any natural thing…').[54] Even in their final version, these lines feel brief, a willed coda of orthodoxy after a powerful and troubling directness. Partly, this is because of the change of meaning in the use of the second-person pronoun: from 'All that you have done, and been' (where 'you' is particular, and can't be ducked) to 'Where you must move in measure' (where 'you' is no more than 'one', or, as Ricks might put it, 'all of us').

The language of *Little Gidding* II, its poetic movement and style, are at a deliberate distance from Yeats. But even in Yeats's developing styles

[50] Eliot, 'Yeats', *On Poetry and Poets*, 258.   [51] Eliot, *Collected Poems and Plays*, 195.
[52] *Antony and Cleopatra*, III. xi. 35–6.
[53] Gardner, *The Composition of* Four Quartets, 195.
[54] W. B. Yeats, 'Sailing to Byzantium', *The Variorum Edition of the Poems of W. B. Yeats*, ed. Peter Allt and Russell K. Alspatch (London: Macmillan, 1956), 408.

Eliot knew that there was a process as painful and difficult as any purgation: the 1940 lecture speaks of 'the gradual purging out of poetical ornament'.[55] 'Our concern was speech,' according to the ghost; but it is worth considering how this concern differs from animadversions from earlier in the *Quartets*. In *Burnt Norton*:[56]

> Words strain,
> Crack and sometimes break, under the burden,
> Under the tension, slip, slide, perish,
> Decay with imprecision, will not stay in place,
> Will not stay still.

And in *East Coker*:[57]

> Trying to learn to use words, and every attempt
> Is a wholly new start, and a different kind of failure
> Because one has only learnt to get the better of words
> For the thing one no longer has to say, or the way in which
> One is no longer disposed to say it. And so each venture
> Is a new beginning, a raid on the inarticulate
> With shabby equipment always deteriorating
> In the general mess of imprecision of feeling,
> Undisciplined squads of emotion.

Both passages, in what can hardly be a planned irony, are awkwardly prolix: the commas in the *Burnt Norton* lines emphasize a halting quality to the thought, an inability to get past the verbal motif as phrases stumble back over each other; in *East Coker*, Eliot misjudges fatally the effect of so insistently repeated a use of 'one', and ends up sounding unidiomatically and awkwardly over-formal. By comparison, *Little Gidding*'s ghost is briskly to the point: 'For last year's words belong to last year's language | And next year's words await another voice'. The words here do not belong to anyone exactly—they are not agents in some profoundly personal, and intolerable, wrestle; they are indeed strange to the individual, as the ghost admits, preparing to deliver Eliot's admonition:[58]

> So I find words I never thought to speak
>   In streets I never thought I should revisit
>   When I left my body on a distant shore.
> Since our concern was speech, and speech impelled us
>   To purify the dialect of the tribe

[55] Eliot, 'Yeats', 259.   [56] Eliot, *Complete Poems and Plays*, 175.
[57] Ibid. 182.   [58] Ibid. 194.

> And urge the mind to aftersight and foresight,
> Let me disclose the gifts reserved for age
> To set a crown upon your lifetime's effort.

In its purgatorial afterlife, the ghost is above all the vehicle of a style, the vessel of words; that style, and those words, are not those it would have used in life, and the shock of this is partly in the realization that the link between our lives and personalities, and the language that we pass off as ours, is nothing more than a comfortable illusion. While it is true that Eliot was less addicted than Yeats to 'personality', the lesson remains a chilling one.

It is well known that the compound ghost passage gave Eliot a great deal of trouble in its protracted process of composition; the poet's pains (amply documented in Helen Gardner's edition of the *Four Quartets* manuscript material)[59] were in the cause of a style which would feel strikingly different from that of the discursive passages in the second sections of the other three poems. Of course, the 'model' for Eliot here was to be Dante; but Dante did not write English. Eliot's rhymeless, accentually patterned *terza rima* was a flash of genius, allowing the poem to catch the English speed and momentum of work like Shelley's 'The Triumph of Life', without the chains of rhyme leading the poet's argument in directions of its own. But beyond this formal shape, a lot depended still on the naturalness of Eliot's English. At times in the drafts, the poet can be seen departing from this, as when he asks John Hayward whether 'strode' is ever pronounced 'strod'.[60] But more generally, it is on the persuasive force of the style that the poem's success relies. In a lecture composed at the same time as the final Quartet, Eliot dwells on poetry's tonal proximity to the language of its time:[61]

But there is one law of nature more powerful than any of these varying currents, or influences from abroad or from the past: the law that poetry must not stray too far from the ordinary everyday language which we use and hear. Whether poetry is accentual or syllabic, rhymed or rhymeless, formal or free, it cannot afford to lose its contact with the changing language of common intercourse.

This 'contact' is not achievable through exercise of personality, or vision, or any more general originality. Near the conclusion of his

---

[59] The transcriptions of and comments on the drafts for the compound ghost portion of *Little Gidding* II take up pp. 171–96 of Gardner's book.

[60] Gardner, *The Composition of* Four Quartets, 181.

[61] Eliot, 'The Music of Poetry', *On Poetry and Poets*, 29.

lecture, Eliot spells out the impersonality of language in relation to the individual user:[62]

Forms have to be broken and remade: but I believe that any language, so long as it remains the same language, imposes its laws and restrictions and permits its own licence, dictates its own speech rhythms and sound patterns. And a language is always changing; its developments in vocabulary, in syntax, pronunciation and intonation—even, in the long run, its deterioration—must be accepted by the poet and made the best of. He in turn has the privilege of contributing to the development and maintaining the quality, the capacity of the language to express a wide range and subtle gradation, of feeling and·emotion; his task is both to respond to change and make it conscious, and to battle against degradation below the standards which he has learnt from the past.

Language is bigger than a poet, and Eliot's summary of the poet's responsibilities and opportunities with regard to language keeps step with the compound ghost, the acknowledgement of constant change giving the reason for urgency, for getting things right now rather than hereafter. Poets cannot ignore tone: perhaps this is what expresses itself blandly in Eliot's very late interview with Donald Hall, where he hopes for 'a greater simplification of language and . . . speaking in a way which is more like conversing with your reader'.[63] Yet the other side of this particular coin is the knowledge that 'the communication of the dead | Is tongued with fire beyond the language of the living'.[64] If the first hope voices Eliot's need for 'tone', the other registers the irruption into that tone of an uncontrollable—and finally Yeatsian—power, something which the image orchestration of *Little Gidding* does not successfully tame or quite make conformable to religious orthodoxy.

A high value has been given to the ghost's admonishment, as though it were indeed T. S. Eliot's self-admonishment 'For things undone, and done to others' harm'. It may indeed be this, though the poem cannot tell us, and, in any case, we will never be sure of how far this changes matters. In terms of religion, Eliot's redemption is his own business, and *Little Gidding* II does not make us privy to dealings between the poet and his God. Still less, indeed, does the poetry fulfil a 'redemptive' function for the reader, unless we stretch (as Eliot assuredly would not have

[62] Ibid. 37–8.
[63] T. S. Eliot, interviewed by Donald Hall, *Writers at Work: The Paris Review Interviews* (New York, 1965), 104–5.
[64] Eliot, *Collected Poems and Plays*, 192.

done) 'redemptive' to cover areas far removed from the salvation for eternity of the individual soul. Purgation, though, is perhaps a term capable of wider application. It is interesting that Anthony Julius compares Eliot's lines with the Yeats of 'Vacillation' section V, a poem that is 'simply realistic about the poet's inability to make good the harm that he has done, and the regret that he feels as a result'. 'It is a hard thing', Julius continues, 'to have to accept that it is too late to remedy the injustices one has committed':[65]

Eliot just doesn't see this, and 'Little Gidding' is an aggravated version of this misreading. It refuses to acknowledge any responsibility to those the poet has injured and thereby seeks to avoid just that tone of 'regret' Eliot so disliked in Yeats's poem. 'Vacillation' looks back to a landscape filled with those wounded by the poet; 'Little Gidding' looks forward to the poet's purgation in the 'refining fire'.

But the compound ghost is rather tight-lipped on the question of what Eliot—'you'—must do to be purged; it is the language's purgation that exercises him most, and most compellingly, throughout the passage. Perhaps Julius's argument must regard such distinctions as quibbles; Tom Paulin, as this advocate's advocate, declares all too simply that 'like a true politician Eliot never apologizes and he never explains'.[66] But the kind of purgation in which this passage of *Little Gidding* deals is neither forensic nor political, and cannot be judged in those terms without distortion: it is poetic.

How far is this a lesser thing, a distraction, a side issue, even (if we want to put it like this) an excuse? In comparison with the other items on the critical and political agendas, how serious is poetry? Curiously, the turn in critical and academic fashions, which necessitates the downwards revision of Eliot's reputation, may prove—however spurious most of its own intellectual credentials—to make clearer the conditions upon which poetry in general is tolerated. The knowledge of limitations—of all the things poetry cannot do, and must not delude itself that it might do—is still the test of a poet, the proof and condition of whatever authority his or her poetry might command. In Britain, Auden's example has come to seem more acceptable than Eliot's, his version of poetic humility less threatening and more familiar. For some,

---

[65] Anthony Julius, *T. S. Eliot, Anti-Semitism, and Literary Form* (Cambridge: Cambridge University Press, 1995), 202.
[66] Tom Paulin, 'T. S. Eliot and Anti-Semitism', 160.

Auden has come to be celebrated as an embodied paradox: he was the greatest poet, and the most sceptical about poetry; he was the most celebrated English poet, and the most misunderstood. Such critical beliefs are closer to religion than they would care to acknowledge; but it is an impoverished religion. James Fenton's paean to Auden is a remarkable—and singularly revealing—document:[67]

Auden had the greatest gifts of any of our poets in the twentieth century . . . And it was given him to know this, and to doubt it, to know and to doubt it. The sense of being *primus inter pares,* the sense of always being the youngest person in the room, the spirit that could say to posterity 'You did not live in our time—be sorry'—all this was given him. And then, to be conscious but to refuse to understand, to live not in a fine but in a lean country, to hold to what was most difficult, to face that which was most hostile—this too was given him. To make mistakes, to cling to impossible ideals, to fail, to find himself hated, to know humiliation—this too was given him. To find himself wronged or in the wrong, to find his courage taken for cowardice, to find himself human in short—all this was given him.

By whom was all this 'given' to Auden? Fenton's list celebrates a lot of things, including posterity, impossible ideals and mistakes, but it is primarily a hymn to a personality. For Fenton, Auden is a man of sorrows, and acquainted with grief, to whom all things are given. He came down among us, and was one of us; and we rejected him. Auden's poetry, in this account, is fundamentally a brilliant accomplishment of his personality—and more brilliant, more securely at the top of the list of all-time greats, than that of rival contenders. Fenton may be extreme, but is not wholly unrepresentative of Auden's contemporary English advocates. Yet Auden is not—not in fact, or in any accountable sense once the lecture is over—capable of 'saving us'.

If we want a final paradox, we might assemble it like this: poetry is capable of saving us; the poetry does not matter. But to read poets like Eliot and Auden for the poetry, and not for something else, makes paradoxes like these redundant, and puts poetic language back into the world where sense has to be made, truths (like lies) can be told, and clarity of meaning is possible. It is perhaps a frightening world, and it offers no cheap redemption or easy salvations; but it is at least a real one, in which both poets can occupy an honourable place.

---

[67] James Fenton, *The Strength of Poetry* (Oxford: Oxford University Press, 2001), 249.

CHAPTER 6

Yeats, Form, and Northern Irish Poetry

I

'He became his admirers': W. H. Auden's reflection, in his poem 'In Memory of W. B. Yeats', was perhaps unduly sanguine.[1] Poets do indeed become their admirers in their posthumous careers; they become their critics too, a rule which Yeats's artistic afterlife illustrates particularly well, not least in the context of the 'mad Ireland' which Auden's poem tries to account for and transcend. The name of Yeats means a number of different things in the discourses of contemporary Irish literary criticism, some of them a very long way from what might be understood by admiration. A sense of this may be gained quickly from the following selective (but not unrepresentative) gathering of remarks:[2]

An idea of art opposed to the idea of utility, an idea of an audience opposed to the idea of popularity, an idea of the peripheral becoming the central culture— in these three ideas Yeats provided Irish writing with a programme for action. But whatever its connection with Irish nationalism, it was not, finally, a programme of separation from the English tradition. His continued adherence to it led him to define the central Irish attitude as one of self-hatred...The pathology of literary unionism has never been better defined.

In Ireland, it is fair to say, Yeats is resented...because he claimed to speak in the name of 'the indomitable Irishry.'...In the present confusions, readers of

[1] W. H. Auden, 'In Memory of W. B. Yeats', in *The English Auden: Poems, Essays and Dramatic Writings 1927–1929*, ed. Edward Mendelson (London: Faber and Faber, 1977), 241–3.

[2] Seamus Deane, *Heroic Styles: The Tradition of an Idea* (Londonderry: Field Day Publications, 1984), repr. in *Ireland's Field Day* (London: Hutchinson, 1985), 49–50; Denis Donoghue, *We Irish: The Selected Essays of Denis Donoghue* (Brighton: Harvester Press, 1986), 66; John Wilson Foster, in *The Irish Review*, 2 (1987), 111; Declan Kiberd, 'The War against the Past', in Audrey S. Eyler and Robert F. Garratt (eds.), *The Uses of the Past: Essays on Irish Culture* (Newark: University of Delaware Press 1988), 38.

Yeats resent his appeal to Irishness, and his assertion that he knows the quality of Irishness when he meets it. That resentment is so inclusive that little or nothing survives in its presence.

The battle with Yeats is beginning to resemble the eternal fight. He is the nationalist the Irish critics want and the higher class Protestant they don't want.

Nowhere is this more obvious than in Yeats's hopeless rehabilitation of the modes of Irish deference . . . The deepest insults could now be happily internalized in the postcolonial mind . . . Despite repeated resolutions to 'walk naked' he [Yeats] found it impossible to commit the ultimate revolutionary deed of speaking with his own face instead of performing through a rhetorical mask.

'Now Ireland has her madness and her weather still': again, Auden's ironic observation, however light in its urbanity, might still be said to hold good after more than half a century. 'The battle with Yeats', which the remarks above both witness and embody, continues in literary criticism within and outside Ireland; it is a serious debate, sometimes a learned and stimulating one, and different in kind as well as intensity from the widespread, but seldom explicit, deprecation of Yeats in England. However, the fact of the debate, its intensification in recent years, and the inevitable transformation of Yeats from a corpus of finished poems into a complex system of historical and critical meanings, which the debate effects and thrives upon, are important elements bearing upon any discussion of a Yeatsian influence on Northern Irish poetry, especially if that influence is considered to be, at least in part, a 'formal' one.

The recognition that the forms of poetry can have something to do with other aspects of its literary significance needs to be made by any intelligent critical writing; but a crude version of such an awareness, in which poetic form becomes simply a cypher for ideological content or historical placing, is a danger attendant on some of the more spirited and committed contributions to Irish critical debate on Yeats. In this respect, it is possible to notice a measure of the pervasive suspicion being directed, not just at Yeats's forms themselves, but at the very idea of poetic form as something unamenable to the more urgent kinds of ideological demand. A concern with poetic form may thus be refracted to become 'formalism', and this theoretical position, rather than the precise and particular concerns which gave rise to its labelling, can now be the thing addressed by the post-structuralist, historicist, or postcolonial critic. Against the background of this kind of argument, it is necessary to insist that poetic form remains distinct from 'formalism', and that Yeats's forms, as they are transmitted to subsequent Irish poetry, are more significant and fertile than the other meanings—critical, historical, or ideological—which the name Yeats, like the notion of 'formalism', has accrued. Just as 'Yeats' can mean, under certain circumstances, 'The pathology of literary unionism' or a 'hopeless rehabilitation of the modes of Irish deference', so 'form' can be represented as a set of theoretical assumptions and impositions rather than the lines, timings, rhymes, and stanzas which (unlike pathologies or deferential modes) can be heard and seen openly in the poetry.

The question of form in contemporary theory has a special relevance for Northern Irish poetry since the early 1960s, and the various curiosities and anomalies in the theoretical ways of addressing form might well be said to have their bearing upon the wider reception of poets like Derek Mahon, Michael Longley, and Seamus Heaney. One of the many studies of poets from Northern Ireland begins with a chapter on 'The Politics of Poetic Form', and sets out certain problems with a useful clarity:[3]

Poetically, the difficulty with both the postmodernist and 'Irish identity' readings of the significance of poetic form is that the poetry is thereby reduced either to symptomatic or reactive status. The form of the work is deemed to arise out of a particular set of social co-ordinates, but its function is considered to be a reflection in the realm of the aesthetic of an image of future possibilities in the social arena.

The unease evident here is justified and, even if the author's concern with form does not lead her to discuss or examine any actual poetic forms in the chapter, she does begin here to show how poetry and its critical function can be at odds, especially at the level of formal attention and understanding. The mismatch between critical intelligence and poetic formal resource is often evident in criticism of Yeats, as when David Lloyd, a theorist of the post-colonial school, addresses 'A Dialogue of Self and Soul' and its use of 'remorse':[4]

We need, I believe, to understand remorse as that emotion which, beyond the predetermined gyres of Yeatsian time, chooses to assert that things might have

---

[3] Clair Wills, *Improprieties: Politics and Sexuality in Northern Irish Poetry* (Oxford: Clarendon Press, 1993), 26.

[4] David Lloyd, *Anomalous States: Irish Writing and the Post-Colonial Moment* (Dublin: Lilliput Press, 1993), 80.

been otherwise. It is an appeal to the history of the possible, of what might have been . . . The loose ends produced by such a history are incompatible with the formal drive of Yeats's poetic, as indeed they are equally with any representative aesthetic, asserting the irruption of a content that is in excess of any form and unassimilable to narrative time.

Like the 'image of future possibilities' in the insistence upon form as function, Lloyd's 'history of the possible' in Yeats must be 'in excess of any form', the inevitable 'irruption of a content'. But the 'formal drive' can bear closer scrutiny than Lloyd provides, for the shapes of Yeats's stanzas, their accommodations of rhyme and syntactic structure, allow for an irruption of something inherent in, rather than in excess of form. To take the last stanza of the 'Dialogue', upon which Lloyd concentrates:[5]

> I am content to follow to its source
> Every event in action or in thought;
> Measure the lot; forgive myself the lot!
> When such as I cast out remorse
> So great a sweetness flows into the breast
> We must laugh and we must sing,
> We are blest by everything,
> Everything we look upon is blest.

Yeats's eight-line stanza unit subdivides in terms of its rhyme pattern, holding two four-line shapes within its *abbacddc* scheme. Yeats completes his first sentence within three lines, with the result that the rhyme for 'source' will, in terms of syntax, figure in a new sentence, and lead into a second sequence of rhymes (*cddc*). 'When such as I cast out remorse', the new syntactic start which carries along the rhyme of the sentence it succeeds, prepares for the irruption of new rhymes to conclude the stanza; Yeats accommodates the 'excess' that is his theme here in the stanza's formal renewal towards completion: the stanza is, after all, a pattern of rhyming which, in repeating its shape, changes its rhymes (*abba* repeats as *cddc*). It is part of Yeats's rhetorical achievement here to involve the syntax in this plotting of renewal, changing in the process the personal pronouns, from 'When such as I . . .' to 'We must laugh . . .'. Lloyd's 'loose ends' are only incompatible with Yeats's 'formal drive' here in that they are nowhere to be found; the

---

[5] W. B. Yeats, *The Variorum Edition of the Poems of W. B. Yeats*, ed. Peter Allt and Russell K. Alspatch (London: Macmillan, 1956), 479.

stanza's completeness, its reconciliation of argument, syntax, and rhyme scheme, ensures that 'remorse' is inseparable from 'sweetness'.

A full engagement with Yeats's poem, and with Lloyd's reading of its 'formal drive', would of course require much more detailed analysis of the patterns of formal arrangement and complication in evidence there. For the present purposes, the point to be noted is that 'form' is a perilous critical category when employed in its more abstract or theoretical senses; to invoke 'a content that is in excess of any form' is to risk very serious underestimation of how much form can do in poetry: it is also, of course, to invest in notions of 'content' which are dangerously disembodied. Yet such approaches to Yeats's poetic forms are not at all uncommon, and it is noteworthy that many combative engagements with what Yeats represents tend to allow the poems themselves to fade off the page and become aspects of a 'discourse' in which the boundaries between poetic texts and their surrounding elements of history, reception, and ideology simply dissolve away.

A critique of this principled neglect of actual poetic form, with the consequent substitution of the bogey of formalism in its place, is certainly necessary in Yeats studies and will result, it is safe to suppose, in a more complex sense of the poet's various kinds of achievement. However, the inadequacy of the de-formed version of Yeats may be made manifest by more than just literary-critical discussion, and it is within Irish poetry itself that some of the most significant understandings of Yeats, and engagements with him, are to be found. In poetry from Northern Ireland, in particular, such kinds of reception are often to do with form, and can be traced through study of the kinds of formal resource exploited by poets in the course of the 'influence' Yeats has provided. This chapter raises one formal concern in particular, that of the stanza, and traces Yeats's importance in this respect through some work by Seamus Heaney, Derek Mahon, Michael Longley, and (more briefly) Paul Muldoon. First, however, it is necessary to sketch some preliminary propositions regarding Yeats and stanzaic form.

II

Yeats's most influential stanzaic poems come, broadly speaking, from later in his career; they begin with the volume *The Wild Swans at Coole* (1919) which, besides its title-poem, includes the formal stanzaic elegy 'In Memory of Major Robert Gregory'. Of course, Yeats had been writing in stanzas before this, but with the Gregory elegy a new sense of formal resource is drawn upon, one which comes to dominate the last two decades of the poet's career. Stanzas in the earlier Yeats had often featured refrains, and were made up of shorter lines than the five-footed measure of the poet's more rhetorically elevated voices: many such stanzaic poems gestured back, in one way or another, towards ballad form. Where the early Yeats does use larger stanzas, it is as a means of narrative structure: 'The Man who Dreamed of Faeryland', for example, employs its three twelve-line units as containers for distinct phases of the story being told, with repetition of syntax adding to the sense of structural similarity between stanzas: these twelve-line units in fact pull together a sequence of rhymes in which one pattern simply repeats (*abbacddceffe*). This straightforward progression of rhymes is often present in Yeats's narrative verse, and it is to be distinguished from the more artfully interlocked patterns of rhyme employed in the later stanzaic poems. The later Yeats relies especially upon the *ottava rima* stanza which, with its *abababcc* rhyme scheme, seals up a repeating progression of two rhyme sounds with a last, and importantly a new rhyme in the concluding couplet. Byron's *Don Juan* shows how well this form is suited to the staging and pacing of narrative, but demonstrates also how the *ottava rima* stanza can be used to contain personal reflection and digression without allowing such things to overrun. If one tries to imagine a poem like *The Prelude* written in this stanzaic form, the meaning (and perhaps also the attractiveness) of such containment becomes clear; it was just this capacity of the stanza which Yeats seized upon and made his own in poems of highly structured and performative meditation.

The Yeatsian stanza is a means of both compression and rhetorical launching, and in this respect it moves further away from what might be thought of as narrative utility. A comparison with Byron's *ottava rima* shows this usefully; first, Byron on European-Gothic:[6]

> Huge halls, long galleries, spacious chambers, join'd
>   By no quite lawful marriage of the Arts,
> Might shock a Connoisseur; but when combined,
>   Form'd a whole which, irregular in parts,
> Yet left a grand impression on the mind,
>   At least of those whose eyes were in their hearts.

---

[6] Byron, *Don Juan*, Canto XIII (1823), in *The Complete Poetical Works*, ed. Jerome J. McGann, vol. v (Oxford: Clarendon Press, 1986), 544.

> We gaze upon a Giant for his stature,
> Nor judge at first if all be true to Nature.

Next, Yeats on Anglo-Irish Classical:[7]

> O what if gardens where the peacock strays
> With delicate feet upon old terraces,
> Or else all Juno from an urn displays
> Before the indifferent garden deities;
> O what if levelled lawns and gravelled ways
> Where slippered Contemplation finds his ease
> And Childhood a delight for every sense,
> But take our greatness with our violence?

Byron's procedure is one of narrative description, and the stanza serves him perfectly well, its *ababab* progression of rhymes accommodating a clear syntactic ordering of the evidence, and the final couplet allowing a generalized reflection which, in completing the whole sentence, also completes the significance of what the sentence and the stanza have presented for the reader's attention. The rhymes enact a similar economy, for 'Arts' and 'parts' are indeed 'join'd' and 'combined' in the rhyming 'hearts' of the beholders, and the final direct linking of 'stature' and 'Nature' comes as a resolution provided for by the preceding conjunctions of rhyming words, even though the syntactic meaning of that couplet maintains its reservations. For Yeats, the same stanza form serves a different purpose: the whole sentence with which he fills the stanza is a single rhetorical question, 'O what if . . . ?', and all the description is contained within the syntactic structure this generates, with the important verb occurring in the last line: 'What if [xyz] take our greatness?' Yeats thus shifts the tone of his stanza from the expository and reflective to the exclamatory and disruptive, partly by changing the balance between the alternating *ab* rhymes of the first six lines and the conclusive weight of the final couplet, which must introduce a new rhyme, on 'sense'. The syntax of Yeats's sentence runs into the final couplet, so that the stanza's penultimate line, 'And Childhood a delight for every sense', as well as being governed by 'what if . . .', requires the reader to carry forward the verb 'find' from 'slippered Contemplation finds his ease'. Syntactically, this seventh line is fully a part of the rest of the stanza, but its now final rhyme sound looks for an answering rhyme,

[7] Yeats, *Variorum Poems*, 418.

and Yeats ensures that this is one fully at odds, rather than at its ease, with what has come before: 'But take our greatness with our violence?' The arrival of the verb to resolve the sentence brings with it an unsettling idea and introduces, with the surprise of rhyme, its own element of disruption, the 'violence' that underwrites what has seemed ordered and peaceful. Here, the *ottava rima* stanza is made to function rhetorically and dramatically, its syntax and rhyme patterns in subtle and energetic counterpoint.

The rhyme schemes of all Yeats's stanzas, and not just those of his *ottava rima*, are made to work as elements of the composition which embody, rather than simply contain the rhetorical energies of the authorial will. An alternative eight-line pattern, which Yeats uses in 'In Memory of Major Robert Gregory', 'A Prayer for my Daughter', the second section of 'The Tower', and 'Byzantium', has the rhyme scheme *aabbcddc*: here, the change in the rhyming sequence, which comes with the fifth and sixth lines, often accommodates an important turn in syntax or thought. The ten-line stanza of 'All Souls' Night', the second and third sections of 'Nineteen Hundred and Nineteen', and the second section of 'Meditations in Time of Civil War', which rhymes *abcabcdeed*, again establishes a division within itself, between the first six and the last four lines, which syntax can either echo or override. Another aspect of Yeats's stanzaic practice of significance here is his tendency to balance longer against shorter lines, a further resource which works alongside syntax and rhyme in the formal configuration of his stanzas. Yet this kind of configuration is seldom a matter of unforced arrangement and accommodation, and is more often a system of pressures and counter-pressures as syntax, rhyme, and line-length set up competing patterns and energies inside the stanza.

In the last stanza of section three of 'Nineteen Hundred and Nineteen', Yeats considers desolation and powerlessness, but the stanza he uses enables him to do something with the futility he sets out to contemplate:[8]

> The swan has leaped into the desolate heaven:
> That image can bring wildness, bring a rage
> To end all things, to end
> What my laborious life imagined, even
> The half-imagined, the half-written page;

---

[8] Ibid. 431.

O but we dreamed to mend
Whatever mischief seemed
To afflict mankind, but now
That winds of winter blow
Learn that we were crack-pated when we dreamed.

The complex counterpointing here is to powerful rhetorical effect, and it relies upon the basic shapes that make up this ten-line stanza structure, if only to transcend and reform them. The clear syntactic break occurs between lines five and six, while the change in rhyme pattern from *abcabc* to *deed* comes a line later; what is more, the *d* rhyme, 'seemed', is sounded early in line six, 'O but we dreamed to mend', and the last line of the stanza returns to that same pre-emptive word for its rhyme in 'when we dreamed'. Earlier in the stanza also, Yeats works to reduce the initial symbolic spectacle through internal rhyme: 'That image can bring wildness, bring a rage' sounds out the 'rage' in 'image', and its shifting of emphasis from the visible symbol to the personal will is intensified by the chain of internal echoes that join 'end', 'end', 'imagined', and 'half-imagined' in the next three lines. The weakness of 'even', stranded at the end of the fourth line, is an important one, for its faint rhyme and its unemphatic rhythmic position in the line help to throw emphasis on to 'The half-imagined'. The effect of Yeats's stanza is to transcend the already apparently transcendent image of desolation with which it began: when 'The swan has leaped into the desolate heaven' is fed into this ten-line matrix, it is transformed into a drama of rage, finality, and imagination in which the ordering authorial voice is the victor, triumphant in its disillusion.

Yeats's stanzaic patterns are dramas of order, and it is vital that they make their formal procedures visible if the poems' rhetorical projects are to succeed. If the Yeatsian stanza makes a point of form, so to speak, then Yeats's authorial voice also has to be seen to win out over the patterns of inevitability which such forms might embody: the poet's determination confronts, as it were, the determined patterns of his stanzas. Thus, Yeats will not shift away from, say, *ottava rima* to a different eight-line configuration within a poem, or vary the sequence of rhymes from one stanza to another; the sense of closure, of formal completeness, which critics often notice (and sometimes deplore) in his poetry, is always a battle won rather than an accommodation easily engineered. For Yeats, stanzaic form is a matter of performance, and his stanzas acknowledge the design they carry.

III

When modern Irish criticism chafes under the designs which Yeats's poetry seems too palpably to have upon it, it tends to see form as an issue that can be dealt with straightforwardly. A crude simplification of the common argument might be that Yeats forces himself upon the reader by using, with great rhetorical skill, those strict forms which have their corollaries in the social and political orders for which the poet was, by the end of his career, a keen partisan. Ronald Bush's useful answer to this kind of argument, that 'despite Yeats's conservative themes, it was from the beginning clear to at least some readers that his art was rooted not in totalitarian poetics but in structures enacting the competition of value',[9] might well be applied to the specifically Irish turns which the quarrel with Yeats has taken. Yet the attraction of this argument from corollary is very strong, for it enables critics to locate certain values in contemporary literature by reference to Yeats as a negative example. Thus, Seamus Deane's *Celtic Revivals* (1985) employs its profound scepticism with regard to Yeats's claims on Irish critical and literary practice in readings of contemporary poets like Heaney, Mahon, and Thomas Kinsella, all of whom are shown to have escaped from the dangerous legacy in one way or another; David Lloyd's *Anomalous States* (1993), which attacks Yeats in one chapter (quoted above), attacks Heaney in another for his supposed investment in the kinds of 'identity' so discredited by the older poet. There is commonly a sense amongst critics that Yeats's poetry is somehow implicated in contemporary Irish poetry, whether for good or ill, and that present artistic phenomena, no less than present political troubles, need to be measured critically against ideas and tendencies which Yeats is seen especially to represent.

   Northern Irish poetry since the 1960s has been interpreted as unusually technically controlled, a critical observation which can easily slide into the backhanded compliment, or worse, particularly when form is understood as a kind of political limitation. If Northern Ireland produces a formalist poetry, then the political shortcomings of the place itself can be associated with the lowered revolutionary horizons of the verse and the insufficient awareness of, or rather suspicion of the

[9] Ronald Bush, 'The Modernist under Siege', in *Yeats: An Annual of Critical and Textual Studies*, 6 (1988), 5.

notions of form and order which that poetry reveals. In his 'General
Introduction' to *The Field Day Anthology of Irish Writing*, Seamus Deane
looks with irony towards Northern Irish respect for poetic order; in
delineating what he calls 'The aesthetic ideology', with its high valuation
of 'reconciliation' in art and 'a harmonious and triumphant wholeness',
he gives short shrift to ideas of 'order':[10]

> The idea that that which is chaotic, disorganized and 'rude' can be converted to
> order and civilization was shared by English colonial writers and English literary
> critics, at least until very recent times. It is also shared by those who see a
> connection between Northern Irish violence and the Northern Irish literary
> 'revival'. The literature—autonomous, ordered—stands over against the polit-
> ical system in its savage disorder. The connection here is as interesting as the
> contrast. Ultimately, any key political term is exchangeable with any key literary
> term.

Deane's caricature here would seem to relate to his conception of
Northern Irish critics (such as Edna Longley perhaps, who has discussed the precise placing of a main verb in a Derek Mahon poem as
something which 'enacts art's therapeutic transformation').[11] Order in
literature, in Deane's account (or parody), becomes merely a bolt-hole
from the 'disorder' of the 'political system'. But Deane's parting shot—
'any key political term is exchangeable with any key literary term'—
describes his own practice better than that of any supposed antagonist,
and ignores the implications of the 'autonomous, ordered' idea of
literature which he sets out to mock. It is Deane, and not the critics
who pay attention to poetic form, who links 'the northern Irish literary
"revival"' with ideas of autonomy and order, as though with those of
self-government or strong policing.

Nevertheless, Deane's arguments are as influential as they are representative with regard to Northern Irish writing, and their foundation in
the nationalist (or post-colonial) critiques of Yeats are unmistakable.
Against such a background, the position of a poet of such contemporary
eminence as Seamus Heaney is bound to be an interesting, and in some
ways a delicate one. The 'best Irish poet since Yeats' tag can become a
journalistic convenience which causes some critical embarrassment in

---

[10] Seamus Deane, 'General Introduction' to Seamus Deane (ed.), *The Field Day Anthology of
Irish Writing* (3 vols., Londonderry: Field Day Publications, 1991), vol. i, p. xxvi.

[11] Edna Longley, 'The Singing Line: Form in Derek Mahon's Poetry', *Poetry in the Wars*
(Newcastle-upon-Tyne: Bloodaxe Books, 1986), 179.

this context, and Heaney's less discriminating critical enthusiasts do little to help matters: as one American fan has written, 'Mantles obfuscate as well as illuminate, and Yeats's mantle on Heaney is both burden and honor.'[12] Heaney, for his part, has honoured the burden of Yeats with considerable aplomb; while his 1978 essay 'Yeats as an Example?' combined acute appreciation of Yeats's formal essence with entertaining meditation on Heaney's own poetic development and needs, more recent writing by Heaney has set itself in relation to the prevalent use of Yeats as a symbol for extra-literary anxieties and resentments. It is significant that Heaney's attentions now have turned to the issue of Yeats and form, something addressed explicitly in poem xxii of the 'Squarings' sequence in *Seeing Things*:[13]

> Where does the spirit live? Inside or outside
> Things remembered, made things, things unmade?
> What came first, the seabird's cry or the soul
>
> Imagined in the dawn wind when it cried?
> Where does it roost at last? On dungy sticks
> In a jackdaw's nest up in the old stone tower
>
> Or a marble bust commanding the parterre?
> How habitable is perfected form?
> And how inhabited the windy light?
>
> What's the use of a held note or held line
> That cannot be assailed for reassurance?
> (Set questions for the ghost of W. B.)

This is a poem in touch with recent Irish critical debates on the subject of Yeats, but it is also a piece of writing which carefully ironizes such debates as a series of 'set questions' which the dead poet, addressed by them as if he were a schoolboy with something to prove, will of course never answer. The questions are, then, like Yeats's own questions in poems, not intended for response (compare 'What's water but the generated soul?' in 'Coole Park and Ballylee, 1931'); rather, they set up a series of uncertainties, or possibilities, of relevance to Heaney himself. The central question, 'How habitable is perfected form?', touches on the most delicate point, the issue on which Yeats's harshest critics settle, but

---

[12] Henry Hart, *Seamus Heaney: Poet of Contrary Progressions* (Syracuse, NY: Syracuse University Press, 1992), 1.
[13] Seamus Heaney, *Seeing Things* (London: Faber and Faber, 1991), 78.

about which Heaney, as a poet of real substance, cannot entertain such unhesitating prejudices.

In a series of lectures in honour of Richard Ellmann, published as *The Place of Writing* in 1989, Heaney turns to the issue of Yeats's forms, and in particular the *ottava rima* stanza, where 'the place of writing is essentially the stanza form itself, that strong-arched room of eight iambic pentameters rhyming *abababcc* which serves as a redoubt for the resurgent spirit'.[14] Heaney's metaphoric line of thought here runs on the 'habitable' qualities of Yeatsian form (playing of course with the Italian root of 'stanza' as 'room'), and the use of 'redoubt' is felicitous, bringing together an evocation of Thoor Ballylee and the implications of the 'redoubtable' inhering in the poetic attitudes Yeats chose to house there. It may be a further dimension of Heaney's phrasing here to play the 'redoubt' of Yeats's form against the doubts which it faces down. Heaney continues by praising the felt physicality of the stanza form in Yeats's poems:[15]

In these poems, the unshakably affirmative music of the *ottava rima* stanza is the formal correlative of the poet's indomitable spirit. The complete coincidence between period and stanza which he had begun to strive for compounds utterance with architecture, recalls Milton's figure of the poet as one who builds the lofty rhyme and also recalls Yeats's own stated desire to make the tower a permanent symbol of his poetic work, 'plainly visible to the passer-by.'

The 'indomitable' Yeats (who of course demanded of future Irish poets that they should keep the race itself 'indomitable') is formally protected in Heaney's reading, having 'created a fortified space within the rooms of many powerfully vaulted stanzas'.[16] To follow Heaney's metaphor, it seems that inside such fortifications Yeats can be 'assailed', whether 'assailed by the mocking echo of his own doubting mind'(p. 15) or perhaps by assailants with critical or political doubts of their own about the Yeatsian enterprise. 'What's the use of a held note or held line | That cannot be assailed for reassurance?': to assail can be 'to make a violent hostile attack upon' (*OED* 2), but this does not sit comfortably with 'reassurance'; the word can mean also to 'speak or write directly against' (*OED* 4) or 'to attack with reasoning or argument' (*OED* 5), and it may be that the line Yeats holds in his stanzaic fortifications can, for Heaney, withstand such questioning reassuringly. And yet, of course, this very idea is itself placed within the context of a never-to-be-answered

---

[14] Seamus Heaney, *The Place of Writing* (Atlanta, Ga.: Scholars Press, 1989), 29.
[15] Ibid.   [16] Ibid. 35.

question, one addressed to a spirit rendered indomitable in its stanzaic redoubt.

The delicate balances described and put into operation in Heaney's metaphorical dealings with Yeats are in contrast to the formulations of the critical assailants: Deane, for example, writes of how 'in the end the actuality overbore the symbolism, and left [Yeats's] poetry hysterical when he let his feeling run free of the demands of form, and diagrammatic when he imposed wilfully formal restraints upon his feeling'.[17] This is very confident criticism, not just with regard to its command of 'actuality', but also about the distinction between 'demands of form' and 'formal restraints', the first good, the latter wilful. Introducing the selection from Yeats in *The Field Day Anthology of Irish Writing*, Heaney was presented with a task requiring considerable diplomatic gifts, not least in the matter of Yeats's redoubtable forms, regarded elsewhere as sinister and wilful. Nevertheless, Heaney makes a point in his Introduction of celebrating the Yeatsian command of form: 'poems like "Among School Children" and "A Dialogue of Self and Soul" go beyond the lyric's usual function of giving perfected form to a privileged state of mind and achieve an effulgent, oracular impersonality'; 'Yeats's essential gift is his ability to raise a temple in the ear, to make a vaulted space in language through the firmness, in-placeness and undislodgeableness of stanzaic form.'[18] Far from functioning as a code-word for a set of ideological positions (including formalism), Yeats is here insisted upon as a producer of palpable—and valuable—poetic forms which possess in themselves a degree of 'oracular' authority. Like Auden, Heaney maintains a distance from the Yeatsian posturings in politics and culture that did not, perhaps, quite find their monumental forms, and in which the poet is 'silly like us'; but he does insist on the legitimate authority of the perfected forms of the poems themselves:[19] 'It is an impersonal command that is obeyed when a poet seeks to make the poem a thing, thrown free of inchoate inwardness. It is an impersonal law that enforces itself when the ear recognizes a rhythm as inevitable.' This does not accord at all well with the widespread suspicion of form elsewhere in evidence in Irish literary theory, but it does constitute, all the same, an

---

[17] Seamus Deane, *Celtic Revivals: Essays in Modern Irish Literature 1880–1980* (London: Faber and Faber, 1985), 38.
[18] Seamus Heaney, 'William Butler Yeats (1865–1939)', *The Field Day Anthology of Irish Writing*, ii. 788.
[19] Ibid. 790.

extremely important theoretical contribution to the debate among critics on the significance of form in poetry, whether the poetry being assailed is that of Yeats himself or the work of his too-visibly orderly successors in Northern Ireland. Heaney links the issue of form with the values of impersonal authority and artistic inevitability, and in so doing he lays bare his own identification with the Northern Irish 'revival' and the kinds of poetic practice which the poets of Heaney's place and generation can be seen to prize.

The earlier writings of Derek Mahon and Michael Longley, like those of Heaney himself, emerge from what might be called a broadly formalist school of poetic value. Influences which poets of this generation had in common, besides Yeats, could contribute to an interest in stanzaic form: Philip Larkin, Louis MacNeice, and Robert Graves seem all to have had significant roles in the early poetry of the Northern Irish poets. (The significance of Graves in particular is prone to be overlooked, just as Graves remains underestimated by many critical assessments of British poetry in general.) Both Mahon and Longley make use of stanzaic form in their early writings in ways that clearly owe something to Yeatsian precedent, even if the poets remain far from Yeats in their rhetoric and subject-matter. It would be possible to argue that the formalism of both Mahon and Longley in their earlier work is a consequence of a sense of the 'impersonal command' which Heaney was to formulate much later in his pondering of the Yeatsian example; but it is necessary also to notice that Longley in fact moved *away* from the Yeatsian big stanza in his later writing, and that Mahon complemented his larger stanzaic structures with other, miniaturized forms, in which Yeatsian 'impersonality' is put under very severe strain. Where Heaney has moved closer to the idea of poetic form as the poet's 'redoubt', both Mahon and Longley seem to have started from this point, and moved on from it to other destinations.

The stanzaic art of the early Mahon is one of extraordinary assurance and accomplishment, and the poetry of his first volume, *Night-Crossing* (1968) is distinguished by its ability to match stanzaic form with syntactic period, and to counterpoint these concerns with rhyme, a technical assurance which is altogether in keeping with the book's overall tone of nonchalant disillusion. Mahon's forms in this work do seem to announce their own defensive, or protective function in a mode of performance, of self-drawn rule and limitation, which has its own precedent in Yeats's tendency to make stanzaic form acknowledge the design it embodies. In a poem like 'Day Trip to Donegal', for example, a very simple pattern of rhyming couplets is gathered into six-line stanzas (*aabbcc*), and the poem's procedure is thus structured in a way compatible with narrative progression (each stanza presenting a new, encapsulated stage in the gradual retelling of the day's events), but also, with its containment of syntax within the six-line unit, offering the stages of a narrative as the stages of a lyric argument or meditation. Within each stanza, an initial statement of narrative information ('We reached the sea ...', 'We left at eight ...') gives way to reflection by the third couplet, as here in the poem's second stanza:[20]

> Down at the pier the boats gave up their catch,
> Torn mouths and spewed-up lungs. They fetch
> Ten times as much in the city as there,
> And still the fish come in year after year—
> Herring and whiting, flopping about the deck
> In attitudes of agony and heartbreak.

The wonderful, offbeat rhyme of the last line is all the better for the stanzaic discipline which will enforce a snapping-back to narrative sequence afterwards, as a new stanza gets under way ('We left at eight, drove back the way we came ...'). In this respect, at least, Mahon's subsequent excision of the 1968 third stanza improves the poem, cutting away as it does six lines of reflection on the fate of the landed fish. Each stanza of 'Day Trip to Donegal' shapes itself to a diminuendo, and the staging of the stanza is as a series of narrative events that diminish to the point of paralysis; by the final stanza (where the poet has passed from a narrative of the events to a recollection of sleep), the poem's structure drifts open, into a 'mindless' reception of the elements:[21]

> By dawn I was alone far out at sea
> Without skill or reassurance (nobody
> To show me how, no promise of rescue)
> Cursing my mindless failure to take due
> Forethought for this, contriving vain
> Overtures to the mindless wind and rain.

[20] Derek Mahon, 'Day Trip to Donegal', *Night-Crossing* (London: Oxford University Press, 1968), 22.
[21] Ibid. 23. Mahon's later revisions of this stanza are found in *Poems 1962–1978* (Oxford: Oxford University Press, 1979), 17, *Selected Poems* (Harmondsworth: Penguin Books, 1993), 21, and *Collected Poems* (Oldcastle: Gallery Press, 1999), 25.

Mahon's couplets are distinctly unclosed by now, and his syntax hurries across the rhymes and line-endings to produce a final resolution which is almost the antithesis of a Yeatsian certainty and determination: where Yeats's elaborately interlocked rhyme schemes propel his stanzas towards the declarative, Mahon's hushed couplets fade down towards the repeating 'mindless' with a fine-tuned artistry.

Mahon's stanzaic assurance, then, is visible early in his career: poems like 'In Carrowdore Churchyard', 'Preface to a Love Poem', and 'An Unborn Child' display an acute sense of the stanza as not merely a container for a series of lines but as itself a vital aspect of the poetry's meaning. In absorbing—ultimately from Yeats—the performative energies of stanzaic organization in poems, Mahon succeeds in accommodating a rhetorical elevation which, without its resource of stanzaic pattern, might run astray. Edna Longley, in an essay on Mahon's use of poetic form which displays powerfully the extent of the poet's reliance on and mastery of the stanza, writes of how his 'stanzaic skill serves a poetry of statement pushed to prophetic extremity: not full-throated Yeatsian declamation, but the rhetoric Yeats might have produced had he entered more fully into either the *fin de siècle* or the modern city'.[22] The point is an important one, for Mahon's poetry shows how the stanza, understood as a performative element in poems, can shape the rhetorical diminuendo as readily as the Yeatsian crescendo. The central point in Mahon's writing where this understanding of poetic form is put to proof is 'A Disused Shed in Co. Wexford', a poem which might well be seen as his finest single achievement, and one which is unmistakably in contact with Yeats, on the level of form as well as the more obvious level of its subject-matter.[23] The poem confronts one of the later Yeats's most characteristic places of attention, the Big House, but it does so from the angle of the marginal, the neglected, and the decayed. The mushrooms waiting out decades of history in their shed 'Deep in the grounds of a burnt-out hotel, | Among the bathtubs and the washbasins' constitute a radically reduced version of Yeats's 'delicate feet upon old terraces'. However, Mahon's procedure in the poem, though it accommodates and, in a way, transfigures this reduction, is to adopt the ten-line stanza of Yeats's grandest constructions. On the other hand, it is also possible to observe that Mahon's stanza deforms

---

[22] Edna Longley, 'The Singing Line: Form in Derek Mahon's Poetry', 175.
[23] Derek Mahon, 'A Disused Shed in Co. Wexford', *Collected Poems*, 89–90.

that of Yeats by mutating his rhymes, then scrambling their regular orders. The rhymes of 'A Disused Shed' are often frail ('hotel'/'key-hole', 'washbasins'/'rhododendrons'/'silence', 'star'/'desire', all in the second stanza alone), and the patterns of their deployment through the stanzas are not regular ones. The vaulting of the chamber, to adopt Heaney's metaphor, has been replaced by something apparently ram-shackle, though in its own way resilient.

Yeats's stanzas are crucially dependent on regularity of rhyme scheme; partly, this is because their rhetorical direction is itself reliant on the clinching effect of the seemingly conclusive, or (as it were) the inevitable rhyme. For Mahon, on the other hand, the rhymes will not necessarily arrive on time: the absence of pattern in Mahon's ten-line stanza is wholly in keeping with the attention which the poem pays to things which have failed to find a place in other patterns, whether these are the forgotten inhabitants of the shed itself, or the 'Lost people of Treblinka and Pompeii', who also have their place in the poem. The fourth stanza offers a good example of Mahon's ability to discover an energy in rhyme and its stanzaic distribution that can almost reverse the Yeatsian rhetorical drive:

> There have been deaths, the pale flesh flaking
> Into the earth that nourished it;
> And nightmares, born of these and the grim
> Dominion of stale air and rank moisture.
> Those nearest the door grow strong—
> 'Elbow room! Elbow room!'
> The rest, dim in a twilight of crumbling
> Utensils and broken pitchers, groaning
> For their deliverance, have been so long
> Expectant that there is left only the posture.

The fullest rhymes here have to make contact over a long distance— 'strong'/'long', 'moisture'/'posture'—while other rhymes are carefully etiolated: 'flaking'/'crumbling'/'groaning', 'Nourished it'/'moisture'. There is a fineness of technical self-awareness in Mahon's structuring of the stanza, where the final word, 'posture', itself takes up a proud and resilient position, having been 'so long | Expectant' of its much-delayed rhyme with 'moisture'. Allowing for the designed frailty of Mahon's rhymes, this stanza might be described in terms of its rhyme scheme as *abcbdcaadb*; comparing this with Yeats's ten-line pattern (*abcabcdeed*) reveals how completely Mahon scrambles Yeats's more regular design, but it also shows that Mahon works to set up connections between the beginning and the end of the stanza, rather than to complete an initial sequence of rhymes with a final—and potentially conclusive—new pattern. Mahon reserves this conclusiveness for the end of his poem, where the mushrooms find their voice in a full rhyme:

> 'Let the god not abandon us
> Who have come so far in darkness and in pain.
> We too had our lives to live.
> You with your light meter and relaxed itinerary,
> Let not our naive labours have been in vain!'

The intrusive 'light meter' is also, perhaps, the light metre whose tenuous rhymes the mushrooms' 'pain'/'in vain' speaks up against: here, as in Yeats's stanza, the seventh and the tenth lines rhyme, sealing an elaborate rhetorical construction. But the conclusive energy in Mahon's poem is at least partly, and painfully, ironic: it carries a plea that speaks from a condition of near-ultimate weakness and vulnerability. The poem's form both protects and embodies a 'good faith' which announces and enacts its own precariousness and frailty.

'A Disused Shed in Co. Wexford' might well make Seamus Deane's description of Northern Irish literature—'autonomous, ordered'— seem heavily ironic, for it opens up an aspect of form in poetry where the order of stanzaic form relates obliquely to all but the most extreme autonomy. Again, the Yeatsian forms create the possibility of Mahon's technical discovery, while they remain quite distinct from it. Deane has written of how 'the formal control of [Mahon's] poems is one expression of a kind of moral stoicism, a mark of endurance under pressure',[24] but this seems better to describe Yeats's formal procedures: in Mahon's case, 'formal control' is apart from the stoicism it serves to contain, always a potentially ironic frame for the kinds of endurance to which the poems bear witness. Thus, the musicality of Mahon's poetry can be an unsettling property, just as its syntactic flexibility and command may sometimes contrast starkly with the bleakness of perspective actually on offer. To say that these things redeem such bleakness, or even abolish it, is to miss the irony implicit in Mahon's performative order. Seamus Heaney is so well attuned to the liberation offered by Yeats's different formal command that he misses, like Deane, the full irony of Mahon's

---

[24] Deane, *Celtic Revivals*, 165.

practice; in reading the conclusion of 'A Disused Shed', for example, Heaney takes for granted Mahon's freedom from the situation the poem embodies:[25]

Here he makes the door of a shed open so that an apocalypse of sunlight blazes onto an overlooked, unpleasant yet pathetic colony of mushrooms. What they cry out, I am bold to interpret, is the querulous chorus that Mahon hears from the pre-natal throats of his Belfast ancestors, pleading from the prison of their sectarian days with the free man who is their poet-descendant.

The reading here is not 'bold', merely inadequate, not least because it is hardly free itself from 'sectarian' reflexes; it also reads Mahon's poem as if it were the staging of a Yeatsian 'apocalypse'. The echo of Auden on Yeats ('In the prison of his days | Teach the free man how to praise')[26] perhaps indicates where Heaney's critical attention really lies. However, the failure of the reading here, which like Deane's interpretation conflates Mahon's forms with Yeats's, also suggests that the issue of form in Northern Irish poetry, along with the problem of Yeatsian precedent which is always carried in its wake, remains perilously close to a variety of extra-literary corollaries and analogues, such as those which Heaney's remarks let slip.

Simply to protest against the critical stirring-up of such analogues and corollaries in Northern Irish poetry would be disingenuous in some respects, for they do exert degrees of pressure upon writing since the 1960s which mean that they cannot be ruled out of discussion of the achievements of poets like Heaney, Mahon, and Longley. However, the kinds of autonomy, or of order, which poetic form carries into this poetry are various, and embody different aspects of the Yeatsian performative modes which are (sometimes ironically) their precedents. In the case of Michael Longley, an early exploration of stanzaic form gave place, through the 1970s and after, to an approach which sought simpler kinds of poetic architecture. *No Continuing City* (1968), Longley's first full volume, presented a poet of astonishing technical self-confidence, its rhymed and meticulously measured stanzas owing debts to George Herbert as much as to Yeats. In several poems, Longley's typographical layout, with its symmetries of variously indented lines in rhymed stanzas, serves to emphasize the tight order of the writing itself, and an element of self-consciousness inheres in such feats of balance. In one

---

[25] Heaney, *The Place of Writing*, 49.
[26] Auden, 'In Memory of W. B. Yeats', *The English Auden*, 243.

stanza of 'The Hebrides', for example, Longley seems to measure the distance between his aesthetic practice and the world in which it has to be exercised:[27]

> Dykes of apparatus educate my bones
> To track the buoys
> Up sea lanes love emblazons
> To streets where shall conclude
> My journey back from flux to poise, from poise
> To attitude.

Where Mahon's 'Day Trip to Donegal' brings flux into the stanza and unsettles the balance of order which it accommodates, Longley here makes a display of form in an accommodation of the flux which the sea represents, ending in the 'poise' and 'attitude' of urbane, conclusive poetic shape and rhetorical control. This 'journey back' is mapped out in terms which suggest very clearly what might be understood as a Yeatsian faith in the resources of poetic form: from the 'flux' of the given thing, the disordered world which the imagination perceives, to the 'poise' of a learned discipline and verbal self-control, finally to the 'attitude' which will combine all the elements of the poet's enterprise in one performative act of self-definition. This long and intricate poem is much concerned with the proper point of observation for the poetic eye, and with the correct degree of 'poise' for the poetic voice to adopt; like others of Longley's earlier poems, its rationale is in part a programmatic impulse, a gaining of bearings for the poetic excursions still to come. In the light of this, the extent to which 'The Hebrides' needs to examine its own procedures, its own degree of 'poise', is important, revealing as it does the irony, or anxiety, which is already implicit for Longley in such displays of order. By the end of the poem, all balance is precarious as formality and formalism both come into view:[28]

> Granting the trawlers far below their stance,
> Their anchorage,
> I fight all the way for balance—
> In the mountain's shadow
> Losing foothold, covet the privilege
> Of vertigo.

[27] Michael Longley, *Poems 1963–1983* (Edinburgh: Salamander Press, 1985), 42, repr. in Michael Longley, *Selected Poems* (London: Jonathan Cape, 1998), 16.
[28] Longley, *Poems 1963–1983*, 43; *Selected Poems*, 17.

Here the achieved formal balance of the stanza holds within it the ambition of the poetic voice to lose its balance—and these two things are themselves, so to speak, put into a kind of 'balance' in the poem's formal containment and resolution. Almost every phrase in the stanza might bear an ironic charge: is the poet really 'Losing foothold', for instance, and does he indeed 'fight all the way for balance' if 'vertigo' remains a coveted 'privilege'? Here, at a time before the full force of the word 'order' could have become apparent for Northern Irish poets in its extra-poetic senses, Longley is already fighting shy of the Yeatsian formal 'stance', even in the process of proving himself capable of it.

There are many aspects to Longley's development after his first volume which, while they are often suggested or foreshadowed there, take his characteristic modes of writing away from the 'poise' and 'attitude' contemplated in work like 'The Hebrides' towards forms less obviously structured and self-conscious. One aspect of this development is the change in Longley's stanzas from rhymed to unrhymed arrangements of lines. In a 1985 interview, the poet looks back on these changes in terms which show how far the issue of form, and its vocabulary, have become charged with tensions elsewhere perceptible in the matter of the poetry itself:[29]

In terms of what's happening now I would be regarded as very conservative and traditionalist. I resent being called that. I do believe that poetry releases the tendencies of the language, and two of those tendencies are a drift towards patterns and rhyme. Rhyme is one of the attributes of language. I rhyme very little now, I don't know why that is. I don't think there are arguments for or against rhyme. It's a basic fact that it's one of the things that words do, and when I'm writing I like to embrace as many of the things that words do as possible . . . My interest in form is a bit like the devotion of those monks in their cells illuminating manuscripts in the Dark Ages.

The idea that 'poetry releases the tendencies of language' is a character-istically benign insight, but 'a drift towards pattern' suggests that poetry also controls those tendencies; Longley here presents his development away from overt forms of control as a move towards greater acceptance of what are essentially impersonal forces and tendencies. Yet there is a sense here of 'poise' in the acceptance of this impersonal activity, and Longley's alignment of 'interest' with 'devotion' suggests how far the

---

[29] Longley, 'The Longley Tapes' [interview with Robert Johnstone], *The Honest Ulsterman*, 78 (1985), 19.

issue of poetic form might be seen as resonant in a poetry which does, inescapably, have its dealings with 'Dark Ages', of one kind of another, nearer home. In allowing that rhyme can be present or absent in poetic expression, Longley still insists upon the 'patterns' which give rise to the poet's formal devotion; the observation that the poems on the page are still 'the same old oblongs and squares' does mean that 'It's almost as if the formal sense is now built-in.'[30] The acceptance of 'the formal sense' entails, for Longley, a rejection of the more overtly violent forcings of language into form which the Yeatsian precedent embodies; it does, however, continue to provide for other kinds of patternings which are not without their own performative dimensions.

The control of syntax in the lines of poems, its shaping, turns, delays, and conclusions across the lines and within the regulated gatherings of lines into stanzas, may be all the more marked in Longley's later work for its being so often unrhymed. The absence of rhyme removes from many of Longley's poems the powerfully dramatic aspects of Yeats's stanzaic forms, as well as the capacity for calculated let-downs and surprises of Mahon's unstable, scrambled rhyme schemes. Instead, Longley conveys a sense of the self-generating sentence, of 'the things that words do', in his precisely timed unravellings of syntactic structure, producing very often a coincidence between syntactic period and stanza. In 'Carrigskeewaun', for example, five separately titled stanzas each deploy a sentence over six lines, and the tight uniformity of the poem's design is rendered almost unobtrusive by the absence of rhyme. In the fourth stanza, for instance:[31]

The Wall

I join all the men who have squatted here
This lichened side of the dry-stone wall
And notice how smoke from our turf-fire
Recalls in the cool air above the lake
Steam from a kettle, a tablecloth and
A table she might have already set.

This is exquisitely paced, and subject to a strict understanding of syntax, line, and stanza: the sentence which the six-line unit contains allows subordinate elements to assume prominence by their position within the

[30] Longley, 'The Longley Tapes' [interview with Robert Johnstone], *The Honest Ulsterman*, 78 (1985), 20.
[31] Longley, *Poems 1963–1983*, 97.

stanza, so that the ordered statement from outside ('I notice how smoke recalls steam') is counterpointed by a domestic interior ('She might have already set a table'). The control here creates a balance between the outdoor site of the initial declaration ('I join all the men') and the indoor world mapped by the sentence's subordinate clause; the pivotal point comes in the middle of the stanza, when after the third line 'notice how' finds its verb in 'Recalls': the symmetry between wall and turf-fire, steam and table, is vital to the equilibrium of the whole. Without rhymes, syntax and shape become shaping elements, even if what they perform here is a balancing act rather than a rhetorical declaration.

However personal their accents and emphases, Longley's poems take their forms in the knowledge that form in poetry is something more than personal. Heaney's formula ('It is an impersonal law that enforces itself when the ear recognizes a rhythm as inevitable') might well be applied also to Longley's unfolding syntactic periods and their timed conclusions. In *Gorse Fires* (1991), *The Ghost Orchid* (1995), and *The Weather in Japan* (1999), the insistently individual voice is couched in increasingly elaborate syntactic structures, and in Longley's adaptations of Homer (where the personal and the narrative voices coincide), complex lyric constructions are housed within single sentences: 'The Butchers', for example, carries a sentence over twenty-eight long lines. Seldom, if ever, are Longley's procedures in this respect visibly forced; however, the artistic success of his poetry consists in a sense of rightness, of achieved measure and balance, at which each poem seems to arrive, and this is a point where the affinities between 'inevitability' and 'order' in perfected form are of some importance. Longley's formal containments are by now very far removed from Yeats's dramatic performances, but their calm insistence upon order, even though it is an order presentable in some ways as one inherent in the properties of words themselves and their structures in speech, is nonetheless a gesture with aspects of 'impersonal' meaning and authority.

Longley's forms are 'habitable' then, and more often the poetic equivalents of the stone-built cottage than the architecturally imposing Big House. Of all the poets of his generation, it is Longley who comes closest, in his handling of formal design, to an absence of self-consciousness; though even this must be, of course, itself an achievement of artistic purpose, and as such might perhaps be said to remain complicit with the view of literature as 'autonomous, ordered' which still fuels critical suspicion of Yeats and others. Like other poets from

Northern Ireland, Longley has done something with the formal influence of Yeats which differs greatly from simple mimicry and which precludes, at the same time, wholesale acceptance of Yeats on the terms he offered to posterity. In learning to 'Sing whatever is well made', Longley and Mahon learned that the 'well made' can allow for modes in which Yeats's performances are scrambled and re-pitched. In his poem 'Architecture', another piece made up of separately titled stanzas, Longley presents four habitations which miniaturize Yeatsian grand dwellings and bring them into close contact with the nature Yeats occasionally scorned: thus, there are different small houses 'on the Seashore', 'on the Bleach Green', and 'Made out of Turf'. The six-line stanzas do rhyme (unusually for Longley in the late 1970s):[32]

The House Shaped Like an Egg

> Do you pay for this house with egg money
> Since its whitewashed walls are clean as shell
> And the parlour, scullery, bedrooms oval
> To leave no corner for dust or devil
> Or the double yolk of heaven and hell
> Or days when it rains and turns out sunny?

Longley's rhyme scheme here (*abccba*) seals his stanza into a tight circle, and is a long way from the rhyme progressions, always complicit with the moving-forward of argument, of Yeatsian stanzas. Here the last line, with its own movement from darkness to welcome light, provides in its rhyming connection to the point of departure in the first line a liberating contrast to the fifth line ('Or the double yolk of heaven and hell') with its packed Neoplatonic riddle once used by Yeats to cap a stanza of 'Among School Children' ('Or else, to alter Plato's parable, | Into the yolk and white of the one shell').[33] Longley's house shaped like an egg presents in itself an image of order and self-containment which neglects altogether Yeatsian architecture but which, like Longley's poetry itself in miniature, encloses and preserves a clean space, formal and impersonal.

The impersonalities of Paul Muldoon's poetry mingle, like those of Longley, with autobiographical elements; yet Muldoon, from a younger generation of poets, is also a more challenging critical case as regards his understanding of, and uses for poetic form. For Muldoon, the line between form as perceived stylistic pattern and form as impersonal

---

[32] Longley, *Poems 1963–1983*, 153.   [33] Yeats, *Variorum Poems*, 443.

intellectual grid is often deliberately unclear: in early collections like *Quoof* (1983) and *Meeting the British* (1987) the formal concerns of stanza and rhyme are never far from view, but their function, or the relation between them and the business in hand of their respective poems is often problematic. Muldoon's later work, and especially *The Annals of Chile* (1994) and *Hay* (1998) invests heavily in form: poems sometimes feel like illustrations in an encyclopedia of forms, and patterns of amazing (or possibly monstrous) intricacy generate long poems like 'Yarrow' and 'The Bangle (Slight Return)'; beyond separate poems, rhyme schemes are shared in patterns that stretch between whole books. The resource of form, whatever its Yeatsian connotations, seems in later Muldoon to have been replaced by a mania for form, and form as mania: something well beyond any orbit known even to Yeats's most feverish visions.[34] Even in earlier long narratives like 'The More a Man Has the More a Man Wants', Muldoon uses the fourteen-line stanza which, often standing alone as a sonnet, is his most common formal unit. These sonnet stanzas can have lines of any length and can rhyme, according to highly individual and often apparently improvised criteria, in any order. Form is paraded in front of the reader, blatantly emphasized as something created or imposed, while at the same time a show of offhand nonchalance surrounds the various feats of unlikely rhyme and sometimes apparently arbitrary stanzaic organization. Are Muldoon's sonnets more properly parodies of sonnets, or even, so to speak, 'deconstructed' sonnets? On the larger scale, in his book-length *Madoc* (1990), Muldoon produced a narrative which makes a display out of its 'meaning' by giving square-bracketed titles to each of its many short sections, in the form of philosophers' names. As with the shapes of his poems themselves, this makes authorial working and shaping so visible as to become problematic, and form can start to appear as, rather than an enabling means, a hermetic and continually self-defining end.

Difficulties such as these may seem to stand at a considerable distance from the issue of Yeats's influence; yet Muldoon represents a point in Northern Irish poetry at which the reception of Yeats has been pursued all the way to an elusive (and allusive) irony. Whether this irony can enable serious creative work is still, despite Muldoon's most recent writing and its mammoth forms of relation, an open question. Certainly,

---

[34] For description and discussion of Muldoon's large formal structures in these collections, see Clair Wills, *Reading Paul Muldoon* (Newcastle-upon-Tyne: Bloodaxe Books, 1998), chs. 7 and 8.

Muldoon follows poets like Longley and Mahon, taking their ways with poetic form a stage further, to a situation in which the full implications of poetic form as poetic performance can be readdressed.

Here, Yeats is inescapably present, and Muldoon allows him to enter the long, self-circling '7, Middagh Street' in *Meeting the British* as a shifting, flexible, and richly adaptable point of reference of the different speakers whose monologues make up the poem. It is one of '7, Middagh Street''s numerous ironies that the poem is set inside a house which is for all the speakers a temporary home, a makeshift address far from the architectural embodiments of 'deep-rooted things'. Instead of being 'Rooted in one dear perpetual place', then, the seven voices of Muldoon's poem find themselves thrown together to share moments of transition, and their surroundings are almost incidental to this situation: 'In itself, this old, three-storey brownstone | Is unremarkable' ('Carson').[35] In the monologue given to 'Wystan', Muldoon's Auden reflects on how 'The roots by which we were once bound | are severed here', and finds himself contemplating the recently deceased W. B. Yeats in terms which resituate the poet in a 'ruined tower' rather than the 'malachited Ballylee' of the Irish poet's ideal/real dwelling. As often in '7, Middagh Street', engagement with Yeats happens through allusion and quotation:[36]

> As for his crass, rhetorical
>
> posturing, 'Did that play of mine
> send out certain men (*certain* men?)
>
> the English shot . . . ?'
> the answer is 'Certainly not'.
>
> If Yeats had saved his pencil-lead
> would certain men have stayed in bed?

Yeats's question in 'Man and the Echo' is rendered 'crass, rhetorical' here partly by formal intervention, as 'Wystan' fractures the original iambic tetrameter couplets of Yeats, deploying his own truncation and full rhyme to interrupt their all too 'certain' momentum. The last question here parodically adopts a regular tetrameter couplet of its own to expose the outlandishness of Yeats's 'posturing'. Other snippets

---

[35] Paul Muldoon, *Meeting the British* (London: Faber and Faber, 1987), 52.
[36] Ibid. 39.

from Yeats are subjected to similar distortion through quotation (or near quotation) throughout the poem: 'Gypsy' [Rose Lee] for example, remembers advice as 'Never, he says, give all thy heart; | there's more enterprise in walking not quite | naked'.[37] The effect is in part parodic and satirical, but it is achieved by locating the Yeatsian raw material in a formal element to which it is not equal: Muldoon's relentless formalism can devour Yeats's original forms, often here to comic effect.

7, Middagh Street in 1940 presents Muldoon also with a suggestive parallel to other poetic addresses and dates—most of all, perhaps, to 'Coole Park and Ballylee, 1931', for Muldoon's cast are aware of their own roles as 'the last romantics' of their period, and are all casting backward glances over finished phases of their lives and careers. The 'old, three-storey brownstone' is the site for a debate in which Yeats provides one topic, as well as a near-constant subtext, and the terms of this debate are drawn from the issues raised in (the real) Auden's 'In Memory of W. B. Yeats', especially the quarrel between the idea of art as autonomous and that of art as agent, which seems to be present in the famous line 'For poetry makes nothing happen'. 'Wystan' elaborates on one reading of this apparent statement throughout his monologue, but later 'Louis' [MacNeice] is made to throw the idea into reverse: 'poetry *can* make things happen— | not only can, but *must*'.[38] It is worth noting that, just as Muldoon's Auden develops his rejection of history from his rejection of the 'crass, rhetorical' Yeats, Muldoon's MacNeice produces his endorsement of art's capacity for action after quoting Yeats's 'In dreams begin responsibilities'. The two stances (each, in its way, 'rhetorical') seem to be set poles apart, just as they are situated at opposite ends of the poem itself; but Muldoon's formal design means that the poem is potentially circular rather than linear: the last line of 'Louis' runs back into the first of 'Wystan', in the same way that each of the seven monologues picks up its predecessor and runs into its successor, by starting, and completing, a quotation. As Edna Longley has observed, 'This suggests that the poet's dilemmas endlessly circumnavigate, rotate on their own axis, perne in their gyres';[39] this spiralling is in part perhaps parodic of Yeats, but it might be said just as well to be authentically Yeatsian in its ability to make form enact a complexity, disarming the

---

[37] Ibid. 44.

[38] Ibid. 59.

[39] Edna Longley, 'The Aesthetic and the Territorial', in Elmer Andrews (ed.), *Contemporary Irish Poetry: A Collection of Critical Essays* (Basingstoke: Macmillan, 1992), 65–6.

demands for a kind of fixity and coherence which art cannot satisfactorily supply.

Muldoon's 'gyres', like Mahon's and Longley's stanzas, and like Heaney's critical constructions of vaulted stanzaic rooms, offer a use of Yeats's forms which is something other than either ideological grudge or formalist imitation. The various ways of absorbing Yeats as a formal precedent in Northern Irish poetry show how unworkable and unsatisfactory is the critical attempt to see form as narrowly symptomatic in the writing of poetry, whether of political attraction to 'order' or cultural delusions of 'autonomy'. Much of the misunderstanding of Northern Irish poetry sees in a supposed formalism only a set of abstractable assumptions and prejudices, and these can be perceived in Yeats as well, given the same quality of misunderstanding. But the central fact which such approaches ignore is that of the flexibility and the changing nature of poetic form: in Yeats's hands, as much as those of his successors, form and performance are constantly moving, shifting modes that set the authorial will a fresh challenge each time a new poem has to be written. Poetic form is in that sense 'living' rather than 'dead', dynamic rather than static, for its kinds of order do not stand still, and they are never finally 'perfected' while they can still be inhabited. In the context of the critical quarrel with Yeats, and in contrast to the empty, unserviceable rooms of theoretical distrust and resentment, poets from Northern Ireland have demonstrated just how 'habitable' his forms remain.

CHAPTER 7

Louis MacNeice's Posterity

I

In his volume *Visitations* (1957), Louis MacNeice published the short poem 'To Posterity', in which a speaker in mid-career (MacNeice was 50 years old) tries to look beyond the horizon of his own contemporary reception. In fact, that career was closer to being over than either the poet or his readers could reasonably have supposed, for MacNeice was to publish only another two collections, *Solstices* (1961) and the (just) posthumous *The Burning Perch* (1963), dying a week or so short of his fifty-sixth birthday. 'To Posterity' addresses a far future with an open question:[1]

> When books have all seized up like the books in graveyards
> And reading and even speaking have been replaced
> By other, less difficult, media, we wonder if you
> Will find in flowers and fruit the same colour and taste
> They held for us for whom they were framed in words,
> And will your grass be green, your sky be blue,
> Or will your birds be always wingless birds?

It is a subtle and a haunting poem, one which sets the terms and (crucially) the tone for MacNeice's late lyric achievement. 'To Posterity' considers the future as an open book, but remains alert to the image of the 'books in graveyards', solidified in the opened volumes that adorn the work of monumental masons, frozen open and unreadable for ever. As in so much late MacNeice, the terms of hope and the terms of nightmare inhabit the same register, and the poem's carefully pitched question is not presuming on an answer. 'To Posterity' may be speaking up for words, but it is also a poem which has taken the measure of time's

---

[1] *The Collected Poems of Louis MacNeice*, ed. E. R. Dodds (London: Faber and Faber, 1966; corr. repr. 1979), 443.

way with words, and knows the odds against which, as a poem, it is operating.

That Louis MacNeice's poetry has not yet 'seized up', and persists in British and, especially, Northern Irish literature as a living influence, does not answer completely the kinds of question which 'To Posterity' raises. Partly, this is because MacNeice's sights are fixed on more distant futures than anything which our own present time might constitute; but partly too the substance of MacNeice's influence on contemporary poetry is to be found in the kinds of anxiety—and also kinds of confidence—with which poems admit the matter of their own posterity. When Peter Porter writes of Derek Mahon and other Northern Irish poets that they 'seem outside time, to be playing up to some committee preparing a Pantheon',[2] he perceives a characteristic angle of approach which derives from MacNeice (and which MacNeice derived in part from Yeats); in similar vein, Declan Kiberd notes of Mahon's poetry in *The Field Day Anthology of Irish Writing* that 'he writes not just of, but for posterities'.[3] Both comments have an edge of complaint, as though the poets concerned were in some way opting out by fixing their gazes habitually upon such far horizons (and, perhaps, in so doing missing out on things closer to hand and to view). In these respects, too, the late MacNeice might seem to be a presiding spirit, and the conclusion of his 'Memoranda to Horace' to provide an apt epigraph for a whole tradition:[4]

> To opt out now seems better than capitulate
> To the too-well-lighted and over-advertised
> Idols of the age. Sooner these crepuscular
>
> Blasphemous and bawdy exchanges; and even
> A second childhood remembering only
> Childhood seems better than a blank posterity,
> One's life restricted to standing room only.

This is, of course, no simple or naive opting-out, and MacNeice's horror of 'blank posterity' is well aware of those 'Idols of the age' from whom 'remembering only | Childhood' might be the last refuge. Like *The*

---

[2] Peter Porter, review of Derek Mahon, *The Hunt by Night*, *Observer*, 19 Dec. 1982, quoted in Edna Longley, *Poetry in the Wars* (Newcastle-upon-Tyne: Bloodaxe Books, 1986), 71.

[3] Declan Kiberd, 'Contemporary Irish Poetry', in Seamus Deane (ed.), *The Field Day Anthology of Irish Writing*, 3 vols. (Londonderry: Field Day, 1991), iii. 1380.

[4] MacNeice, *Collected Poems*, 543.

Burning Perch as a whole, 'Memoranda to Horace' is in the business of transmitting messages over and beyond the noise and fuzz of the quotidian conditions of its own time. In Northern Irish poetry, the sending of messages like these has had important aesthetic consequences.

Posterity is perhaps best seen in two different lights: as a trope in poetry itself (flourishing since Horace), and as a category or value invoked by criticism. A poem's most modest posterity comes in its second reading, but more generally also in its life as a written object beyond the time of its publication or writing. That afterlife is where the critics come in, but their work and success should not be confused with the figures open to the poet himself in considering what lasts in poems. And poems get written along the lines of memory: a poet's voice pitches, paces, and times itself in a lyric poem so as to make its movements feel inevitable, and capable of repetition. At the same time, all such movements are engaged in hearing again other patterns of repeated sound and rhythm, from other poems, that echo into the new work. A critic's notion of posterity is not attuned to such things. Much that is apart from the mechanisms of memory and memorability enters this kind of posterity; as Edna Longley writes, 'The odds against which a poem operates include the noise of history as well as the silences of oblivion or dissolution.'[5] Weak poets (and these may include, at any time, a number of very successful and celebrated contemporary figures) take critical posterity as the measure of their ambition, and try to listen in to history's 'noise' in order to second-guess the future. It is a mark of artistic immaturity which some poets never outgrow; but we cannot recommend ourselves to posterity by planning ahead, and we certainly cannot hope to win it over by showing the testimonials collected from our contemporaries.

MacNeice's most mature writing does not warm to the idea of posterity, but feels it like a chill in its bones. In this, his late work particularly braces itself against time, without hopes of a future life. MacNeice's late manner combines vivid (at times, surreal) close-up with unnervingly open vistas, and a book like *The Burning Perch* is marked by this juxtaposition of insistent contemporaneity with an equally insistent sense of posterity. As a result, MacNeice's characteristic perspectives are doubly shadowed, allowing a vividly lit present to be dwarfed by the future, just as it is also, on occasion, loomed over by the past. The poem

---

[5] Edna Longley, *Poetry and Posterity* (Tarset: Bloodaxe Books, 2000), 20.

entitled 'Perspectives' begins with the knowledge that 'The further-off people are the smaller', and instances 'the tax-collector | Or the dentist breathing fire on one's uvula' as figures who can dwarf 'Grandparents, | Homeric heroes or suffering Bantu' in immediate perception. But the poem's second half returns on this given situation, and reverses it:[6]

> Yet sometimes for all these rules of perspective
> The weak eye zooms, the distant midget
> Expands to meet it, far up stage
> The kings go towering into the flies;
>
> And down at the end of a queue some infant
> Of the year Two Thousand straddles the world
> To match the child that was once yourself.
> The further-off people are sometimes the larger.

This provides a subtle variation on the notion of 'a second childhood remembering only | Childhood', since the child in the future comes in 'To match the child who was once yourself'. Both these infant figures— the one known intimately, the other unknowable—undermine the stability of the self that must speak of, and in, its present time. The dizzying effect is one achieved in many of the poems of *The Burning Perch*, and notably in its opening poem 'Soap Suds', which begins with a croquet ball rolling 'back through a hoop | To rest at the head of a mallet held in the hands of a child', but which comes to an end with something else:[7]

> And the grass is grown head-high and an angry voice cries Play!
> But the ball is lost and the mallet slipped long since from the hands
> Under the running tap that are not the hands of a child.

The Burning Perch profits from MacNeice's sense of the strange economy of his life's work, and the 'running tap' here restates, in a more mundane register, the rushing water of streams and rivers that had carried a preoccupation with flux through some of his earliest poetry. Writing about the volume in the last month of his life, the poet noted the relevance of 'poems I was writing thirty years ago', and added how 'I myself can see both the continuity and the difference.'[8] In a sense, the

---

[6] MacNeice, *Collected Poems*, 519.   [7] Ibid. 517.

[8] Louis MacNeice, 'Louis MacNeice writes...', *Poetry Book Society Bulletin*, 38 (Sept. 1963), repr. in *Selected Literary Criticism of Louis MacNeice*, ed. Alan Heuser (Oxford: Clarendon Press, 1987), 248.

volume is haunted by the poet MacNeice once was, as well as the child that was once himself; it is charged, too, with a sense of the poet he is becoming, and the future this poet faces.

The doubled perspectives of late MacNeice seem to be vital to the kinds of influence which, at least in this early part of his posterity, the poet has exercised. In order to take the measure of this, what is needed is a kind of critical two-way thinking, as opposed, perhaps, to the kinds of 'one-way' thought diagnosed by MacNeice when, still in his twenties, he considered the pitfalls of posterity:[9]

Posterity affects to put dead poets and movements in their place; to tell us their real significance and cancel out their irrelevances. This habitual procedure of posterity is, like other affectations, useful in that it is tidy and saves thinking (I do not mean one-way thinking). Most people can only afford the time to see contradictions in their contemporaries. The self-contradictory is what is alive, therefore for most people the most living art is contemporary art. Yet people are ungrateful; they prefer the dead to the living and try to kill even their contemporaries by looking a hundred years forward. I continually hear people saying 'Yes, but I wonder what people will say of him a hundred years hence', or 'I dare say, all the same, posterity will think more of Mr X.' They herein miss the point. If we do our duty by the present moment, posterity can look after itself. To try to anticipate the future is to make the present past; whereas it should already be on our conscience that we have made the past past. . . . If poetic criticism is to develop, it must give up one-way thinking.

In 1935, when this was written, MacNeice was much concerned with the need for writers to do their duty by the present moment, and his own fullest attempt to perform this duty was to come in the contemporary panoramas of *Autumn Journal* in 1939. However, by the end of his life MacNeice felt less confident that posterity could be put effectively beyond the bounds of a writer's present attention to 'look after itself', and a 1960 review of George Seferis is alert to the ways in which the present, in poems, is always on the verge of becoming something *other* than the present:[10]

The voyagers keep asking (unanswerable?) questions:

> But what are they looking for, our souls that travel
> On decks of ships outworn . . .

[9] Louis MacNeice, 'Poetry To-day', in Geoffrey Grigson (ed.), *The Arts To-day* (London: Bodley Head, 1935), repr. in *Selected Literary Criticism*, 13.
[10] Louis MacNeice, review of *Poems* by George Seferis, *New Statesman*, 17 Dec. 1960, repr. in *Selected Literary Criticism*, 222.

The poem which begins like this ends:

> We knew it that the islands were beautiful
> Somewhere round about here where we are groping,
> Maybe a little lower or a little higher,
> No distance away at all.

Which perhaps *is* an answer; on a plane just a shade above or below our own or just round the corner which after all is our own corner, so near and yet so far in fact, lies something which might make sense of both our past and future and so redeem our present.

The aspiration here is not (to use MacNeice's 1935 terms) to make the present past; however, both past and future are here being admitted to the present in what is perhaps an application of creative two-way thinking. By 1960, MacNeice is less inclined to dismiss the 'habitual procedure of posterity' as an 'affectation'; at the same time, he continues to distrust the notion of posterity as a simply envisaged future: the register of his speculations is that of a (cautious) confession of faith, albeit a faith which holds on tight to its every reservation.

The MacNeice of 1935 and the late MacNeice share the common sense that posterity entails the death of the present, but what the younger man rejects, the older man knows that he has to accommodate. The tone of the specific acknowledgement of this in the Seferis review is unstable: it moves uneasily into cliché ('so near and yet so far in fact', where 'in fact' flatly fails to save the day), and formulates its hopes in finally too neat a manner, so that in the end the meaning of MacNeice's clinching verb 'redeem' is somewhat disingenuously unclear. However, 'just round the corner which after all is our own corner' is taken from near-platitude to something different in one of the poems of *The Burning Perch*: in 'Round the Corner', MacNeice begins with the simple recollection of how 'Round the corner was always the sea', and carries on from 'Seaweed to pop and horizon to blink at' to 'Round the corner where Xenophon crusted with parasangs | Knew he was home' (in the *Anabasis* which the poet would have read at school) to Columbus and the Bible, with its promise (or threat) of 'no more sea'. This realm is just out of reach and always on the brink of recollection:[11]

> . . . which we remember as we remember a person
> Whose wrists are springs to spring a trap or rock

---

[11] MacNeice, *Collected Poems*, 518.

A cradle; whom we remember when the sand falls out on the carpet
Or the exiled shell complains or a wind from round the corner
Carries the smell of wrack or the taste of salt, or a wave
Touched to steel by the moon twists a gimlet in memory.
Round the corner is—sooner or later—the sea.

In this poem, 'the child that was once yourself' provides the meaning of the 'something' which MacNeice's 1960s review cannot name. The simplicity of this meaning—what is, and was, around the corner is the sea—frames a poetic progression, or spiralling movement, in which past and present are vividly intercut, and where perspectives keep opening backwards and forwards. The future in the poem comes to transform simple recollection into a contemplation of something which will survive that recollection by persisting beyond it: 'there will be always a realm | Undercutting its banks . . .', and the symbolic meaning of the sea which continues in the future goes deliberately unmentioned. In part, this is because there is simply *no need* for any such meaning; the significance of the sea is its presence in the past, and its continued presence in the future, so that past and future are both immanent for the writing voice in the present. The poem's simple opening and closing sentences shift from 'was' to 'is', but this final present 'is' feels more like a future tense, with its promise of what will come 'sooner or later'. Even the child in the poem is shadowed by the image of 'springs to spring a trap or rock | A cradle'; like other children in *The Burning Perch*, the child in 'Round the corner' puts the past in touch with a cold future. In this sense at least, the past's other name is posterity, and the cost of admittance is known all the more surely for its being unspoken.

II

MacNeice's characteristic perspectives on posterity, though they may seem sombre enough, are by no means the bleakest of those possible, and the proof of this comes (ironically perhaps, though logically too) in certain aspects of MacNeice's artistic legacy. Derek Mahon, who has identified his elegy for MacNeice, 'In Carrowdore Churchyard', as the moment at which his own poetry first found its independence, has pursued MacNeice's sense of posterity further in poetry than any of his contemporaries. In biographical terms, links between Mahon and

MacNeice are (at first sight anyway) minimal ones, as a 1991 interview makes clear:[12]

I've always had a thing about MacNeice. We met twice, once in a Dublin pub after a rugby international at Lansdowne Road, and once at his house in London, where he was watching rugby on TV and didn't have much to say. He took no notice of me (why should he?) but I felt some connection had been made.

Even these casual-sounding remarks, however, seem curiously secure in their sense of 'some connection'; and the reality of that connection as well as its extent are plainly set out in a great deal of Mahon's poetry. Like his contemporary Michael Longley (who did not get as far as even the modest meetings recorded here), Mahon knows about an artistic connection and intimacy with MacNeice for which biographical coin-cidings are strictly irrelevant. Both Mahon and Longley are more inter-esting for the ways in which they remain in touch with MacNeice than for any contact they might once have had with him; in this respect, their poetry registers in subtle and revealing ways MacNeice's life in posterity.

The notion of such a 'life', of course, while it is always edged with dark shadows in MacNeice, is for Mahon an idea flooded with the bitterest of ironies. If MacNeice's verse shudders in the prospect of posterity, Mahon's poetry is hardened to the cold of that particular region, having adopted it almost as its native element. The similarities and differences come into focus with regard to one of MacNeice's perennial themes, that of flux and change, which has an obvious applicability to the whole issue of verse and posterity. MacNeice's poetry is preoccupied with expres-sions of flux from its earliest stages; where in his earlier work the poet is inclined to celebrate the dazzle and change of quotidian perception, by the time of the later poetry this perception of reality in flux has become more of a challenge to a more closely observed force of finality. Cru-cially, the later MacNeice finds ways of absorbing the quick-change, many-angled sense of experiential flux in the texture of the verse itself, and in its varying speeds and tricks of perspective. In 'Variation on Heraclitus' (from *Solstices*), the Greek philosopher's remarks that 'all things are flowing' and that 'one cannot step into the same river twice' are refigured within a framework where the speaking voice is itself riding the rapids of constant change:[13]

---

[12] Derek Mahon, interview in *Poetry Review*, 81/2 (Summer 1991), 5.
[13] MacNeice, *Collected Poems*, 502.

> Even the walls are flowing, even the ceiling,
> Nor only in terms of physics; the pictures
> Bob on each picture rail like floats on a line
> While the books on the shelves keep reeling
> Their titles out into space...

The stability, or rather persistence, of the 'I' who observes all this is at issue in the poem, and is put in a problematic relation to the writing in which the first-person voice engages: 'nor can this be where I stood— | Where I shot the rapids I mean—when I signed | On a line that rippled away with a pen that melted...'. The permanence of writing is in no way a settled matter here, and the poem's long lines, with all the twists and turns in their continued acceleration, build towards a conclusion in which the idea of the 'static' is rejected most emphatically at the moment when (ironically) the verse's movement comes to a dead halt:

> No, whatever you say,
> Reappearance presumes disappearance, it may not be nice
> Or proper or easily analysed not to be static
> But none of your slide snide rules can catch what is sliding so fast
> And, all you advisers on this by the time it is that,
> I just do not want your advice
> Nor need you be troubled to pin me down in my room
> Since the room and I will escape for I tell you flat:
> One cannot live in the same room twice.

The vitality of 'I will escape' is, like other prospects of the future in the later MacNeice, hedged with the ironies it is determined to push beyond. The voice's escape route in flux is exhilarating; it is also one in which the implications of 'One cannot live' are understood. The poem's energy and exhilaration outweigh the sombre burden which the suddenness of its ending nevertheless steadfastly acknowledges.

When Derek Mahon approaches this Heraclitean theme, it is with MacNeice's poem whispering in his ear. 'Heraclitus on Rivers', however, replaces MacNeice's helter-skelter movement with a measured, largely end-stopped pace. Shaped like a sonnet which has become slightly too large for itself (as nine lines followed by seven), Mahon's poem begins with a level acknowledgement of inherent change:[14]

> Nobody steps into the same river twice.
> The same river is never the same

---

[14] Derek Mahon, *Collected Poems* (Oldcastle: Gallery Press, 1999), 114.

> Because that is the nature of water.
> Similarly your changing metabolism
> Means that you are no longer you.
> The cells die, and the precise
> Configuration of the heavenly bodies
> When she told you she loved you
> Will not come again in this lifetime.

From one angle, this might seem like a restatement of MacNeice's position; but it does not, crucially, *sound* like one, for the voice of this poem has exchanged speed for stability, and it is no longer experiencing, but now observing the effects of flux. The 'I' of MacNeice's poem, which is at once its voice and its (disappearing) subject has been replaced by an address to 'you', as though the poem spoke directly to its reader or even (by extension) addressed its own poet. In its second, sestet-like section, Mahon's poem turns upon the kind of poet who might write a poem like this, and dismisses notions of survival in a measured, and rigorously calm, appeal to an unreachable posterity:

> You will tell me that you have executed
> A monument more lasting than bronze;
> But even bronze is perishable.
> Your best poem, you know the one I mean,
> The very language in which the poem
> Was written, and the idea of language,
> All these things will pass away in time.

Supplying as it does an elaboration on the second half of the Heraclitus tag ('All things are flowing, and nothing remains'), Mahon's poem here opens up a vista on to a posterity which is more in the nature of eternity. In the process, it makes Horace's boast ('exegi monumentum aere perennius') matter for a dourly ironic sermon. In so far as 'Heraclitus on Rivers' revives a strongly MacNeicean theme, it enters into the kind of intertextual conversation in which MacNeice's artistic posterity consists; to the extent that it argues against MacNeice's revered Horace, and insists on ultimate decay and disappearance, it makes explicit elements which the MacNeice poem works by keeping (just) out of sight.

Mahon's choice of Horace is unlikely to be one uninfluenced by his reading of MacNeice. *The Burning Perch* has 'Memoranda to Horace' as its longest poem, in which issues of posterity and survival are to the fore. Furthermore, Mahon has engaged with MacNeice on Horatian territory in what looks like open competition, with his translation of *Odes* 1.11

('How to live', in Mahon's version, 'Carpe diem' in MacNeice's posthumously published translation). Neither the Latin, nor the two translators' versions have much time for the future; it is interesting, all the same, that Mahon should choose this canonical instance of the distrust of posterity as the site for an engagement with MacNeice. Again, Mahon's verse here chooses stability over the MacNeicean speed, as may be seen from the two poets' versions of the poem's concluding sentiment. For Mahon:[15]

> the days are more fun than the years
> which pass us by while we discuss them. Act with zest
> one day at a time, and never mind the rest.

And for MacNeice:[16]

> While we chat, envious time threatens to give us the
> Slip; so gather the day, never an inch trusting futurity.

Mahon's contained and neat chattiness may well miss the purchase MacNeice's more intricate pacing and diction gain on the 'chat' which time overshadows. Oddly, Mahon's verse here lacks the 'zest' it chooses to mention, while MacNeice's rhythm and glaring enjambment achieve something fittingly zestful.

The paradox that Horace's disdain for posterity is an important element in his *actual* posterity, a part, that is, of any monument more lasting than bronze which his poetry might constitute, is of course one well known to MacNeice. It is also important to the poetry of *The Burning Perch*. Writing on his 'conscious attempt to suggest Horatian rhythms' in 'Memoranda to Horace', MacNeice added a revealing observation:[17]

This technical Horatianizing appears in some other poems too where, I suppose, it goes with something of a Horatian resignation. But my resignation, as I was not brought up a pagan, is more of a fraud than Horace's: 'Memoranda to Horace' itself, I hope, shows this.

'Resignation' is very much at issue in late MacNeice, and in *The Burning Perch* in particular; MacNeice's reservations about his own resignation are relevant to this late poetry in ways that have a bearing on the poetry's

---

[15] Ibid. 78.

[16] MacNeice, *Collected Poems*, 550.

[17] Louis MacNeice, 'Louis MacNeice writes...', *Selected Literary Criticism*, 248. For more on MacNeice and Horace, see Peter McDonald, '"With eyes turned down on the past": MacNeice's Classicism', in Kathleen Devine and Alan J. Peacock (eds.), *Louis MacNeice and his Influence* (Gerrards Cross: Colin Smythe, 1998), 34–52.

particular kinds of success. In using Horace against MacNeice in 'Heraclitus on Rivers', Mahon perhaps registers some of the ironies implicit in MacNeice's own attitude towards Horace. Certainly, 'Memoranda to Horace' is one of the poems which Mahon's critical writing singles out for praise: deploring the poem's absence from Michael Longley's 1988 selection from MacNeice, Mahon calls the poem 'the last really good work he did', and characterizes it as 'mordant and valedictory',[18] while the much earlier (and critically consequential) essay 'MacNeice in Ireland and England' (which Mahon published in 1974) quotes the stanza on 'blank posterity' and observes that 'It must have been clear to [MacNeice], in his last years, that the things he valued were being daily outnumbered by the things he feared.'[19] The attitude to posterity is evidently crucial to Mahon's evaluation here, as it is more generally to his representation of 'the poems MacNeice left us, their intimate whispers still echoing somewhere in the ether'.[20] Mahon seems to welcome the 'resignation' in late MacNeice in so far as this conditions MacNeice's perspectives on the contemporary world; but with regard to the older poet's reservations about that 'resignation', Mahon perhaps is less well placed to pick up the specific frequencies that are involved.

It is noteworthy that Mahon has allowed himself to be more often critical of the late MacNeice than of the poet's 1930s and wartime writings. 'Budgie', one of the poems from *The Burning Perch* for which Mahon has expressed enthusiasm, perhaps represents one kind of 'resignation' which is particularly congenial to the younger poet. The poem's depiction of a budgerigar in a cage, 'Its voice a small I Am', makes the pet bird into an entertainer of sorts, whose performances take on unexpectedly expansive symbolic range as it sings to 'Galaxy on galaxy, star on star, | Planet on planet, asteroid on asteroid, | Or even those four far walls of the sitting room', oblivious to all but its own image in a mirror. In the poem's conclusion, MacNeice opens up a series of ultimate horizons, only to return to the tame bird, which in its attitudinizing and self-regard becomes a kind of dark parody (or, perhaps, an exceptionally perceptive reading) of Yeats's 'golden bird' at the end of 'Sailing to Byzantium':[21]

---

[18] Derek Mahon, *Journalism: Selected Prose 1970–1995*, ed. Terence Brown (Oldcastle: Gallery Press, 1996), 47.

[19] Ibid. 28.

[20] Ibid. 42.

[21] MacNeice, *Collected Poems*, 539.

> The mirror jerks in the weightless cage:
> *Budgie, can you see me?* The radio telescope
> Picks up a quite different signal, the human
> Race recedes and dwindles, the giant
> Reptiles cackle in their graves, the mountain
> Gorillas exchange their final messages,
> But the budgerigar was not born for nothing,
> He stands at his post on the burning perch—
> I twitter Am—and peeps like a television
> Actor admiring himself in the monitor.

The last things scattered through this conclusion seem prophetic of many of Mahon's apocalyptic perspectives, while the bird's persistence in the face of destruction sounds a central theme in *The Burning Perch*'s recurring concerns. The budgerigar's self-regard is refigured as its duty, and its repetitive attitudinizing becomes a kind of heroic perseverence in the face of the future's impossible odds. It is important that *both* of these possibilities remain in play throughout the poem and at its conclusion; like other pieces in the volume, 'Budgie' combines satire with a finally tragic vision, resignation with reservation.

Derek Mahon complained at the absence of the 'tremendous' poem 'Budgie' from Michael Longley's *Selected* MacNeice, and both the complaint and the omission are revealing. Interestingly, Mahon's advocacy of 'Budgie' concentrates on its satirical aspect: calling it 'one of [MacNeice's] last and bitterest poems', he has seen it as an attack on 'the hegemony of television', adding that 'perhaps, more disturbingly, it is a satire on the poetic vocation'.[22] While Mahon sees this poem's 'tone' as central to its value, his laconic observation that 'it is the tone that is symptomatic' links his reading of 'Budgie' to his larger interpretation of MacNeice's later years as exhibiting a series of 'distressing symptoms'.[23] But 'tone' seems too level a term to catch the unnerving oscillations of MacNeice's late poetry, and its edgy pitch. Alert to MacNeice's distress in this poetry, Mahon seems to be (in part) deaf to its resilience and determination. To some extent, this may be due to the complementary influence exerted on Mahon by Samuel Beckett, whose 'tone' takes

---

[22] Derek Mahon, 'Louis MacNeice, the War, and the BBC', in Jacqueline Genet and Wynne Hellegouarc'h (eds.), *Studies on Louis MacNeice* (Caen: Société Française d'Études Irlandaises, 1988), 76. The phrases quoted here were removed from the version of this piece which appears in Mahon's *Journalism*.

[23] Mahon, *Journalism*, 41.

over where MacNeice's leaves off. In terms of ways of facing posterity, Beckett allows Mahon to pursue artistic 'attitudinizing' (to adopt a term from 'Budgie') to colder and grimmer extremes than late MacNeice will countenance. In Mahon's 'Burbles', which is subtitled 'after Beckett', this posture is struck through stylistic ventriloquism:[24]

> silence such as was before
> forever now will never more
> be broken by a murmured word
> without a past of having heard
> too much unable now to do
> other than vow so to continue

Yet poetry like this is perhaps *no more than* attitudinizing in the end, and it is lacking finally in the power of reservation that checks internally (so to speak) the impulse to routine resignation. Rather than taking its measure, the poem has given up on posterity. MacNeice's admiration for Beckett in 1963 was tinged with certain reservations: these are of limited value now as criticisms of Beckett himself, but may be illuminating as observations on the Beckettian element in Mahon. MacNeice compares Beckett's *Malone Dies* with William Golding's *Pincher Martin*, praising the resistance embodied in the latter, in which the hero 'fights his way to defeat by every kind of delaying action'. With regard to Beckett, MacNeice approaches him by quoting lines of Browning ('I hardly tried now to rebuke the spring | My heart made, finding failure in its scope') and adding a commentary which tells us as much about the poet of *The Burning Perch* as it does about the author of *Malone Dies*:[25]

Just as the absence of God implies the need of God and therefore the presence of at least something spiritual in man, so to have failed in living implies certain values in living, however much Beckett's characters may curse and blaspheme against it and behave like clowns in a clownish universe. As with any other blasphemy, the other side of the coin is an act of homage.

If this side of the late MacNeice is effectively written out, or written over, by Mahon's understanding of his work, it is understood nevertheless by other, no less influential, figures in the poet's immediate posterity.

---

[24] Derek Mahon, *The Hudson Letter* (Oldcastle: Gallery Press, 1995), 22.
[25] Louis MacNeice, *Varieties of Parable* (Cambridge: Cambridge University Press, 1965), 142.

III

The 'zest' which Derek Mahon supplies at the end of his translation from Horace (albeit as part of a couplet which is somewhat lacking in that quality) is a word marked with MacNeicean associations. Michael Longley picks up on this in the conclusion to the Introduction to his 1988 *Selected Poems* of MacNeice, where he reports how his own rereading of the poet has left him 'overwhelmed and exhilarated':[26]

What other twentieth-century poet writing in English explores with such persistence and brilliance all that being alive can mean? Perhaps only Yeats. Certainly, when MacNeice honours Yeats's 'zest', he betrays a kinship. We can say of Louis MacNeice's poetry too: 'there is nearly always a leaping vitality—the vitality of Cleopatra waiting for the asp.'

Longley's receptiveness to 'vitality' in late MacNeice is indicative of his own particular response to the poet's preoccupations and techniques. It is tempting to oversimplify, and say that Longley reads with exceptional acuteness the MacNeice who 'explores . . . all that being alive can mean', whereas Mahon reads with a special clarity the MacNeice who explores all that being dead can mean; but such schematic differences distort the subtlety of the different relationships involved. It is certainly true that Longley's admiration of, and uses for MacNeice's poetry respond more readily to the 'leaping vitality' involved in the later work as it fights its way to defeat. Longley has described the poems of *The Burning Perch* as 'poems of the winter solstice', in which 'the nightmares of childhood fuse with the real nightmare of growing older', and has pointed out that they are 'also powered by metaphysical urgency'.[27] The ways in which nightmare is transmuted into power (and Longley's accounts of Mac-Neice make it plain that this is a power which continues posthumously) are involved also in MacNeice's strange 'vitality' and 'zest'.

Some of MacNeice's later lyrics seem to carry poems by Michael Longley deep in their structures. In 'Hold-up' (from *Solstices*), MacNeice makes a poem about going nowhere into a way of artistically getting somewhere. Like others among his late poems, its progress is at best equivocal, or something of a two-way affair; the phrase in the first and last lines, 'refused to change' is, in one sense, an obdurate and unmoved

---

[26] Michael Longley, 'Introduction', *Louis MacNeice: Selected Poems*, ed. Michael Longley (London: Faber and Faber, 1988), p. xxiii.
[27] Ibid., pp. xxi–xxii.

obstacle, though in another it is itself changed in meaning by the time of its repetition. Plainly, a lot depends on the reader's angle of approach; at the same time, MacNeice is here engaging in his own experiments in tilting and arranging line- and syntactic units so as to outflank things that refuse to shift. A 1963 review speaks approvingly of Robert Frost as a 'master of angles' in this respect, and quotes Edwin Muir on how in Frost 'starting from a perfectly simple position we reach one we never could have foreseen'.[28] 'Hold-up' shows how deeply MacNeice had absorbed such strategies:[29]

> The lights were red, refused to change,
> Ash-ends grew longer, no one spoke,
> The papers faded in their hands,
> The bubbles in the football pools
> Went flat, the hot news froze, the dates
> They could not keep were dropped like charred
> Matches, the girls no longer flagged
> Their sex, besides the code was lost,
> The engine stalled, a tall glass box
> On the pavement held a corpse in pickle
> His ear still cocked, and no one spoke,
> No number rang, for miles behind
> The other buses nudged and blared
> And no one dared get out. The conductress
> Was dark and lost, refused to change.

It may appear difficult to perceive the vitality in this particular night-mare, but the poem is not reducible to weary resignation alone, and this is due in some measure to the carefully timed stop-start in the dispos-ition of the verse itself. The strongly marked enjambments common to MacNeice's late style are used here to point up slight (but definite) anticlimax—'The bubbles in the football pools | Went flat', for example, first creates a metaphor out of a mundane term, then, having given the reader slight pause, directs that metaphor towards disappointment in a staged let-down. The nightmare of 'Hold-up' is that of complete stasis, and several of its images for this recur also in *The Burning Perch*: engines stall, for example in 'The Pale Panther' from that volume, while the 'corpse in pickle | His ear still cocked' in the phone-box returns in

---

[28] Louis MacNeice, review of *The Poetry of Robert Frost* by Reuben Brower, *New Statesman*, 12 July 1963, repr. in *Selected Literary Criticism*, 245.

[29] MacNeice, *Collected Poems*, 503–4.

'October in Bloomsbury', and 'what we miss most | In the callbox lifting a receiver warm from the ear of a ghost'.[30] But the poem's real horror, while it is implicit in the verse's structure, is also to a degree alleviated by the sureness of that structure; by the end, the tiny semantic space opened by the alteration in meaning of 'refused to change', though it hardly promises escape, offers perhaps at least a glimpse of daylight. In even the most nightmarish of all his visions of complete stasis, MacNeice ensures that the specifically architectonic energies of verse remain live and active.

The 'zest' encoded deep in a poem like 'Hold-up', which is implicated in its particular kind of 'metaphysical urgency', may become clearer by comparison with Michael Longley's poem 'Detour'. Here, MacNeice's location (probably London) is replaced by a 'small market town' in Ireland, and the traffic involved has become the poet's own funeral cortege. In place of a hold-up, there are now merely pauses in the procession:[31]

> I want my funeral to include this detour
> Down the single street of a small market town,
> On either side of the procession such names
> As Philbin, O'Malley, MacNamara, Keane.
> A reverent pause to let a herd of milkers pass
> Will bring me face to face with grubby parsnips,
> Cauliflowers that glitter after a sunshower,
> Then hay rakes, broom handles, gas cylinders.

Where MacNeice pitches all of his structural resources into the out-flanking of his static surroundings, Longley converts stasis into pause, an arranged and sustained balance in which things are seen 'face to face', and in which (as elsewhere in his poetry) they are arranged in orderly lists. As 'Detour' continues, the imagined funeral, and the speaker in his coffin, take in more and more of the surroundings:

> Reflected in the slow sequence of shop windows
> I shall be part of the action when his wife
> Draining the potatoes into a steamy sink
> Calls to the butcher to get ready for dinner
> And the publican descends to change a barrel.
> From behind the one locked door for miles around

[30] Ibid. 529.
[31] Michael Longley, *Gorse Fires* (London: Secker and Warburg, 1991), 7.

> I shall prolong a detailed conversation
> With the man in the concrete telephone kiosk
> About where my funeral might be going next.

The funeral, by the end of the poem, has the feel of a party that is only just beginning; the procession's detour seems to be open-ended, and its various delays are celebrated as the means by which 'I shall be part of the action'. The balance here is ensured in the unperturbable level tone which Longley's verse establishes (in marked contrast to MacNeice's edgy and angled lines), while the final notion of the deceased's conversation (a *prolonged* conversation) with 'the man in the concrete telephone kiosk' neatly inverts MacNeice's image of 'a corpse in pickle | His ear still cocked' where 'no one spoke, | No number rang'. As a way of imagining posterity, 'Detour' converts MacNeice's horror of stasis into a celebration of what can be prolonged, protracting as it does (in common with much of Longley's poetry) an ideal balance of observed elements.

Longley's reading of the later MacNeice (or at least that reading which is transmitted through the medium of his own poetry) is influenced heavily by his own response to some lines from MacNeice's earliest writing which have assumed for him a talismanic function. The couplet from MacNeice's poem 'Mayfly' discloses, according to Longley, 'the nucleus of his imagination', but is also the nucleus for Longley's poetry: 'But when this summer is over let us die together, | I want always to be near your breasts'.[32] Death and love are refigured in these lines as a wish for perpetuation of one intimate moment. In a way, Longley's poetry has been truer to that wish than MacNeice's writing finally managed to be, and one condition of this has been a less threatened, and certainly less horrified posture in the face of posterity. The absence of poems like 'Memoranda to Horace' and 'Budgie' from Longley's selection of MacNeice is indeed, as Mahon supposed, a revealing one, and reflects a reading of the late MacNeice in which posterity's presence in poetry is ultimately benign. Longley's 1995 volume *The Ghost Orchid* includes a rare explicit engagement with the question of survival, in a short poem entitled 'The White Garden':[33]

> So white are the flowers in the white garden that I
> Disappear in no time at all among lace and veils.

---

[32] MacNeice, *Collected Poems*, 14, quoted and discussed in Michael Longley, 'Introduction', *Louis MacNeice: Selected Poems*, p. xxii.
[33] Michael Longley, *The Ghost Orchid* (London: Cape, 1995), 52.

> For whom do I scribble the few words that come to me
> From beyond the arch of white roses as from nowhere,
> My memorandum to posterity? Listen. 'The saw
> Is under the garden bench and the gate is unlatched.'

In its delicate way, the poem is engaged in the contemplation of what will remain when 'I | Disappear', and the speaking voice here is placed somewhere just out of reach of the point of view it creates, 'among lace and veils', 'beyond the arch of white roses as from nowhere'. 'My memorandum to posterity' conflates part of a MacNeice title with one of the most important words in the poem concerned; whether or not this can be construed as an allusion, it marks a point at which Longley crystallizes the benign aspect of MacNeicean stasis as a continuity of care and loving attention, in the quotation of ' "The saw | Is under the garden bench and the gate is unlatched." ' In fact, the poet is here reproducing the text on a shard from ancient Greece, preserved in an Athens museum, and is in the process finding the words for a 'memorandum' which will make posterity something other than 'blank'. That these are not *Longley's* words is important to the poem, for the posterity envisaged is one in which the everyday is protracted and preserved after the speaking self has withdrawn.

Where Derek Mahon has picked up signals from MacNeice in such a way as to develop the loneliness and cold distance in his poetry, Michael Longley has attended to aspects of MacNeice so as to realize new expressions of the 'vitality' of the older poet. Both poets respond to elements that are present in MacNeice's poetry, and especially his later poetry; if the 'readings' their own writing provides are inevitably partial ones, they are also illuminating. As episodes in MacNeice's artistic influence, Mahon's and Longley's work constitutes, of course, only a part of a picture that remains far from finished; in Northern Irish poetry alone, there are other poets (Paul Muldoon, for example, or Ciaran Carson) and other aspects of that influence which continue in a complex and fascinating pattern of development. Another, complementary, pattern could be traced in English poetry written over the past three decades, in which MacNeice's significance has increased steadily, and has steadily consolidated itself as a matter of technique, and angle of approach, rather than the more ideas-dominated area covered generally by the word 'influence'. Successful during his own lifetime in the USA, MacNeice has not fared so well there since his death; there are many reasons for this, but it is true that one of the things which distinguishes modern British and Irish from American poets is that they have Mac-Neice's poetry running in their veins. Such things—like all things—may change. Yet perhaps the central point to be made now is that Mac-Neice's work is not merely one among a number of available influences for contemporary British and Irish poets, but has become more clearly one of the indispensable conditions for their poetry's existence. The posterity MacNeice distrusted as he fought his way to defeat in the poetry of his last years has proved to be (in artistic terms) real, while both his resignation and his reservations have been, in their different ways, exemplary realities for the best poets in Ireland and elsewhere. In 1963, things looked altogether different. Literary history seems to have carried off one of those tricks of perspective which MacNeice relished and practised in the shapes and turns of his best writing, and in registering his presence in contemporary poetry it has made critical two-way thinking imperative: the further-off people are, indeed, sometimes the larger.

CHAPTER 8

The Pitch of Dissent: Geoffrey Hill

I   *Hill's timing*

Writing about his version for the stage of Henrik Ibsen's *Brand*, Geoffrey Hill voices some powerful (if presently discomforting) ideas about the nature and significance of verse as being 'at once character and enactment . . . itself both absolute will and contingency'.[1] 'Will', however we interpret 'absolute', is a matter central to the writing of poetry, though it is arguably something less accessible for poetry criticism; 'contingency'—a term which can (and possibly might) encompass everything that is, or appears to be, outside the poem, is sometimes a matter for critical attention, but seldom figures as one of the cruxes of poetic preoccupation. 'It is the precise detail', Hill adds in a footnote, 'of word or rhythm, which carries the ethical burden; it is technique, rightly understood, which provides the true point of departure for inspiration.'[2] An entire *ars poetica* is implicit in these remarks, but while this is certainly and recognizably Hill's, its power and importance follow from its being something more than just a personal account of one poet's experience; the insistence on 'the ethical burden' carried by 'the precise detail' is one which applies itself to poetry (and to writing) in general, and which makes large claims on those issues of 'will and contingency' exerting pressure on more than just the individual writer or reader. That is, Hill is here presuming not to speak for himself—or not simply so, in the midst of a poetic culture where the 'simply' personal account of the poet's art has become accepted (and perhaps often expected) as a gesture of paradoxically authoritative modesty.

[1] Geoffrey Hill, 'Preface to the Penguin Edition', *Brand: A Version for the Stage* (1978; 3rd edn. Harmondsworth: Penguin, 1996), p. x.
[2] Ibid., p. xi.

To put aside—if only for a moment—the strength or weakness of Hill's particular contentions here about poetic language, it is clear that his directness on the matter is liable to hostile construction. Isn't there, for instance, more than a shade of arrogance in this unembarrassed loftiness, and doesn't Hill's central contention amount to an unacceptable insistence on obscurantist (and effectively elitist) repudiation of the accessible in poetic communication? 'The precise detail', you might say, is one thing; to insist on it as carrying some kind of 'ethical burden' is quite another, and may amount to no more than reading far too much into mere details. But such objections are themselves, in the end, full of the very 'arrogance' they try to expose; it is an important fact of British cultural life that 'reading too much' into things, like allowing difficulty in the substance of literary work, can be routinely identified as elitist, and therefore unacceptable to the presumed reasonableness of the intelligent reader, while at the same time these very identifications, and those who make them, rely absolutely on a sense of cultural authority which both derives from and assiduously polices its own more actually located, and perhaps self-deluding, elitism.

To say this is, of course, to read rather a lot into what passes for common sense. But common sense, like a shared opinion, depends completely on the conditions of its own time in order to 'pass': and what passes for sound judgement in these terms, or even succeeds in passing itself off as such, is also subject to its own inevitable passing away with the passing of its time. Literary language and composition depend on more than this, even if they are never simply apart from it, and their times include the precision of other conceptions of timing on which they also rely. Hill's poetry is in this sense answerable to his criticism and the standards intuited there, so that, however shy they may be of identifying the 'ethical burden' of words in imaginative literature, his readers are still confronted by a poetry whose details are intended to be load-bearing in serious ways.

Questions like these are questions of authority—how it is defined, how far it is accepted, and how it is actually exercised—which Hill's writing has posed, with increasing explicitness, all through his career. And to distinguish in this context between literary and other forms of authority would be as naive as strategic: plainly, the manner of Hill's writing, like its matter, insists upon certain obligations—intellectual, social, ethical—that bind us to each other and to the dead, and these obligations are at odds with a number of prevailing modes, and moods, of thought. The notion that time and attention might need to be spent on certain things, and that the more these are spent the more these things repay them, is likely to be seen as an idea of difficulty, which a rhetoric of democratic openness finds hard to stomach; and this, in turn, is often perceived as being now in league with a host of unacceptable positions—'elitism', 'arrogance', and the like—with which few contemporary commentators would wish to have themselves associated.

In an interview following the publication of *The Triumph of Love*, Hill responded to the identification of his work as 'difficult':[3]

Let's take difficulty first. We are difficult. Human beings are difficult. We're difficult to ourselves, we're difficult to each other. And we are mysteries to ourselves, we are mysteries to each other. One encounters in any ordinary day far more real difficulty than one confronts in the most 'intellectual' piece of work. Why is it believed that poetry, prose, painting, music should be less than we are? Why does music, why does poetry have to address us in simplified terms, when, if such simplification were applied to a description of our own inner selves, we would find it demeaning? I think art has a right—not an obligation—to be difficult if it wishes. And, since people generally go on from this to talk about elitism versus democracy, I would add that genuinely difficult art is truly democratic. And that tyranny requires simplification.... any complexity of language, any ambiguity, any ambivalence implies intelligence. Maybe an intelligence under threat, maybe an intelligence that is afraid of consequences, but nonetheless an intelligence working in qualifications and revelations... resisting, therefore, tyrannical simplification.

Hill's insistence that difficulty must be retained as one of the conditions of the truly open and accessible in art could not be more markedly against the grain of its time. The interview is in tune, though, with a great deal of Hill's poetry: authority here depends on the intelligence—and this is Milton's 'simple, sensuous, passionate' intelligence, rather than the philosopher's or the theorist's 'intellect'. To *define* this intelligence further is to risk missing the point: the capacity of Hill's poetry is to *exemplify* it, and much of his writing since *Canaan* (1996) has this as its ambition. As Milton's triple definition might already indicate, however, such an exemplification in poetry is not a matter of singleness, but of complex and contingent combinations. If this results in 'difficult' materials, then we must remember that difficulty is a necessary attribute of ourselves and our understandings (and misunderstandings) of one

---

[3] Geoffrey Hill, interviewed by Carl Phillips, *The Paris Review* 42/154 (Spring 2000), 275.

another: to put it in terms of literary performance and what we make of it, this parallels Hill's observation that 'Lyric utterance stands as witness to a faith in "sheer perfection" even while it is standing scrutiny as a piece of evidence in the natural history of such belief.'[4] The poem's 'simple, sensuous, passionate' resources and performances make up a fact in the worlds from which it arose and in which it is experienced—they do not just record or report on those facts. It is inevitable that 'lyric utterance' should, in some measure, result in difficulty when considered in the complexity of its relations to those elements—its author, its readers, their time(s), and the language they share or contend over—that remain extrinsic to its own controlled space or moment of performance. To encounter and acknowledge this kind of difficulty is to be an honest and responsible critic. But it is wrong to confuse this with a gratuitous or purposeless difficulty, whether deliberated or inadvertent, in the poem itself. For Hill, the time and timing of the 'lyric utterance' are to be measured against Milton's 'simple, sensuous, passionate' criterion, rather than against some scale of intellectual demand and display. The poem may embody or include intelligence; it is only a poor medium, on the other hand, for the expression or transmission of an 'intellect' which can be separated from its language's particular dynamics.

To find in Hill's poetry intelligence rather than intellect is a point of semantics, though not—as a good many would have it—*merely* a semantic point. The sensuousness of the intelligence is put to special tests and uses in poetry, and Hill's work shows how far language's capacity for 'lyric utterance' is involved with the working of intelligence in, and against, and with its time. The poetry's sense of timing, too, is a matter of importance here, and more than just a way of speaking about particular patterns of syntax and metre: for Hill—and especially in *Canaan* and subsequent work—poetry's timing is set against the abrupted or disruptive rhythms in the language of its time, so that the poet's ear accommodates both music and discord, the timed utterance of verse and the comically bad timing which it may simultaneously seem to evince. With *The Triumph of Love* and (even more) *Speech! Speech!*, Hill brings the rhythmic pacing and sureness of his own best writing in the past up against a screeching, insistent, cat-calling element of interruption and staccato challenge, creating in the process a series of forms

---

[4] Geoffrey Hill, *The Enemy's Country: Words, Contexture, and Other Circumstances of Language* (Oxford: Clarendon Press, 1991), 101.

which seem to exhibit profound instabilities of many kinds. These do not make for easy reading, and to maintain that 'easy reading' is a part of the problem with which they contend will not really be enough to account for their difficulty. However, it is worth giving some thought to the strange turn of events whereby Hill, whose work had often been read as a development and refinement of the 'impersonality' recommended to Modernism by T. S. Eliot, has caused confusion by his embrace of elements that appear confessional in their personal frankness, at the same time making these parts of a new kind of poetry in which the transparency generally accorded to autobiographical confession is a problematic business.

Further levels of complication need to be taken into account when coming to terms with Hill's later poetry. Most importantly, perhaps, a reader of later Hill finds himself engaging with modes of poetry which are not always, and almost never consistently, lyric modes. This is a rarer occurrence at present than it may at first sound. While it is probably true that we pay little conscious attention to the lyric nature of most of the commonly read and discussed contemporary verse (and in this sense the genre has become, so to speak, owing to its very pervasiveness an invisible one), the case for remembering that poetry's generic capacity has extended beyond lyric in the past ought to remain strong. The lyric poem may exact, as well as reward, patience in its readers; but the obvious call on readers' time made by a poem of greater length, or of plainly different genre (whether narrative, satirical, or didactic) is seldom familiar. The satisfactions of lyric are potent, and Hill's earlier writing proves them so with a particular (and perhaps, in his generation, an unmatched) fullness and persuasiveness. The poet of *The Triumph of Love* knows all about the possibilities of the lyric mode he is leaving behind, and the lyric poet's exposure in that work to elements of recalcitrant hostility, objection, and doubt, all of which stand stubbornly in the way of any attempted lyric assimilation or transcendence, is Hill's attempt to wrestle against his own strengths.

If, as Hill has maintained, technique is indeed the point of departure for inspiration, the changes in matters of technique so evident in his work since *Canaan* give some indication of a newly directed purpose in the poetry which addresses itself less centrally to the fields of reference we attribute to the lyric (broadly, the individual voice, measured and measuring, that absorbs and transforms a given world), and more to the areas of attention where discourses compete, voices interrupt, and self-containing measurement—whether of genre or poetic form—is not easily achieved. In *Canaan*, the poise of lyric is already under strain. Partly, this is proved in the progressive dismantling of the poetic line which many of the poems display: the sustained, end-rhymed lines of which Hill is a master are changing here into something else, and this change is registered by the stepped lineation of the poems, the gaps in a poem's disposition over a page which may—and may not—indicate deliberative pauses, points of silence, or changes in voice or direction. 'Of Coming into Being and Passing Away' seems to be peppered with holes in its lyric fabric:[5]

> Rosa sericea: its red
> spurs
>   blooded with amber
> each lit and holy grain
> the sun
>   makes much of
> as of all our shadows –
>
> prodigal ever returning
> darkness that in such circuits
> reflects diuturnity
>   to itself
> and to our selves
>   yields nothing
> finally –
>
>   but by occasion
> visions of truth or dreams
> as they arise –
>   to terms of grace
> where grace has surprised us –
> the unsustaining
>   wondrously sustained

It should be obvious that the poem's gaps of layout are not—or are not quite—marks of rhythmic stalling, then starting up again; instead, they present us with a series of turning-points, or pivots, where one way of reading, or hearing, the lyric measure changes into another way of so hearing or reading the lines. Thus, the rhythmic possibility of a line like 'its red spurs blooded with amber', though real, is one that can only be

---

[5] Geoffrey Hill, *Canaan* (Harmondsworth: Penguin, 1996), 4.

realized by the voice's passing over other possibilities, moments of pause that are also points of focus, in the isolation of 'spurs', and in the gaps before and after that word on the page. What interrupts the natural lyric line here is not another sound but another way of seeing the words; it is as though Hill arranges for the reader to be aware simultaneously of the rhythm that can be made and of the making involved in that process, the word itself and the word as co-opted into the poetic line. Another poem in *Canaan* speaks of 'the knowledge | of sensuous intelligence | entering into the work',[6] and it is just this 'knowledge' of which Hill's writing here gives evidence, as the poem develops away from its intricate and precise beginnings towards a meditation on the process of time and existence which underlies its title.

The poem is a metaphysical gaze into light and shadows—seeing things in one light, from one angle, and seeing them from another—and it is therefore both absorbed in and absorbed by the precarious but sustained balance between shadow and substance, truth and dreams, religious grace and the terms on which such a thing might be offered or recognized. Coming into being is distinct, as a perception, from passing away; yet the two phrases, and two perceptions, describe the same process from different ends, or with an eye to beginning and an eye to ending. In the romantic and post-romantic tradition, the directed and measured line of the lyric is one which begins and ends as part of a structure, or a process, that also goes from its beginning to its ending, with its development and completeness capable of an organic self-containedness and wholeness. Much as such ways of regarding the lyric have been challenged in the last thirty or more years, they remain nonetheless essentially accurate as an account of the requirements most readers of poetry feel most at ease in applying to poems. And these are requirements which Hill's writing has fulfilled time and again. What is new about a poem like this is its accommodation of the powerful forces in and on language itself, the weight of semantic possibility and pitch determination which might be—for the singing line of pure lyric—an inertial drag, to the shape and coherence of what is still finally a lyric structure.

A poem's rhythm can be at odds with both determining the precision of, and ambiguity in, the words making that rhythm. Putting this another way, we might say that the reader of a line of poetry does not

---

[6] 'That man as a rational animal desires the knowledge which is his perfection', ibid. 2.

stop the poem in its tracks to consult the dictionary. However, Hill's poetry has from the very beginning been in the habit of pulling itself up, and stopping itself short, as it experiences the ambiguities and indeterminacies of its own language: the two 'Annunciations' poems in *King Log* are concentrated instances of this, and the phenomenon is still to be seen in the smoother rhythmic environment of *The Mystery of the Charity of Charles Péguy*:[7]

> To dispense, with justice; or, to dispense
> with justice. Thus the catholic god of France,
> with honours all even, honours all, even
> the damned in the brazen Invalides of Heaven.

The intimacy between syntax, timing, and meaning is on display in these lines, and in the process the pentameter breaks down as anything other than a theoretical matrix for that display. The comma (and therefore the voiced pause) of 'To dispense, with justice' is set against a cruel enjambment, in 'to dispense | with justice', where the eye makes a pause which the voice cannot (and at a cost) accommodate. Hill repeats the trick almost immediately, in 'honours all even' and 'honours all, even | the damned'. The effects here do not depend on, or find their own deeper origins in, Hill's governing rhythm; instead, they make an interruption in that rhythm, as though the language of the lyric line were, for a moment, to spring back against the line's momentum and level force.

There is no reason at all, as has long been understood, why multiple levels of ambiguity, like different inflections of meaning through syntax or punctuation and pause, should be incompatible with the self-containing lyric. But 'self-containing'—like the more notorious 'organic'—is one of those metaphors whose figurative essence is a little too easy to forget, and it is true that those mid-century critics whose enthusiasm for lyric self-containment went furthest made themselves, in the course of time, easy prey for the kind of approach to poetry which sees all such valorization of completeness as inherently suspect. We do not need to reject poetry in favour of deconstructible 'text' in order to acknowledge the impossibility of a poem's being in actuality a self-regulating, naturally self-ordering and implicitly self-reading verbal arrangement. It is in this respect that Hill's 'difficulty' has been an aspect of his poetry's intelligence, since the verse has always made it possible for the reader to

---

[7] Geoffrey Hill, *Collected Poems* (London: André Deutsch, 1986), 190.

register—like the poet—the contingent pressures on and in its language, as the contexture against which Hill's music is conscious of playing. In 'Of Coming into Being and Passing Away', this involves bringing together the process of duration, which the rhythms mimic and take part in, and the indeterminacies of pitch and meaning, which the words consider and embody. 'Prodigal ever returning | darkness' is what 'reflects diuturnity | to itself | and to our selves | yields nothing | finally': in these lines, Hill's verse makes possible quite incompatible interpretations, as it balances on 'finally', which determines the pitch of 'yields': we can read it as 'producing nothing in the end', or as 'gives up nothing definitively', and with a number of shades of meaning between these two points. The darkness that is 'ever returning' puts pressure on 'reflects' (which must be figurative, though we are perhaps faintly troubled by the possible tautology of reflecting *to* the self rather than intransitively reflecting); this pressure is made more acute by 'reflects diuturnity'. 'Diuturnity' ('Long duration or continuance; lastingness', according to the *OED*) is a word that stops short of permanence, even though it gestures towards a longevity that is still strictly beyond us—the *OED* cites Charles Lamb in 1829: 'I promise myself, if not immortality, yet diuturnity of being read.' The word is not ambiguous, but the idea it denotes can be seen from two ends: longer than life, but shorter than eternity. Coming into being is also, seen as it were from the other end, coming into passing away; there are no shadows without the sun, and there is no sun where there is a shadow. In the context of paradoxes like these, the poise of 'finally –' on the page is important, and the three lines that follow it, not in parenthesis, yet in a kind of suspension, take up the possibility of 'visions of truth or dreams' as things that 'arise' 'by occasion'. 'An intelligence working in qualifications and revelations'[8] (as Hill puts it) is one that knows the complexity and contingency of its 'occasion' at the same time as it opens itself to the revealed light: thus, the sun 'makes much of' the rose's red spurs—makes them into something, and makes too much out of nothing; and (as we wait to find out in the long suspension of syntax and movement) the darkness yields nothing finally 'to terms of grace | where grace has surprised us'. Grace does not, as Hill knows, offer terms, but offers itself; these 'terms' then are also the words for grace (such as, perhaps, 'Rosa sericea'), and the poem's rhythms approach a regularity here, in the run of 'to terms of grace |

[8] Hill, interview in *Paris Review*, 274.

where grace has surprised us', and the final pentameter, broken only to the eye, of 'the unsustaining | wondrously sustained'. However, that visual (but also voiceable) break could relate 'wondrously sustained' back to the 'visions of truth or dreams'.

Clearly, the possibilities of connection in this poem cannot be decided one way or the other; nor indeed can they be said to be in any simple sense opposed possibilities in an either/or system of ambiguity. Instead, Hill's metric allows different inflections and possibilities to exist each in the other, and in doing so enables us to hear the simultaneity of purpose and cross-purpose in rhythm and cross-rhythm. Long before *Canaan*, Hill had written profoundly about language, rhythm, and poetry, in his essay 'Redeeming the Time':[9]

An enquiry into the nature of rhythm must first attempt to account for the inertial drag of speech. Language gravitates and exerts a gravitational pull. Oastler is not 'compelling' but compelled. Social locutions which to others might be scarcely more than half-comic irritants impose upon the Nottingham framework-knitters a force as shiftless as that of nature herself. In Wordsworth's 'Ode: Intimations of Immortality...', published in 1807, the line

> Heavy as frost, and deep almost as life!

is a weighted acknowledgement of custom's pressure; stanza eight is allowed to settle onto this line. However, the poet immediately breaks continuity, thrusts against the arrangement, the settlement, with a fresh time-signature

> O joy! That in our embers
> Is something that doth live...

It has been pointed out that in this poem 'the prevailing rhythm is merely iambic' and the Ode has been further described as 'broken-backed'. Saintsbury may be technically correct; but Wordsworth's strategy of combining a pause with a change of time-signature within the 'merely iambic' prevailing rhythm overrides both the propriety and the pressure. It could be suggested, in response to C. C. Clarke's criticism, that the Ode is indeed broken but that the break, far from being an injury sustained, is a resistance proclaimed. If language is more than a vehicle for the transmission of axioms and concepts, rhythm is correspondingly more than a physiological motor. It is capable of registering, mimetically, deep shocks of recognition.

The breakages of rhythm in *Canaan* owe a great deal to this extraordinary insight into the power of Wordsworth's 'Ode', and they make sense

---

[9] Geoffrey Hill, *The Lords of Limit: Essays on Literature and Ideas* (London: André Deutsch, 1984), 87.

as part of the 'resistance proclaimed' which that book sets out to voice and embody—a resistance which, as the reception given to the volume tends to confirm, is not something which the ear can judge easily when it is most attuned to the predominating sounds of much contemporary verse. Hill locates the impetus for his insight into Wordsworth in a letter of Gerard M. Hopkins, where he praises Wordsworth's 'Ode' as the poem in which 'his insight was at its very deepest', making him one of those men who 'had something happen to them that does not happen to other men,' who had '*seen something*, whatever that really was . . . human nature in these men saw something, got a shock . . . in Wordsworth when he wrote that ode human nature got another of those shocks.'[10]

For all the brilliance of Hill's quotations and remarks in his essay, it is possible still to feel a little excess pressure being applied to Hopkins (and also, perhaps, to sense Hopkins himself applying an excess of pressure to the particular lines of Wordsworth). The 'sudden shock' at issue here is real enough: but it is the 'shock' administered by one major poet as he makes a deep discovery about his own art in the work of another—Hopkins finds his own deepest rhythmic intuition in Wordsworth; Hill finds his in Hopkins, or at least in Hopkins's intuition of 'shock'. The 'recognition' in question, then, is a poet's recognition of himself in another's arrangement of sounds and stress. Hill's capacity to hear language—language, that is, both as it is used in literary and historical texts, and language as it is circulated, broadcast, and exchanged in the commerce of contemporary popular and intellectual discourse—makes him an abnormally acute receiver of Hopkins's sense of the tension between poetic language and rhythm and the language of the world. In terms of literary criticism and evaluation, it is possible that Hill, like other critics reading poetry in the mid-twentieth century and after, does perhaps accord to Hopkins a problematically high significance; but this would be to miss the point of Hill's attraction, which is to do with both poetic self-discovery (in terms of language), and, further along the line, with poetic development (in terms of technique).

Given Hill's insistence of the value of 'pitch' in literary language, it is worth remembering that the term carries distinct marks of Hopkins, for whom pitch is (as Daniel Brown summarizes it) 'the intensive measure of both the cumulative stresses of grace and the subject's affirmation

---

[10] Gerard M. Hopkins, letter to R. W. Dixon, 23 Oct. 1886, *Selected Letters*, ed. Catherine Phillips (Oxford: Oxford University Press, 1991), 240.

and instressing of them'.[11] It is Hopkins, too, whose 'sprung rhythm' provides Hill with an example of deliberated break with convention, a sense of verse which sets out to revivify and refresh the muffled, slurred, or artificially synthesized language of the time. In a letter of 1885, Hopkins writes:[12]

Sprung rhythm gives back to poetry its true soul and self. As poetry is emphatic- ally speech, speech purged of dross like gold in the furnace, so it must have emphatically the essential elements of speech. Now emphasis itself, stress, is one of these: sprung rhythm makes verse stressy; it purges it to an emphasis much brighter, livelier, more lustrous than the regular but commonplace emphasis of common rhythm as poetry in general is brighter than common speech.

Perhaps it was not until some of *Canaan* that Hill began to find the creative ways of registering the 'deep shock of recognition' that Hop- kins's sense of rhythm represents, and this is in the often painful admission of the world's cacophony into the measures of verse; where Hopkins had to redeem a smoothed out and monotonously lulling poetic line, Hill eventually has to salvage a language that threatens to become something closer to *tinnitus aurium*, an insistent and perhaps in the end insidious ringing in the ears.

Hill's most ambitious attempt to make use of breaks in fundamental poetic rhythm comes with *Speech! Speech!* In this sequence of 120 twelve- line poems, Hill is taking to its most extreme point as yet the idea of verse as breaking and self-breaking; this is in part a consequence of his radical reconfiguration of the lyric voice as one which must find its pitch against the instabilities of language in contexture. *Speech! Speech!* is, accordingly, Hill's most difficult volume of poetry to date, and it is likely that critical approaches to it (including, certainly, this present one) will be slow to take its true measure, just as they will have long work in weighing up its different registers and fields of reference. For the moment, however, it is probably relevant to draw attention to Hill's adoption in the poems of a series of printed cues that recall those employed by Hopkins in the notation of his own verse (and which were subsequently adopted in printed editions): these, for Hill, include the marking of emphatic stress, and the indication of caesurae in lines.

---

[11] Daniel Brown, *Hopkins's Idealism: Philosophy, Physics, Poetry* (Oxford: Clarendon Press, 1997), 268.
[12] Hopkins, letter to Everard Hopkins, 5 Nov. 1885, *Selected Letters*, 218–19.

The initial effect of such notations—in Hill as in Hopkins—is to convey
the strenuousness of effort that must direct even what might seem the
free flow of verse and cadence. It is, of course, a short step from this to
identify (and perhaps deplore) evidence of the 'over-strenuous'. However, we might wish to reflect that Hill's subject is—in a sense that needs
to be felt as real—a struggle: we do not complain of the over-strenu-
·ousness of a fighter, and it is clear by now that Hill is not a poet—like
Eliot—for whom the 'wrestle | With words and meanings' can ever be
allowed to become 'intolerable'.[13] Stresses marked on a page point us, as
readers, towards intended meaning; and in Hopkins, of course, the link
between intention and poetic rhythm is fundamental.

It is in the light of this that we should approach Hill's accommodation of broken rhythms in *Speech! Speech!*, remembering that the breakages
are also fractures of the poetic self along with the regularity of the line.
Early in the sequence, Hill sets stress against 'silence':[14]

> Inheritance is a power among powers
> out of its keeping. To these'
> honours, titles, are like wreaths delivered
> in the name of the PEOPLE; that is to say
> in name only. The acclaimed chorus
> overrehearses silence. Listen: I ám—this
> also ís—broken. For instance see *passim*.

The verse here is what makes actual a way of hearing—or of imagining
what it would be to hear—language working free of both contemporary
din, with its endlessly ramified tangles of history, ignorance, and prejudice, and of the defeated 'silence' in which the intellect might seek
refuge from language's corrupted noise. It is one of the central di-
lemmas of *Speech! Speech!* that these two forces, the newspaper-headlined
voice of the 'PEOPLE' and the reserve and withdrawal of art's 'acclaimed
chorus' are in fact in a kind of collusion with one another (a collusion
which is also a recurring irritant for *The Triumph of Love*). Hill's 'Listen'
could do two things at least: it could ask us to listen closely to things
around us—to language around us—and so become receptive to the
'overrehearsed' quality of a staged 'silence' in the face of things said, and
things done, 'in the name of the PEOPLE'; it could also, at the same time,
sound the note of exasperation of a voice pushed to its limits of clarity

---

[13] T. S. Eliot, *East Coker* II, *Complete Poems and Plays* (London: Faber and Faber, 1969), 179.
[14] Geoffrey Hill, *Speech! Speech!* (Washington, DC: Counterpoint, 2000), 7.

by an uncomprehending auditor. The stresses that follow, and the line-break in which a breakage is acknowledged, both announce and enact Hill's struggle, an encounter the consequence of which is to lame the lyric self. Time and again, individual sections finish either with a short line or with a short clause, in a kind of rhythmic limp which Hill identifies at the end of the book with 'the English Limper', the scazon, like 'Catullus's sure-| footed imitation of the Limper'. The *OED* quotes Obadiah Walker in 1673, on 'Archilochus and Hipponax two very bad poets' who 'invented those doggerel sorts of verses, Iambics and Scazons', and this citation is unlikely to have been lost on Hill.

In an essay on Housman, Hill shows his awareness of the kinds of risk which a self-laming, self-breaking art must run. In doing so, he returns again to 'intelligence' as the heart of the matter, and locates the working of intelligence in the 'contest' which must go beyond the merely notional:[15]

Transposing James's concern with drama to my own concern with poetry, I would claim that the poet in the poem is bound to take on the challenge of the 'usurping consciousness'; either he accepts it or he is the ignorant recipient of a destructive burden. There is rarely an unambiguous issue to this contest. To be wholly defeated by the challenge is to be drawn down into 'mere monologue'. Many poems move us with their knowledge of what is being exacted by such confrontation: in this sense there can be a difficult beauty of imperfection; but it is not, in such cases, a beauty of thought. It is a manifest beauty of intelligence—by which I mean, as the *Oxford English Dictionary* means, in one of its several senses of 'intelligence', 'understanding as a quality of admitting of degree'. Eliot concedes that solipsism rests upon a truth; but one would add that, if solipsism is to be redeemed from mere monologue, the intelligence which is brought to bear upon it cannot be simply conceptual. What James called the 'indispensable centre' of such work must be realized within the many dimensions of language itself (though language is never, in actuality, language itself).

Much here makes sense in the context of *Speech! Speech!*, and its pugilistic encounter with varying kinds of 'usurping consciousness'. To see the work of the poet as a 'contest' in, with, and against language and languages, which involves also those forces in the past and present that use, inhabit, appropriate or diminish languages, is to accept 'imper-

[15] Geoffrey Hill, 'Tacit Pledges', in Alan W. Holden and J. Roy Birch (eds.), *A. E. Housman: A Reassessment* (Basingstoke: Macmillan, 2000), 69–70.

fection', but not to resign oneself to it exactly. In Hill's jarring recognition that 'language itself . . . is never, in actuality, language itself' there is an implicit poetic—one difficult as the pugilist is difficult—which *Speech! Speech!* enacts.

The timing that makes verse, its keeping of time, is the element in which Hill's 'contest' takes place; inevitably, this is a 'contest' also with the 'time' we call for convenience, but without actual warrant, 'our' time. Put in this way, Hill's timing could be claimed, in this latest work, as a reinvention of the lyric voice, in which the lived time of the poetic self finds itself in and out of step with the timings of line and rhyme, with their comings and goings, and makes a pattern that can be remade in times that lie beyond the contemporary. Of course, for *Speech! Speech!* this is only half—the good half—of the story. Nevertheless, it is possible to see points at which Hill's technique achieves something extraordinary with the necessarily ambiguous issue to its contest, as in section 52:[16]

> Strange working of the body; how it knows
> its own time. Thát after all¹ and more—
> seventy years near enough—the resin-knurled
> damson tree, crookt at black gable-end,
> stands in the sight of him departing. LÓRD¹
> THÓU HAST BEEN OUR DWELLING PLÁCE—FROM ONÉ
> GENERÁTION¹ TO ANÓTHER (*lento*). So barely
> out of step¹ bow and return. Charles Ives's
> *Ninetieth Psalm*, found late, as grief's thánksgiving;
> as full tide with ebb tide, the one in the other,
> slow-settling bell arpeggios. Time, here renewed
> ás tíme, hów it paces and salútes ús¹ in its wáys.

The rhythms here are brilliantly double; their 'full tide with ebb tide', the coming into being and passing away they describe, are precise and moving keepings of time in a broken and mended verse that hears and responds to 'absolute will' and 'contingency' at once. 'The inertial drag of speech' is refigured here to accord with the pull of the will against time and in time. For all this, the inspiration is, ultimately, in technique; and one might add, in praise, that the technique here most fully achieved is an inspiration, as well as one of those 'deep shocks' by which poetry moves though time.

[16] Hill, *Speech! Speech!*, 26.

II   *'Violent hefts': The Triumph of Love*

'Opinion is not worth a rush':[17] Yeats's line needs to be quoted, and pondered, more often. In contemporary poetry, 'opinion' is generally the motive force behind the rush to consensus: literary critics and journalists, in Britain at least, agree with remarkable swiftness and with impressive certainty on a great many things. In this sense, at least, shared and disseminated opinion is always 'true'. The media excitement surrounding Ted Hughes's *Birthday Letters* is as good an example as any of how literary opinion puts itself around; many other instances could be cited, though, of similar hyperbolic consensus, and of a condition of shared enthusiasm for a number of contemporary poets which seems to reflect a certain anxiety to be seen wearing the right opinions in the company of the British literary media. Arguably, the force of consensus makes itself felt in negative, as well as these apparently positive, ways. If there is one thing, for example, which 'everybody' can agree about just now, it is that Geoffrey Hill has moved beyond the circle of those poets found acceptable by the most influential British critics and critical publications. Hill's indigestibility is sometimes registered with regret, but more often it serves to confirm certain assumptions and preconceptions—about seriousness, about literature and its relation to erudition, and about the nature of language—which give much contemporary literary criticism its opinion-making power and stability.

Geoffrey Hill's book-length poem, *The Triumph of Love*, published in the United States in 1998 and in the United Kingdom early in 1999, is by turns a daunting, baffling, exacerbating, and a provoking work; and this chapter can make no attempt to treat Hill's poem with anything approaching a comprehensive—or perhaps even a partial—explanatory or exegetical agenda; nor will it try to approach the poem as merely an incident in the history of contemporary literary reception. That is, I do not wish to give an account of the unfolding of Hill's specific design, intent, and expression in *The Triumph of Love*, nor to examine the story of the poem's immediate critical reception, though both of these tasks would be taxing and instructive. There is some point, however, in considering a few of the questions Hill raises in the book: questions about language and difficulty, language's difficulty for us, and our difficulty with language; questions too

---

[17] W. B. Yeats, 'Michael Robartes and the Dancer', *The Variorum Edition of the Poems of W. B. Yeats*, ed. Peter Allt and Russell K. Alspatch (London: Macmillan, 1956), 385.

(and perhaps not incidentally) about contemporary orthodoxies in the matter of difficulty, its legitimate bounds and extent, its testing of the limits of our taste, and our reflexes when confronted by the tasteless.

It may be that, as far as the phrasing of these questions is concerned—never mind their substance—we are already sick of hearing this: and being sick is certainly of the essence in Hill's recent work. Nauseous reflex has always been part of Hill's poetic repertoire, as for instance in the pair of sonnets entitled 'Annunciations' where 'all who attend to fiddle or to harp | For betterment, flavour their decent mouths | With gobbets of the sweetest sacrifice'[18]—lines which, as Hill's printed exchanges with his unadmiring Penguin anthologizer Kenneth Allott made clear, suggest in part the literal consumption, by connoisseurs, of 'husk and excrement'.[19] *The Triumph of Love* is more direct in instructing one of its adversaries to '*eat | shit, MacSikker*'.[20] Yet Hill's early feeling for revulsion is more than simply aggressive: the short piece 'The Humanist' (like 'Annunciations', from the 1968 volume *King Log*) stages its own moment of irruptive reaction as a parenthesis which the poem's body may not be able to digest:[21]

> The *Venice* portrait: he
> Broods, the achieved guest
> Tired and word-perfect
> At the Muses' table.
>
> Virtue is virtù. These
> Lips debate and praise
> Some rich aphorism,
> A delicate white meat.
>
> The commonplace hands once
> Thick with Plato's blood
> (Tasteless! tasteless!) are laid
> Dryly against the robes.

It is as though, in regaining its quiet and restrained equilibrium, the poem expels the matter of that reflex exclamation '(Tasteless! tasteless!)', and

[18] Hill, *Collected Poems*, 62.
[19] 'Art is "decent": it "reconciles the irreconcilable"; it serves to pay lip-service to heritage (hence the persistent sense of being at a banquet). It will not soil the decent mouth.' Geoffrey Hill, in *The Penguin Book of Contemporary Verse 1918–1960*, ed. Kenneth Allott (Harmondsworth: Penguin, 1962), 392.
[20] Geoffrey Hill, *The Triumph of Love* (Harmondsworth: Penguin, 1999), 75.
[21] Hill, *Collected Poems*, 69.

feels better at ease, both with the 'delicate white meat' of its consumption, and with the thick blood of which the hands now, after all, are dry.
The complex status of the parenthetical interjection records a complexity
of pitch: are these words, for example, in the same voice as the rest of the
poem? Are they, in part at least, in the voice of a prospective reader of
the poem and, if so, is the poet treating his readers with acute attentive-
ness or a condescending brutality? In raising a voice against itself, does
the poem try out a productive or a finally debilitating strategy? Is the
parenthesis, in fact, a tasteless bit of writing, and in its way too loud, badly
timed, and embarrassing? The parallels with the moments of ventrilo-
quized criticism in *The Triumph of Love* are clear enough:[22]

> Shameless old man, bent on committing
> more public nuisance. Incontinent
> fury wetting the air. Impotently
> bereft satire. Charged with erudition,
> put up by the defence to be
> his own accuser.

But *is* this the defence, or even a strategy of 'the defence' (as almost all
reviewers have assumed)? And who exactly is on trial? As with '(Tasteless! tasteless!)', it is extremely difficult to fix precisely the relation of the
indigestible matter to the larger body that may—or may not—digest
such matter.

   In suggesting a complexity of pitch, however, it may appear that
important questions about what is meant by 'pitch' are being strategic-
ally begged. Since the word has become increasingly important for Hill
(and increasingly useful in writing about Hill) in the burst of poetry
which began with *Canaan* in 1996, and continued through *The Triumph of
Love* to *Speech! Speech!*, and since its usefulness has also been challenged by
hostile critics, some account of it here seems necessary. Reviewing T. S.
Eliot's *The Varieties of Metaphysical Poetry* in 1996, Hill summarizes his
examination of the posthumously printed lectures in these terms:[23]

I have attempted to show that, throughout his argument, Eliot aims at pitch but,
for the most part, succeeds only in tone. I say 'succeeds' because tone is what
people expect and suppose themselves familiar with. It was the pitch of *Prufrock
and Other Observations* that disturbed and alienated readers; it was the tone of *Four
Quartets* which assuaged and consoled them. That is to say, Eliot's poetry

---

[22] Hill, *The Triumph of Life*, 19.
[23] Geoffrey Hill, 'Dividing Legacies', *Agenda*, 34/2 (1996), 22.

declines over thirty years from pitch into tone and these late-published papers contribute significant evidence to the history of that decline.

'What people expect and suppose themselves familiar with' enters our language at the level of its own postures of accommodation—as for a lecturer (like Eliot) it must, the better to enable the communication demanded and attempted in that context. Hill cites Eliot's 'small tonal irritants and irritations: "what many of you will have expected; a neat and comprehensive definition . . . ", "But I think that I warned you . . . ", "You will perhaps think it unjust of me . . ."'. 'The style of Eliot's address to his audience,' Hill adds, 'is a matter of tone; the burden of his analytical criticism is, or ought to be, the question of pitch.'[24] In a bravura performance, Hill proceeds to contrast Eliot's suave references to Richard Hooker's prose with the actual complex energy concentrated in that prose, fixing on Hooker's use for the word 'common', and citing ten distinct senses in *The Laws of Ecclesiastical Polity* to show how 'Hooker's "style" is to a large extent his semantic ingenuity, his ability to make these senses merge and part with equanimity though not always with equity.'[25] If Eliot failed to account for this, his failure was in the cause of his lectures' tone; in detecting and pursuing the failure, Hill's enquiry into pitch is itself an example of the pitch of and in verbal exactingness, something which, he contends, the poet of *Prufrock* knew all about, and which the poet of *Four Quartets* had learned (accommodatingly, as it happened) to overcome.

'Pitch', for Hill, describes a quality of deliberated alertness in the use of a word or phrase, in which even the intended meaning has taken stock of the misconstructions to which it is liable. 'Tone', as Hill employs the term, concerns the degree of collusion between writer and audience, where words and phrases are employed to mark and confirm the degree of that practical and mutually accepted relationship. How far this pair of terms depend upon their context in a critique of Eliot is a moot point; certainly, the significance of Eliot in Hill's adoption and use of them in his writing more generally needs to be borne in mind. A cheap and facile point sometimes made by Hill's critics is that he 'is a parasite upon Eliot's imagination',[26] but it is obvious by now that Hill's poetry not only relates to Eliot's in various ways, but also

---

[24] Ibid. 19.   [25] Ibid. 20.
[26] Tom Paulin, 'A Visionary Nationalist: Geoffrey Hill', *Minotaur: Poetry and the Nation State* (London: Faber and Faber, 1992), 281.

has come to challenge Eliot on a number of levels: the 1996 attack on
Four Quartets is a logical step in a lifelong engagement with Eliot's poetry
and poetics, where Hill has constantly pushed beyond those points (in
terms of artistic procedure as well as aesthetic principle) at which Eliot
left off. *The Triumph of Love* might well be read as a reply to *Four Quartets*,
but one which treats its subject unsparingly, disowning 'tone' and yet, at
the same time—and by the same token—abandoning any aspirations
towards impersonality, or indeed commonality—of address. How completely Hill throws the later Eliot's assumptions into reverse may be
gauged from comparing the 'pitch' of *The Triumph of Love* with what Eliot
has to say about Dryden:[27]

> Perhaps we do not realize how natural the speech of Dryden must have
> sounded to the most sensitive of his contemporaries. No poetry, of course, is
> ever exactly the same speech that the poet talks and hears: but it has to be in
> such a relation to the speech of his time that the listener or reader can say 'that is
> how I should talk if I could talk poetry'.

The Triumph of Love hears this kind of pronouncement in comically
subversive ways: the poem's running gag of mishearing ('For definitely
the right era, read: deaf in the right ear' (CV))[28] and misunderstanding
makes short work of Eliot's 'sounded to the most sensitive', 'the same
speech that the poet talks and hears', and his (already patronizingly
projected) 'how I should talk if I could talk poetry'. The precise verbal
coordinates of Eliot's tone may have passed, but the message they
convey is still with us, and it is easy to imagine how, in contemporary
British poetic culture, Eliot's point might be translated readily into our
own tonal range of relevance, immediacy, and accessibility. Indeed,
Eliot's next sentence could do service as the language of more recent
'poetry is good for you' promotional enthusiasm: 'the best contemporary poetry,' he writes, 'can give us a feeling of excitement and a sense of
fulfilment different from any sentiment aroused by even very much
greater poetry of a past age.' 'Very much greater' would nowadays be
edited out; but now as then, the reasonableness of tone, and the ease of
its consensus, are not guarantees of the soundness of the judgements
being made.

---

[27] T. S. Eliot, 'The Music of Poetry' (1942), *On Poetry and Poets* (London: Faber and
Faber, 1957), 31.
[28] Hill, *The Triumph of Love*, 54.

It takes little acuteness to remark that Hill's work is, as far as many literary commentators are concerned, hard to stomach; but indigestibility is a theme as well as an effect of that work. If Hill's poetry was always alert to its own difficulties in keeping things down, *The Triumph of Love* has shown what happens when they come back, or come up again. In poem LXXV, where a voice addresses the '*Vergine bella*', prayers to whom punctuate the sequence, Hill braves tastelessness and embarrassment, or he seems to:[29]

> *Vergine bella*, now I am half-way
> and lost—need I say—in this maze of my own
> devising, I would go back and start
> again; or not start at all, which might
> be wiser. No. Delete the last four words.
> Talking to oneself is in fact
> a colloquy with occasion—*eppur*
> *si muove*—or so I tell myself.
> Extraordinary how N. and N. contrive
> to run their depilators off the great turbine—
> the raw voltage could flay them. Such
> intimate buzzing and smooth toiletry,
> mingled with a few squeals, may yet
> draw blood from bloodless Stockholm. *Mea culpa*,
> I am too much moved by hate—
> pardon, ma'am?—add greed, self-pity, sick
> scrupulosity, frequent fetal regression, *and*
> a twisted libido? Oh yes—much
> better out than in.

The particular modulations of this 'colloquy with occasion' are perplexing, and the passage, like much else in Hill's recent work, is far from smooth in its flow. The constant self-interruption, the interjections and turnings-back on speech, and the mishearings, all contribute to what we might call a radical instability of tone, had not Hill already made it clear that he rejects what he calls 'tone' in favour of 'pitch'. But poetry like this is less pitched in a key than pitched hurtling in our faces; and its mixture of (not too subtly) coded references to Nobel Prize-winning poets who appear to be shaving their legs, bloody flayings, and a catalogue of personal faults, will not necessarily strike those on the

[29] Ibid. 39.

receiving end as something 'much | better out than in'. What happens
here seems to bring the 'tasteless' into a new dimension of vivid clarity.

So at any rate it has struck many of Hill's critics, and the reception of
The Triumph of Love has been marked by a number of more or less
disgusted reactions to what the poet has chosen to bring up. Few, on
the whole, have paused to consider how immediately they were able to
come up with these reactions. Fewer still, perhaps, have taken the time
to recall Hill's critical book of 1991, *The Enemy's Country: Words, Contexture, and other Circumstances of Language*—a book which itself took, and
takes, time and hard attention on the part of its readers. It is here,
however, that Hill meditates on poets like Dryden and Pound, both
writers 'at bay', in ways that certainly exert pressure of some kind on *The
Triumph of Love*. In his chapter on Dryden, for example, Hill acknowledges that the seventeenth-century writer 'knew that there were liber-
ties which he could not afford to take or would take at his peril', and
juxtaposes two articulations of the poet's stance when he is thus 'at bay',
and up against it:[30]

We weigh ' 'tis dangerous to offend an Arbitrary Master' against 'When a Poet is
throughly provok'd, he will do himself Justice, however dear it cost him' and
conclude that Dryden's own style is a matter of constant vigilant negotiation
among and between 'danger', 'justice', and 'cost'. It may be added that it is one
of the virtues of his style to transform a driven condition into a cadenced
vehemence and that 'however dear it cost him' strikes one as having earned its
place in the syntax of his conviction ...

Ezra Pound's convictions, too, are figured for Hill in the shadow of his
fitness for another, and more judicial, kind of conviction; even so,
Pound's literary 'attention upon the forces of attrition' plays an important part in *The Enemy's Country*, and the necessity of this attention, as well
as the reality of those forces, does not slip from view. When another
writer gives way to 'attrition', Pound's reaction is quoted:[31]

... he could bring himself to suggest, after [Allen] Upward's suicide, that he had
'shot himself in discouragement on reading of [the Nobel] Award to Shaw.
Feeling of utter hopelessness in struggle for values.' Such a timbre is not unlike
Upward's own in his autobiography, which has been defined as one of 'forced
levity and grim desperation ... betraying the lacerated spirit'. ... Such disparities
in fact stem from a coherent emphasis: that the self-same writer may become

---

[30] Hill, *The Enemy's Country*, 69.   [31] Ibid. 85–6.

the helpless and hopeless victim of those circumstances which he has acutely diagnosed and assayed.

Is there a measure of self-identification in this kind of critical writing? If so, it would be a mistake to assume that Hill is simply lining up a series of role models, so to speak, and putting himself, wilfully or wishfully, in their place. Pound's phrase, 'struggle for values', for example, is not one which Hill allows his readers to accept in an unquestioning way, for 'values' are not all self-evidently valuable. But Hill's tenor is plain enough: it is when a writer is most 'at bay', most confronted by those adverse forces in his contemporary surroundings, that he is backed into a position where he must—he can *only*—do himself justice in the pitch of his language, and its way with 'cadenced vehemence'.

But how is this pitch to be judged, and how far should the difficulties of its circumstances dictate its own measures of difficulty and intractability? Is it entirely right, for instance, for such writing to give the appearance of being so worked up on the matter of Nobel Prizes? The adversarial figures in *The Triumph of Love*—critics like MacSikker, Sean O'Shem, and Croker, and laureates like 'N. and N.', are quick to point out the element of 'obsession' is such a recurring concern. Section XLIII is a couplet in which this identification is juxtaposed with a furious—perhaps 'impotent'—snapping-back:[32]

> This is quite dreadful—he's become obsessed.
> There you go, there you go—narrow it down to *obsession*!

There is a doleful comedy in the compression here: the complacency of the first line, and its 'quite dreadful' (only *quite* dreadful?) is counterpointed immediately by the kind of vehemence whose cadence gives it away, as the voice takes on the pitch of a family row, narrowing itself down in the process. The tiny poem has room enough for two matched acts of mutual inattention. Yet Hill's registers remain extremely unstable, and almost helplessly vulnerable to misconstruction: there is irony everywhere, but its pitch is often at odds with its surroundings. In CIII, Hill writes of 'the presiding | judge of our art, self-pleasured *Ironia*',[33] and the implications of this self-pleasuring are taken up at once at the beginning of the next section. The whole section seems important in the context of irony, distaste, and tastelessness:[34]

---

[32] Hill, *The Triumph of Love*, 21. [33] Ibid. 53. [34] Ibid.

> Self-pleasured, as retching on a voided
> stomach pleasures self. Savage indignations
> plighted with self-disgust become one flesh.
> Pasternak, for example: *shesdesyat*
> *shestoy*, they shout—give us the sixty-
> sixth [sonnet, of Shakespeare—ED]. You could say
> that to yourself in the darkness before sleep
> and perhaps be reconciled. Nothing true
> is easy—is that true? Or, how true is it?
> It must be worth something, some sacrifice. I
> write for the dead; N., N., for the living
> dead. No joke, though, self-defenestration.

Like so much in *The Triumph of Love*, this is poetry which is constantly interrupting itself, seeming to change tack, to tear holes in its own fabric. The intrusions of an editorial voice are part of this, but more generally it is necessary to hear the extreme, painstaking heaviness of the progress—if it is progress—as Hill's language impacts the difficulties of its situation: 'Nothing true | is easy—is that true? Or, how true is it?' These questions, and the patience of their unfolding, weigh heavily; again and again, Hill insists on the necessity of attending to the things being said, though they are being heard with an increasing lack of clarity:[35]

> Excuse me—excuse me—I did not
> say the pain is lifting. I said the pain is in
> the lifting. No—please—forget it.
>
>   (XLII)

The poetry challenges its readers—its mishearers—to ignore the difficulties that are, but are never simply, its burden. In section XL, Hill concludes with '*Is that right, Missis, or is that right?* I don't | care what I say, do I?'[36] But this is the note of 'provok'd' vehemence which inhabits the teasing structures of the poetry, and enables Hill to find a level between the incompatible extremes ('*Is that right, Missis, or is that right?*') to which circumstance, and the voice 'provok'd' by circumstance continually threaten to drive him. Again, an earlier observation by Hill on Ezra Pound is pertinent:[37]

The ethical and the aesthetic come together at those points where 'freedom of pitch' and 'freedom of field' perfectly coincide. And when the conjunction is

---

[35] Hill, *The Triumph of Love*, 21.   [36] Ibid.   [37] Hill, *The Lords of Limit*, 158.

bungled we discover the complicity between a solecism and 'a sloppy and slobbering world'.... The desperation of 'I never did believe in Fascism, God damn it', the angry bewilderment of 'everyone's inexactitude very fatiguing', are both pre-judged by 'the tyro cannot play about with such things, the game is too dangerous'. Pound had written this, in 1917, in an essay on Laforgue, 'the finest wrought' of modern French satirists. 'Finest wrought' and 'everyone's inexactitude' are mutually uncomprehending and Pound stands condemned by his own best judgment, the 'tyro' to his own mystery.

Hill's own best judgement is not such as to leave *The Triumph of Love* standing condemned, and on the contrary it makes all the more audible the pressured and sometimes agonized pitch of the poem's self-checkings and self-crossings.

But what about the sheer extravagance of Hill's 'vehemence', and what the poem itself calls his 'splenetics' (LXXXVII)? To return to the bare-knuckle ride of section CIV, how far can the poet's critical perspicuity help with the final, bone-crunching wrench in pitch, from the apparently 'serious' to the nearly gruesome joke that is 'no joke'?

> It must be worth something, some sacrifice. I
> write for the dead; N., N., for the living
> dead. No joke, though, self-defenestration.

To complain about the lack of subtlety in the enjambment here (as some reviewers have done) is to fail to catch the self-consciously awful obviousness of the joke: it is not for nothing that Hill elsewhere in the book makes 'Boom-boom!' answer both to the ceremonial salvo of 'noon guns' and to the accents of Basil Brush—'... boom-boom, boom-boom!' (XXXIV).[38] In a sense, to fall for this is to fall for something where the poem's voice declares itself to be self-propelled in any fall it does take. Not irony, then, but transparency is involved: the critical capacity to handle the former is embarrassed by the presence of the latter. Once again, we seem to be confronted by the 'tasteless'. To reconfigure the living as the 'living | dead' is to nit-pick, and so returns a defiantly transparent response to 'I write for the dead', if that is heard as the voicing of a common complaint. To complain that Hill's codes in *The Triumph of Love* are easy to see through is both to get the point and to fail to get the point: the parallel is with Hill's characterization of Dryden, whose 'insult to Rochester, though in code, could not be more

---

[38] Hill, *The Triumph of Love*, 18.

clear … The deliberated insult has the quality of impenetrable transparency.'[39]

The process of 'self-defenestration', however, is painful for all concerned. The generic positioning which Hill insists upon, that of *laus et vituperatio*, or praise and condemnation, is one which sets out on a deliberately dangerous engagement between language and its 'contexture' in a world of multifarious misconstruction. In section CXXXIX, Hill writes of how there is 'nothing between | election and reprobation, except vertigo', and the poem continues into a dizzy (or at least a dizzying) encounter with precedent, as the poet is joined on his window-ledge by Milton, then Plutarch, then Hopkins, then Herbert, then Joyce … The context for this is precisely that of praise and blame, blessing and 'The deliberated insult':[40]

> Milton writes of those
> who 'comming to Curse … have stumbled into
> a kind of Blessing'; but if you suppose him
> to invoke a stirrup-and-ground-type mercy, think
> again. It's a Plutarchan twist: even our foes
> further us, though against their will and purpose (*up
> yours, O'Shem*). Hopkins gave his two best
> coinings of the self—*inscape*,
> *instress*—to Lucifer for his self-love,
> *non serviam*: sweetness of absolute
> hatred, which shall embrace self-hatred,
> encompass self-extinction, annihilation's
> demonic angelism. Hereditary
> depression is something else again. You
> can draw up Plutarch against yourself; yourself
> the enemy (*do it and be damned*).

This concern with concern for the self marks the point at which Hill's impulse towards self-destruction, doing it and being damned, meets the reflexes and the impacted energies of his rhetoric. In an essay on some notably vituperative writers of seventeenth-century prose, Hill mentions the relation between 'curse' and 'blessing' which language can inscribe as something apart from both Lockean ideas of communication and the counsel of despair in an assumption of inevitable misconstruction:[41]

---

[39] Hill, *The Enemy's Country*, 71.   [40] Hill, *The Triumph of Love*, 75–6.
[41] Geoffrey Hill, 'The Eloquence of Sober Truth', *Times Literary Supplement*, 11 June 1999, p. 11.

. . . I would respond that the perplexed matter of tradition, or custom, as we have received it, gives evidence that to legislate, as 'the end of Speech' 'that those Sounds, as Marks, may make known [our] *Ideas* to the Hearer' is to presume to disconnect language from the consequences of our common imbecility. The Lockean prescription names a legitimate function of language; but its tacit proscriptions turn legitimacy into tyranny. As with other patrimonies, our language is a blessing and a curse; but in the right hands it can mediate within itself, thereby transforming blessing into curse, curse into blessing.

The Triumph of Love is, of course, a poem about the patrimony we inherit, and the extent to which we fail to honour that patrimony: its curses fold within themselves 'blessing', but as a matter of faith. Thus, while the poem laments, sometimes with a wounded rage, the extent of modern forgetting in the kinds of self-congratulatory cultural and historical amnesia that have become dominant in the literary mind, it also refigures those intensities of poetic vision—in personal memory, in love for place, in unrepeatable vividness of perception—in which 'blessing' resides. In none of this can disgust—including self-disgust—be separated from the intensity of vision: curse and blessing are implicate, one in the other; no epiphany can escape from the mire of its contexture. This, one might hazard, is still, as it has always been, Hill's greatest sin against the literary orthodoxies of late twentieth-century England.

There are signs of labour everywhere in Hill's work: his poetry, like his prose, is nothing if it is not worked at, and the point is granted explicitly in *The Triumph of Love*. But the poem also, like Hill's prose, should give us pause in our reflex use of such a term. The series of epigraphs to the book, which present verses from the Book of Nehemiah in Hebrew, Latin, Old German, and English, have been taken as a sign of arrogance, where they are more truly a defence of labour: 'And I sent messengers unto them, saying, I am doing a great worke, so that I can not come down: why should the worke cease, whilest I leave it, and come downe to you?' The point here is that the 'worke' is more important, not just than 'you', but than 'you' and 'I'. Reviewers who have seized on this as a sign of self-importance forget (or do not know) that Nehemiah is being sent for by enemies who wait to murder him: in the meanwhile, he builds his wall. Hill's 'worke', like Nehemiah's, is for a community, and not for himself. The point is elementary, perhaps, but it is of the first importance in understanding *why* this poem has the ambitions it does.

Critics fond of accusing Hill of a kind of literary paranoia seem deaf to the stridency and intensity of their own vehemence. It is tempting to say that, if anything, Hill tends to underestimate the contemporary forces that resist the kinds of 'worke' he favours. In theory, Hill is committed to absorbing this resistance, as poetic language must absorb ultimately that against which it must react. Now 'charged with erudition'—and charged outright by some readers—in *The Enemy's Country*, Hill had put the matter in this way:[42]

> Quotidian language, both casual and curial, is itself highly charged, but charged with the enormous power of the contingent and circumstantial, a 'confused mass of thoughts', a multitudinous meaning amid which the creative judgement must labour to choose and reject. There are 'meanings' which are self-evidently wrong...but the 'meaning' of a poem, its constitution, the composition of its elements, is not so readily abstractable from the constituted opinions and solecisms of the age; and though the grading and measuring of words presupposes the ability to recognize ambiguities, there are some ambiguities so deeply impacted with habit, custom, procedure, that the 'recognition' is in effect the acknowledgement of irreducible bafflement. Dryden and Pound are alike in their feeling for a language that is as expressive of the labour and bafflement as it is of the perfected judgement.

'Labour' is always necessary but, one might say, it is seldom admired by critics whose interests do not encourage self-examination in matters of 'habit, custom, procedure'. Nor is this a phenomenon attached narrowly to the world of modern poetry and its reception: as Hill has repeatedly suggested, the loss of memory and the loss of attention are aspects of a more general change in temper. In 1989, Hill rounded upon the promoters of 'relevance' in biblical translation by writing in praise of William Tyndale's 'diligence':[43]

> If 'the significance of Tyndale as a highly conscious craftsman' remains unestablished, as the new introduction insists, one can only respond that, in the domain of the review-sated intelligentsia, the power of established fact is scarcely distinguishable from the potency of transient reputation. Norman Davis (*William Tyndale's English of Controversy*, 1971) states, by no means rashly, that 'the excellence of Tyndale's translations has been recognized almost from the time they appeared, and has often been analysed and justly praised', but in the world of amnesia and commodity this kind of established fact is no longer thought sufficient. 'Tyndale's ravishing solo' must now be 'heard across the world' as if he were some dissident poet in line for the Nobel Prize.

---

[42] Hill, *The Enemy's Country*, 65–6.

[43] Geoffrey Hill, 'Of Diligence and Jeopardy', *Times Literary Supplement*, 17 Nov. 1989, p. 1274.

Whether the judges in Stockholm impressed Hill more in the years after 1989 must remain extremely doubtful. Nevertheless, 'the world of amnesia and commodity' is not a place to be simply shunned: that is in itself a kind of wilful attempt at forgetting which cannot amend the situation for either side. Rather, Hill knows (and knows especially in *The Triumph of Love*) that he has his work cut out for him in that very world: poetry is not above the fray, nor is poetry merely in the fray: in truth, poetry *is* the fray.

It is worth allowing Hill's 1989 essay more room on this point, for recent criticism especially has been both explicit and unapologetic in its contempt for the kind of self-importance, or elitism, which such an attitude is commonly held to represent. Hill insists on the reality of *difficulty* in our dealings with language:[44]

Those who read my objection as an unjust elitist contempt for what Lord Coggan terms 'intelligibility', or for the needs of worshippers drawn from 'a wide range of ages and backgrounds' might ask themselves how it was that, in 1910, Everyman's Library could bring out its edition of *The First and Second Prayer Books of Edward VI* with a scholarly introduction by Bishop Gibson and with the original Tudor spelling unchanged. J. M. Dent, the founder of the series, and Ernest Rhys, its first editor, were not insensitive to the needs of 'the weak stomachs' among their wide readership but, like some other men of letters at that time, they showed respect for the intelligence of 'ordinary' people by occasionally making demands upon it. To set the old Everyman text and introduction against the introduction and text of the Yale New Testament or to read Lord Coggan's preface to the REB after Bishop Gibson is to begin to understand the irreparable damage inflicted, during the past eighty years or so, on the common life of the nation. 'Intelligibility', 'accessibility', do not make sense, do not cohere, without 'diligence', as Tyndale defines it.

Ironically, it is the very insistence on difficulty, and on the reality of our labouring on and in the matter of words, that has been successfully identified with 'unjust elitist contempt' both in and by the cultural forces that constitute contemporary orthodoxy. This is, indeed, 'no joke'. Hill's conclusion in 1989 is suggestive:[45]

I had intended to say that the Word of God in English could now withdraw from the clamour of its 'promotion' into the 'inaccessibility' of Mombert's edition of Tyndale's Pentateuch or Wallis's edition of the 1534 New Testament or, best of all perhaps, the old Everyman edition of *The First and Second Prayer*

[44] Ibid. 1275.   [45] Ibid. 1276.

Books of Edward VI. But maybe that is too tempting to be right. The alternative
conjecture would be that the Word diligently withdraws *into* the modern world's
jeopardy, the 'captiuite of ceremonies', to make there its 'affirmation of resurrection'.

What are the literary consequences of this? Hill's answer lies partly in his
subsequent (and important) insistence on T. S. Eliot's descent from
'pitch' to 'tone' in the accommodations of *Four Quartets*—a work which
The Triumph of Love at some levels sets out to undermine; partly, too,
Hill's response is in the 'blessing' which, as his long poem insists, cannot
separate itself from the 'curse' it knows to be on its lips, and which it
constantly tastes there.

The Triumph of Love is, then, a poem in which the effort to lift language
out of the mire into which it is constantly being pulled is also, and at the
same time, in the same words, in the same breath, the effort to expel, to
return upon and bring back up the poisonous matter itself. In this
respect, Hill plays the part of Shakespeare's Leontes:[46]

> How blest am I
> In my just censure, in my true opinion!
> Alack, for lesser knowledge! How accurs'd
> In being so blest! There may be in the cup
> A spider steep'd, and one may drink, depart,
> And yet partake no venom, for his knowledge
> Is not infected; but if one present
> Th' abhorr'd ingredient to his eye, make known
> How he hath drunk, he cracks his gorge, his sides,
> With violent hefts. I have drunk, and seen the spider.

It is not just because 'heft' has become a favourite word of Hill's that
these lines have a bearing on the situation of *The Triumph of Love*: they
represent a dramatic moment analogous to the poem's intensity of self-
imagining. In the fury of its combat, with itself and with the world it
knows (and as it cannot then *not* know) is all around it, Hill's book does
not ever entirely forget the fate of Leontes: how things go, and how
things end for him, cruelly mocked by his own words, and cheated
forever by his belief in a 'true opinion'. *The Triumph of Love*, in other
words, is self-lacerating as well as lacerating; far from setting out to be a
crown upon a lifetime's effort, it wears the dunce's cap as well as a crown
of thorns. In its daring and riskiness, in its extraordinary range, and in its

[46] *The Winter's Tale*, II. i. 36–45.

sometimes bewildering tonal unpredictability and inaccessibility, it is part of what may come to be seen as the most remarkable late burst of poetic energy since that of Yeats. Such things do, of course, take time to digest; and time is, at the moment, what most influential ways of reading contemporary literature do not care to spend. And yet, as Hill's poem knows, it is time and not tone that is the ruthless test of all 'true opinion'.

Select Bibliography

ALLOTT, KENNETH (ed.), *The Penguin Book of Contemporary Verse 1918–1960* (Harmondsworth: Penguin, 2nd edn. 1962).

ARMITAGE, SIMON, and CRAWFORD, ROBERT (eds.), *The Penguin Book of Poetry from Britain and Ireland since 1945* (Harmondsworth: Penguin, 1998).

AUDEN, W. H., *The Dyer's Hand and Other Essays* (London: Faber and Faber, 1953).

—— *The English Auden: Poems, Essays and Dramatic Writings 1927–1929*, ed. Edward Mendelson (London: Faber and Faber, 1977).

—— *Collected Poems*, ed. Edward Mendelson (London: Faber and Faber, 1991).

—— *Lectures on Shakespeare*, reconstructed and edited by Arthur Kirsch (London: Faber and Faber, 2000).

COOPER, JOHN XIROS, *T. S. Eliot and the Ideology of* Four Quartets (Cambridge: Cambridge University Press, 1995).

CULLINGFORD, ELIZABETH BUTLER, *Gender and History in Yeats's Love Poetry* (Cambridge: Cambridge University Press, 1993).

DONOGHUE, DENIS, *Yeats* (Glasgow: Fontana, 1971).

ELIOT, T. S., *The Use of Poetry and the Use of Criticism: Studies in the Relation of Criticism to Poetry in England* (London: Faber and Faber, 1933; 2nd edn. 1964).

—— *Selected Essays* (London: Faber and Faber, 1951).

—— *On Poetry and Poets* (London: Faber and Faber, 1957).

—— *To Criticize the Critic and Other Writings* (London: Faber and Faber, 1965).

—— *Complete Poems and Plays* (London: Faber and Faber, 1969).

EMIG, RAINER, *W. H. Auden: Towards a Postmodern Poetics* (Basingstoke: Palgrave, 2000).

EVERETT, BARBARA, *Poets in their Time: Essays on English Poetry from Donne to Larkin* (London: Faber and Faber, 1986; repr. Oxford: Clarendon Press, 1991).

FENTON, JAMES, *The Strength of Poetry* (Oxford: Oxford University Press, 2001).

GARDNER, HELEN, *The Composition of* Four Quartets (London: Faber and Faber, 1978).

HEANEY, SEAMUS, *The Government of the Tongue: The 1986 T. S. Eliot Memorial Lectures and Other Critical Writings* (London: Faber and Faber, 1988).

—— *The Place of Writing* (Atlanta, Ga.: Scholars Press, 1989).

—— *The Redress of Poetry: Oxford Lectures* (London: Faber and Faber, 1995).

—— *Opened Ground: Poems 1966–1996* (London: Faber and Faber, 1998), 464.

HILL, GEOFFREY, *The Lords of Limit: Essays on Literature and Ideas* (London: André Deutsch, 1984).

—— *Collected Poems* (London: André Deutsch, 1986).

—— 'Of Diligence and Jeopardy', *Times Literary Supplement*, 17 Nov. 1989, pp. 1273–6.

—— *The Enemy's Country: Words, Contexture, and Other Circumstances of Language* (Oxford: Clarendon Press, 1991).

—— 'Preface to the Penguin Edition', *Brand: A Version for the Stage* (1978; 3rd edn. Harmondsworth: Penguin, 1996).

—— 'Dividing Legacies' [review of T. S. Eliot, *The Varieties of Metaphysical Poetry* ed. R. Schuchard (1993)], *Agenda*, 34/2 (Summer 1996), pp. 9–28.

—— *Canaan* (Harmondsworth: Penguin, 1996).

—— *The Triumph of Love* (New York: Houghton Mifflin, 1998; Harmondsworth: Penguin, 1999).

—— 'The Eloquence of Sober Truth', *Times Literary Supplement*, 11 June 1999, pp. 7–12.

—— *Speech! Speech!* (Washington, DC: Counterpoint, 2000; Harmondsworth, Penguin, 2001).

—— 'Tacit Pledges', in Alan W. Holden and J. Roy Birch (eds.), *A. E. Housman: A Reassessment* (Basingstoke: Macmillan, 2000), 53–75.

HOWES, MARJORIE, *Yeats's Nations: Gender, Class, and Irishness* (Cambridge: Cambridge University Press, 1996).

JULIUS, ANTHONY, *T. S. Eliot, Anti-Semitism, and Literary Form* (Cambridge: Cambridge University Press, 1995).

LARKIN, PHILIP, *Collected Poems*, ed. Anthony Thwaite (London: Marvell Press and Faber and Faber, 1988).

LLOYD, DAVID, *Anomalous States: Irish Writing and the Post-Colonial Moment* (Dublin: Lilliput Press, 1993).

LONGENBACH, JAMES, *Stone Cottage: Pound, Yeats, and Modernism* (New York: Oxford University Press, 1988).

LONGLEY, EDNA, *Poetry in the Wars* (Newcastle-upon-Tyne: Bloodaxe Books, 1986).

—— *Poetry and Posterity* (Tarset: Bloodaxe Books, 2000).

LONGLEY, MICHAEL, *Poems 1963–1983* (Edinburgh: Salamander Press, 1985).

—— *Selected Poems* (London: Jonathan Cape, 1998).

MACNEICE, LOUIS, *The Collected Poems of Louis MacNeice*, ed. E. R. Dodds (London: Faber and Faber, 1966; corr. repr. 1979).

—— *Selected Literary Criticism of Louis MacNeice*, ed. Alan Heuser (Oxford: Clarendon Press, 1987).

McDIARMID, LUCY, *Auden's Apologies for Poetry* (Princeton: Princeton University Press, 1990).

McDONALD, PETER, 'Believing in the Thirties', in Keith Williams and Steven Matthews (eds.), *Rewriting the Thirties: Modernism and After* (Harlow: Longman, 1997), 71–90.

MAHON, DEREK, *Poems 1962–1978* (Oxford: Oxford University Press, 1979).

—— *Selected Poems* (Harmondsworth: Penguin Books, 1993).

—— *Journalism: Selected Prose 1970–1995*, ed. Terence Brown (Oldcastle: Gallery Press, 1996).

—— *Collected Poems* (Oldcastle: Gallery Press, 1999).

PAULIN, TOM, *Minotaur: Poetry and the Nation State* (London: Faber and Faber, 1992).

—— *Writing to the Moment: Selected Critical Essays 1980–1996* (London: Faber and Faber, 1996).

RAMAZANI, JAHAN, *Yeats and the Poetry of Death: Elegy, Self-Elegy, and the Sublime* (New Haven: Yale University Press, 1990).

RICHARDS, I. A., *Science and Poetry* (London: Kegan, Paul, French, Frubner, 1926).

RICKS, CHRISTOPHER, *T. S. Eliot and Prejudice* (London: Faber and Faber, 1988).

—— *Essays in Appreciation* (Oxford: Clarendon Press, 1996).

SCHUCHARD, RONALD, *Eliot's Dark Angel: Intersections of Life and Art* (New York: Oxford University Press, 1999).

STALLWORTHY, JON, *Vision and Revision in Yeats's* Last Poems (Oxford: Clarendon Press, 1969).

VENDLER, HELEN, 'Yeats and *Ottava Rima*', in Warwick Gould (ed.), *Yeats Annual 11* (London: Macmillan, 1995), pp. 26–44.

WILLS, CLAIR, *Improprieties: Politics and Sexuality in Northern Irish Poetry* (Oxford: Clarendon Press, 1993).

YEATS, W. B., *A Vision* (London: Macmillan, 1937).

—— *Collected Plays* (London: Macmillan, 1952).

—— *The Letters of W. B. Yeats*, ed. Allan Wade (London: Rupert Hart-Davis, 1954).

Autobiographies (London: Macmillan, 1955).

—— *The Variorum Edition of the Poems of W. B. Yeats*, ed. Peter Allt and Russell K. Alspatch (London: Macmillan, 1956).

—— *Mythologies* (London: Macmillan, 1959).

—— *Essays and Introductions* (London: Macmillan, 1961).

—— *Explorations* (London: Macmillan, 1962).

—— *A Critical Edition of Yeats's* A Vision *(1925)*, ed. George Mills Harper and Walter Kelly Hood (London: Macmillan, 1978).

—— Michael Robartes and the Dancer: *Manuscript Materials*, ed. Thomas Parkinson with Anne Brennan (Ithaca, NY: Cornell University Press, 1994).

—— The Wild Swans at Coole: *Manuscript Materials*, ed. Stephen Parrish (Ithaca, NY: Cornell University Press, 1994).

—— The Winding Stair (1929): *Manuscript Materials*, ed. David R. Clark (Ithaca, NY: Cornell University Press, 1995).

Index